THE IRISH BENEDICTINES

Edited   ʾlmán Ó Clabaigh OSB

The Irish Benedictines
A History

the columba press

First published in 2005 by
the columba press
55a Spruce Avenue, Stillorgan Industrial Park, Blackrock, Co. Dublin

Cover by Bill Bolger
Origination by The Columba Press
Printed in Ireland by ColourBooks Ltd, Dublin

ISBN 1-85607-497-8

Acknowledgements

The pictures of the Shrine of St Patrick's arm on the front cover and on page 108 are reproduced with the kind permission of the trustees of the museums and galleries of Northern Ireland.

The illustrations of Macmine Castle (p 134) and Merton House (p 135) are taken from David Rowe and Eithne Scallan's *Houses of Wexford* (Ballinakella Press, Whitegate, 2004), and are reproduced by kind permission of the artist, David Rowe, and Ballinakella Press editor and publisher, Dr Hugh Weir.

Maps on pages 26, 78 and 190 were drawn by Tim O'Neill.

This publication has received support from the Heritage Council under the 2005 publications grant scheme.

SUPPORTED BY THE HERITAGE COUNCIL

LE CUIDIÚ AN CHOMHAIRLE OIDHREACHTA

Table of Contents

6

Foreword

If the history of the Benedictines in Ireland has not quite captured the popular imagination, it is not for want of fine scholarly work. This volume is in a very real sense a work of synthesis presenting, I think, for the first time, the current state of research on all aspects of Irish Benedictine life and history, from its earliest to its current manifestations. We are honoured by the contributions of so many eminent scholars in the disciplines of history, theology and archaeology; and we are grateful to them for sharing with us so freely of their expertise.

In a scholarly but accessible fashion these essays celebrate and explore the Irish Benedictine tradition over a period of 1400 years. Commitment to monastic life brought Irish monks and nuns, 'pilgrims for Christ', through Dark Age Europe, where their monasteries played a vital role in the dissemination of the Christian and Benedictine tradition. Introduced into Ireland as part of the reform movement of the medieval Irish church, their activities provide a fascinating picture of the difficulties of monastic living in an ethnically divided society. The upheaval of the Reformation in the sixteenth century all but extinguished the Benedictine tradition in Ireland but, in exile on the continent, Irish Benedictine nuns, in association with their English colleagues, established a centre that kept the flame alight. The monastic revival of the nineteenth century produced a most significant spiritual writer in the person of the Dublin-born Abbot of Maredsous Abbey, Blessed Columba Marmion. Ireland, in turn, was host to a number of monastic refugee communities driven from the continent by anti-religious legislation and by World War I. All these form the tradition of which we today are heirs.

The shade of one particular monk of Glenstal hovers over this volume with a certain pride, I suspect, and perhaps with some anxiety (if that emotion is a part of the beatific vision). Father Gerard MacGinty OSB was a passionate scholar of monastic life and culture in medieval Ireland. His own contribution to the history of the monastic order in Ireland is best represented by the section on the Benedictines in Aubrey Gwynn and R. N. Hadcock's *Medieval Religious Houses: Ireland*. It is a matter of satisfaction to us, his confrères, to see his work carried forward and this volume is dedicated to his memory.

Christopher Dillon OSB
Abbot of Glenstal

Preface

In the story of Irish monasticism one chapter has been curiously neglected: the Irish Benedictine tradition as a whole has never attracted the historian's attention. This volume seeks to redress this by providing for the first time a comprehensive survey of the ways in which Irish men and women have sought – and continue to seek – God by following the Rule of Saint Benedict.

Most of the chapters in this book are based on papers delivered at a conference held in Glenstal Abbey in September 2002, marking the 75th anniversary of the foundation of that monastery. These have subsequently been revised and a number of chapters added.

The authors bring a wide range of expertise to their subject. Many are professional historians, bringing the critical eye of the academy to bear on the evidence. Others are themselves Benedictines, striving to follow in the same tradition as the men and women about whom they write. A number contrive to be both. Whatever their background they have performed a profound service to the Irish Benedictine community, for which we are deeply grateful.

That tradition is difficult to neatly define, characterised as it is by frequent adaptation and realignment, in response to various internal and external influences. On one level it might seem that there is very little connection between the disparate stories told here and that the very word 'tradition' is itself misplaced. But such a view is mistaken. The account of the Irish Benedictine tradition, as it emerges in this volume, in all its variegated and occasionally eccentric glory, reveals Irish men and women who, listening with the ear of the heart, found wisdom and guidance in the Rule of Saint Benedict for well over a millennium. Therein is the *traditio* – not merely the transmission of a coherent set of facts, but the handing on of a life-giving way. Choosing to live under a Rule and an Abbot or Abbess, their 'running the way of God's commandments with unspeakable sweetness of love' brought them across Dark Age Europe, through Reformation England and the war-torn continent and into modern Africa. In exile and persecution they established centres of learning and refuge. Returning to Ireland they continue to devote themselves to these activities, adapting themselves and their lives to the changed and changing circumstances of the twenty-first century, 'that in all things God may be glorified'.

Martin Browne OSB and Colmán Ó Clabaigh OSB
2 February 2005, Feast of the Presentation of the Lord

Contributors

Aidan Bellenger is Prior of Downside Abbey in Somerset, England. His publications include *The Exiled French Clergy in the British Isles after 1789*, *Princes of the Church: A History of the English Cardinals* and *The Mitre and the Crown: A History of the Archbishops of Canterbury*.

Martin Browne is a monk of Glenstal Abbey. He currently works in the abbey school as a housemaster, a teacher of History and Irish, and school choirmaster.

Celestine Cullen was Abbot of Glenstal from 1980 until 1992, when he was elected Abbot President of the Benedictine Congregation of the Annunciation. He retired from office in 2004.

William Fennelly is a monk of Glenstal Abbey. He currently works in the abbey school as Dean of Boarding and a teacher of History and French.

Peter Harbison is an archaeologist and honorary academic editor with the Royal Irish Academy. His publications include *Guide to the National Monuments of Ireland*, *The High Crosses of Ireland*, *The Golden Age of Irish Art*, and *Ireland's Treasures*.

Placid Murray is a monk and former Conventual Prior of Glenstal Abbey. From 1971-74 he was Chairman of the working committee which produced the English translation of the Divine Office. His publications and editions include *John Henry Newman, Sermons 1824-1843, Volume I*, *Newman the Oratorian* and *The Rule of Benedict: A Guide to Christian Living*.

Mark-Ephrem M Nolan is Superior of the Olivetan Benedictine community in Rostrevor. Born in Belfast, he entered the Abbey of Bec-Hellouin in Normandy in 1979. He was a member of the Bec *cella* in Northern Ireland in the 1980s, later serving as novice master at Bec, before returning to Ireland in 1998 to lead the foundation now established at Holy Cross Monastery in Rostrevor.

Andrew Nugent is Prior of Glenstal Abbey and is a former novice master of St Benedict's Priory, Ewu-Ishan, Nigeria. He is the author of *The Four Courts Murder*.

Colmán Ó Clabaigh is a monk of Glenstal Abbey, where he is the monastery librarian. He is a research fellow of the Mícheál Ó Cléirigh Institute at University College, Dublin and author of *The Franciscans in Ireland, 1400-1534*.

Dáibhí Ó Cróinín is a Professor in the Department of History at the National University of Ireland, Galway. He is the author of *Early Medieval Ireland: 400-1200*. He is Director of the 'Foundations of Irish Culture' Project at NUIG.

Dagmar Ó Riain-Raedel is a member of the Department of History at University College, Cork, and co-ordinator of the 'Sources for Insular Studies' and 'Pilgrimage' projects. She has published widely on the subject of Irish pilgrims on the continent.

Tim O'Neill is an historian and a scribe. He is the author of *The Irish Hand* and *Merchants and Mariners in Medieval Ireland*.

M Angela Stephens is a nun of the Benedictine Congregation of the Adorers of the Sacred Heart of Jesus of Montmartre. She is Superior of St Benedict's Priory, Cobh.

Mark Tierney is a monk of Glenstal Abbey. His books include *Murroe and Boher: A Parish History, Blessed Columba Marmion* and *Glenstal Abbey: An Historical Guide*.

Kathleen Villiers-Tuthill is an historian and writer based in Clifden. Her publications include *Beyond the Twelve Bens: A History of Clifden and District 1860-1923, Patient Endurance: The Great Famine in Connemara* and *History of Kylemore Castle and Abbey*.

CHAPTER ONE

A Tale of Two Rules: Benedict and Columbanus

Dáibhí Ó Cróinín

If the measure of a man's greatness is his capacity to generate controversy, then Benedict and Columbanus are up there with the best of them! That the great Irish saint and scholar should have been the cause of so much difficulty during the years of his missionary activity in Gaul and in Italy would surprise no one who has read his surviving letters.[1] But even if the letters had not come down to us (they did so, after all, only in a single seventeenth-century transcript of a St Gall manuscript, now lost), the principal events of his very eventful career are recorded by his biographer, Jonas of Bobbio.[2] In stark and striking contrast to Columbanus, however, Benedict, a paragon of meekness and virtue, would have seemed, until relatively recently at any rate, to have been a most unlikely candidate for debate amongst historians, and who could have anticipated that the few small niggling suspicions that hung over his career down the centuries would, in our own time, turn into what our RTÉ weather-forecasters like to call 'organised bands of clouds', clouds that threaten to drown the man and his reputation?

It is just over sixty years now since Dom Augustin Génestout startled first his fellow Benedictines of Solesmes, then a meeting of Benedictine abbots at Rome, and finally the academic world at large by announcing what the great Oxford historian of the church, Sir Richard Southern, described as 'one of the greatest surprises in the history of medieval scholarship',[3] namely, that the *Regula Benedicti* (Rule of St Benedict) was not an original work at all, but was, in fact, in large part an adaptation of an earlier rule, the so-called *Regula Magistri* (Rule of the Master), composed by an older, anonymous, Italian

---

1. See G. S. M. Walker (ed & trans), *Sancti Columbani opera*. Scriptores Latini Hiberniae. ii (Dublin 1957), pp 2-59.
2. Bruno Krusch (ed), *Ionae Vitae sanctorum Columbani, Iohannis, Vedastis*, Monumenta Germaniae Historica [MGH] Scriptores Rerum Merovingicarum [SRM], iv (Hannover, 1902), pp 1-152; separatim (1905). The most recent authoritative discussion is in Ian Wood, *The missionary life. Saints and the evangelisation of Europe, 400-1050* (Harlow, 2001), pp 31-39, 41-42, 159-60, 261, 264.
3. Quoted from R.W. Southern, *Western Society and the Church in the Middle Ages* (Harmondsworth, 1979), p. 221, by Marilyn Dunn, 'Mastering Benedict: monastic rules and their authors in the early medieval West' in *English Historical Review*, cv, No ccccxvi (July, 1990), pp 567-94. Dunn's article provides a very useful summary of the literature.

contemporary of St Benedict.[4] Needless to say, this sensational claim caused enormous and instant controversy, and not only amongst the Benedictines. Well over a hundred books and articles have appeared since then on the subject, and the controversy is by no means over yet. However, it is, I think, fair to say, that the balance of probability has tilted markedly in favour of those scholars who have accepted Génestout's case, though the thesis is still meeting resistance to this day (and not all of it from diehard traditionalists).[5] The appearance in 1963 of Dom David Knowles's article 'The *Regula Magistri* and the Rule of St Benedict', in his collection of essays called *Great historical enterprises,* set the seal on the controversy in the English-speaking world.[6] His view was that:

> In our present state of knowledge, the case for the priority of the Master seems stronger by far than the case for the priority of St Benedict as presented by the conservatives. The thesis of the Master's priority may never be proved by demonstration, but it is hard to see that its opponents can ever regain the ground that they have lost in the past twenty-five years.[7]

Opposition to Dom Génestout's revolutionary viewpoint was decisively rebutted in the French-speaking world first in 1964 by the appearance of the magisterial three-volume edition of the *Regula Magistri,* and then finally silenced in 1971 by the no less magisterial six-volume edition of the *Rule of St Benedict,* both from the hand of Dom Adalbert de Vogüé.[8] Since 1971 the controversy surrounding Benedict and his Rule has seen even newer twists, and the texts that once were thought to be rock-solid witnesses to Benedict's life and work have come under renewed scrutiny, not all of it to Dom Adalbert's advantage. In fact, Dom Adalbert, it could be said, has already 'lost' one of the crucial works in this whole debate, and is at present in grave danger of losing a second.

The doubts that lingered concerning the priority of the *Regula Magistri* over Benedict's Rule received unexpected, if indirect, support as a result of a new controversy that has been touched off in more recent times around the person and writings of Benedict's supposed biographer, Gregory I (Gregory

---

4. Augustin Génestout, 'La Règle du Maître et la Règle de S. Benoit' in *Revue d'Ascétique et de Mystique,* xxi (1940), pp 51-112. Génestout had declared his findings already in 1937.
5. *eg,* Marilyn Dunn's article cited above, n. 3.
6. David Knowles, *Great historical enterprises. Problems in monastic history* (London, 1963), pp 135-95.
7. art. cit., p 195.
8. Adalbert de Vogüé (ed & trans), *La Règle du Maître,* Sources Chrétiennes, 105-7 (Paris, 1964); idem (ed & trans), *La Règle de Saint Benoît,* Sources Chrétiennes, 181-6 (Paris, 1971-2). Vol 3 by J. Neufville; vol 7 added in 1977.

the Great). Just as Dom Génestout's sensational thesis rocked the scholarly world of the 1940s and 1950s, so too, in our time, a devastating assault has been launched on the link between Gregory and his *Dialogues* (or 'Miracles of the Italian Fathers', as the work is titled in the manuscripts), a work that for so long has been attached to his name. The second book of that collection comprises Gregory's biography of St Benedict, hence the connection with our subject.

In a paper first delivered to a Gregorian Colloquium at Chantilly in 1982,[9] expanded subsequently and published as a major two-volume study entitled (significantly) *The Pseudo-Gregorian Dialogues* (Leiden 1987),[10] the English scholar, Francis Clark, produced a theory which has had the effect of an atomic bomb on Benedictine scholarship, a theory just as revolutionary in its own way (though not as original) as the earlier one concerning the *Regula Benedicti*, and one which has serious implications for that Rule (which Clark proposed to date to the seventh century). In the manner of the first controversy about Gregory's authorship of the *Dialogues*, which originated with the confessional debates of the Reformation era, Clark's method is polemical and apologetical,[11] his purpose to defend what he considers to be the authentic portrait of Gregory the Great, an outstanding pope, a cultured and sophisticated contemporary of Boethius and Cassiodorus, the last great Father of the Latin Church, a moral and intellectual giant who could never have been responsible for the 'silly' miracle stories that are found in the *Dialogues*:

> The more the true spiritual greatness of St Gregory has been realised anew in the present century, the more the problem of the *Dialogues* has become obtrusive and embarrassing. How could such an inspired yet humble master of divine wisdom be the author of that extraordinary farrago of preposterous tales, which seem to reflect a debased level of religious sensitivity?[12]

In Clark's view, it is necessary above all to detach Gregory from the stories about Benedict and the other Italian saints, and to let the real Gregory

> ...be seen as he truly was: not as a spiritual and cultural schizophrenic, not as a strange mixture of greatness and puerility of soul, but as a man of transparent integrity, of extraordinary mental acuity and of unitary

---

9. Francis Clark, 'The authenticity of the Gregorian Dialogues: a re-opening of the question?' in *Grégoire le Grand, Colloques Internationaux du Centre National de la Recherche Scientifique, Chantilly, 15-19 Sept., 1982* (Paris, 1986), pp 429-43.
10. For a condensed and updated version of this work see Francis Clark, *The "Gregorian" Dialogues and the origins of Benedictine monasticism* (Leiden, 2003).
11. His earliest publication in this vein that I know of is his polemical pamphlet, *The Catholic Church and Anglican orders*. Catholic Truth Society (London, 1962).
12. Clark, *Pseudo-Gregorian Dialogues*, ii, p 749.

vision of reality, as a master of faith and religious experience whom all Christians can honour, without the reservations which so many have felt obliged to make.[13]

By arguing that the *Dialogues* were not composed by Gregory the Great, Clark has set the cat firmly amongst the pigeons – and the pigeons are not doing too well! Despite the fact that the most authoritative handbook of patristic studies has pronounced the verdict: 'Eum non secuti sunt eruditi fere omnes', (*almost all scholars have not followed him*)[14] Clark's case, it must be said, is acutely argued and very substantially documented – whatever may be the eventual outcome of the debate.[15] And it must be said also that one is not necessarily reassured by Dom de Vogüé's defence of the status quo regarding the *Dialogues*,[16] when one recalls that he has recently been obliged to acknowledge that the case for Gregory's supposed authorship of a commentary on the Book of Kings has bitten the dust.[17]

Whatever the eventual outcome of these various debates, one common fact emerges from discussion of Gregory's *Dialogues* and the *Regula Benedicti*: they both emerge into the light of day for the first time in the seventh century, and the Irish connection is significant in both cases.[18] For the record, the four earliest manuscripts of the *Dialogues* belong to the end of the seventh century or beginning of the eighth, and come from 'Luxeuil', 'south France', 'Northumbria', and 'a continental centre with insular connections'.[19] The

---

13. Clark, ibid., p 750

14. Eligius Dekkers and Aemilius Gaar, *Clavis patrum Latinorum* (Steenbrugge, 1951; 3rd rev. ed. 1995), p 586.

15. The verdict of Friedrich Prinz, *Frühes Mönchtum im Frankenreich. Kultur und Gesellschaft in Gallien, den Rheinlanden und Bayern am Beispiel der monastischen Entwicklung (4. bis 8. Jahrhundert)*, 2nd rev ed (Darmstadt, 1988), p 663 n 119: 'In jedem Fall — ganz gleich wie die internationale Forschung zu diesem Werk Stellung nehmen wird — handelt es sich um einen scharfsinnigen und substantiellen Beitrag zur Frühgeschichte des benediktinischen Mönchtums'.

16. Adalbert de Vogüé, 'Grégoire le Grand et ses "Dialogues" d'après deux ouvrages récents' in *Revue d'Histoire Écclésiastique*, lxxxv, pt 2 (March-June, 1988), pp 281-348. This article is De Vogüé's response to Clark.

17. Adalbert de Vogüé, 'L'auteur du Commentaire des Rois attribué à saint Gregoire: un moine de Cava?' in *Revue Bénédictine*, cvi (1996), pp 319-31. See Paul Meyvaert, 'The date of Gregory the Great's Commentaries on the Canticle of Canticles and on I Kings' in *Sacris Erudiri*, 23 (1978-9), pp 191-216.

18. For what follows, see esp Prinz, *Frühes Mönchtum*, esp pp 263 ff.

19 See Paul Meyvaert, 'The enigma of Gregory the Great's Dialogues: a response to Francis Clark' in *Journal of Ecclesiastical History*, xxxix (1988), pp 335-81. Clark in turn has replied to his critics in 'St Gregory and the enigma of the *Dialogues*: a response to Paul Meyvaert' in *Jnl Eccl. Hist.*, xl, No 3 (July 1989) 323-43 (with a response to the response, by Paul Meyvaert, ibid, pp 344-46).

oldest surviving manuscript of the Rule of Benedict is actually late-seventh-century English, and probably of Worcester provenance.[20] However, I do not intend to pursue the question of the *Dialogues* any further;[21] I shall concern myself from here on with the Rule of Benedict and its links with Columbanus and the Irish on the continent.

The Rule disappeared from Italy after the destruction of Monte Cassino in 577 and did not reappear there until the eighth century, when it was re-imported from Francia following the reconstruction of Benedict's famous foundation. It did not make a reappearance in Rome until the tenth century. Long before that, however, the Benedictine Rule is found for the first time in Gaul, at the monastery of Altaripa (Hauterive), near Albi,[22] where it is mentioned in a letter of 628 by abbot Venerandus of Altaripa to Bishop Constantius of Albi. This reference is, however, doubtful (the manuscript of the letter is fifteenth-century, and though its authenticity was championed by no less an authority than the great Ludwig Traube, it must be classed as suspicious).[23] Wherever else the *Regula Benedicti* is mentioned in Gaul in the seventh century, it always appears in the company of Columbanus's *Regula monastica* (monastic rule).

The first monastery (after Altaripa) where it is mentioned is Solignac, near Limoges, in Aquitaine, where the foundation charter of 632 enjoins on the monks to follow the example of the holy men of Luxeuil and to abide strictly by the Rules of the holy fathers Benedict and Columbanus: *'... ut vos et successores vestri tramitem religionis sanctissimorum virorum Luxoviensis monasterii consequamini et regulam beatissimorum patrum Benedicti vel Columbani firmiter teneatis ...'*[24] (in order that you and your successors may follow the path of religion of the most holy men of Luxeuil and firmly hold the rule of the most blessed fathers Benedict and Columbanus). In other words, the first abbot of Solignac had been recruited by its founder Eligius from Luxeuil, the monastery in the Vosges founded by Columbanus, and the community at Solignac was to be administered in accordance with the best

20. See E. A. Lowe, *Codices Latini Antiquiores* [CLA], ii (Oxford, 1934; rev. ed., 1972), No. 240, and Neil Ker, 'The provenance of the oldest manuscript of the Rule of St. Benedict' in *Bodleian Library Record*, ii, No 17 (Dec 1941), pp 28-29. There is a facsimile in E. A. Lowe, *English uncial* (Oxford, 1960), pl XX.
21. It should be noted, however, that Marilyn Dunn has argued for composition of the *Dialogues* in Irish circles on the continent in the mid-seventh century; see 'Gregory the Great, the Vision of Fursey, and the origins of purgatory' in *Peritia*, xiv (2000), pp 238-54.
22. See Prinz, *Frühes Mönchtum*, p 267 ff.
23. Ludwig Traube, 'Textgeschichte der Regula S. Benedicti' in *Abhandlungen der Bayerischen Akademie der Wissenschaften*, philol.-hist. Kl. (München, 1890), pp 600-731, pp 633 ff.
24. See Prinz, *Frühes Mönchtum*, p 268 n. 13 (SRM, iv, p 747 f.).

features of the Benedictine and Irish rules. This formula, *secundum regulam B. Bendicti et ad modum Luxoviensis monasterii* (according to the rule of Bl Benedict and the manner of the monastery of Luxeuil) recurs again and again in the foundation-charters of all the important new seventh-century Frankish monasteries.[25] For example, a few years after Solignac, the monastery of Rebais-en-Brie was founded by three brothers, Ado, Dado and Rado, *ubi monachos vel peregrinos sub regula B. Benedicti et ad modum Luxoviensis monasterii devoti deliberant collocare.*[26] (where holy men resolved to gather together monks and pilgrims under the rule of Blessed Benedict and according to the practice of Luxeuil). Another foundation of one of the brothers, Jouarre (630-7), also followed the joint rule.[27] Likewise the monastery of Moissac, and of Salaberga at Laon (*ex regula beatorum patrum Benedicti et Columbani* (under the rule of the blessed fathers Benedict and Columbanus) while at St Wandrille (Fontanella, founded 649) the *Gesta abbatum Fontanellensium* (Deeds of the abbots of Fontanella) mentions that the monastic library had a codex *in quo continetur regula S Benedicti et S Columbani* (in which is contained the rule of St Benedict and St Columbanus). The fact that Wandregisel spent some time in Bobbio after he had left the services of the Frankish court can leave us in no doubt about the origins of his disciplinary practice.

Jumiéges also followed the same path. Like Wandregisel a former member of the Merovingian royal court at Paris, its founder Filibert had spent some time both at Bobbio and in Luxeuil. He established numerous monasteries in Francia, in Burgundy, and in Italy, and for that purpose he had diligently studied the rules of Basil, Macharius, Benedict and Columbanus (*Basilii sancti charismata, Macharii regula, Benedicti decreta, Columbani institute* – the charismata of St Basil, the rule of Macharius, the decrees of Benedict, the institutes of Columbanus). This pattern was not only repeated in the new Frankish monastic foundations established under royal or aristocratic patronage, but also, at the behest of the Merovingian king Dagobert's wife, later dowager, Balthild, a succession of the older Gallican houses were reformed in accordance with the mixed rule.[28] So, at her new foundations of

---

25. See Prinz, *Frühes Mönchtum*, p 269: 'Die Benediktregel findet sich bald überall im Frankenreich in enger Verbindung mit dem irofränkischen Mönchtum, das von Luxeuil ausging und mit Hilfe vornehmlich des Pariser Hofadels oder des Königs, sich rasch ausbreiten konnte'.
26. Prinz, *Frühes Mönchtum*, p 269. For the brothers Ado, Dado, and Rado, and their connections with Columbanus, see Edward James, *The Franks* (Oxford, 1988), p 132.
27. James, op. cit., pp 132-3. For Irish connections with this monastery, see Dáibhí Ó Cróinín, *Early medieval Ireland, 400-1200* (London, 1995), pp 196 n 1 and 207.
28. Prinz, *Frühes Mönchtum*, p 274.

Corbie and Chelles, as well as in some older houses such as St Denis in Paris, St Germain at Auxerre, and St Medard at Soissons, even St Martin's at Tours, the *sanctus regularis ordo* (the holy rule) was none other than the combined rule of Benedict and Columbanus. The question, then, is: how did this come about?

All the evidence suggests that the early dissemination of the Benedictine Rule went hand-in-hand with the spread of that new brand of Irish-Frankish monasticism which Columbanus had established at Annegray, Luxeuil and Fontaines, and which was continued by his followers and supporters – in particular, those who had served time as royal functionaries at the Merovingian court in Paris and who subsequently featured prominently as monastic founders and patrons. The list is impressive: Autun, Bourges, and Cahors, Laon, Lyon, Meaux, Noyon, Rheims, Rouen, and Verdun, to name only a few. At the same time, with the rise of Columbanan monasticism, the role and influence of the older Gallican centres of monastic influence began to wane: houses like Lérins and Arles, once the centres of a vibrant monastic movement in the south, faded from the picture in the course of the seventh and eighth centuries, for political as well as for religious reasons (though, of course, they never completely disappeared).

But the most striking feature of the evidence from the period before the mid-seventh century, at any rate, is that uniformity of monastic practice was neither expected nor sought amongst the churchmen of Gaul and the new Frankish kingdoms; the Rules of Benedict and Columbanus were only two among a wide variety of monastic precepts from which contemporaries could pick and choose the elements of the religious life that best suited their needs.[29]

This is strikingly illustrated as well closer to home in the case of the Venerable Bede's own monastery at Wearmouth-Jarrow, in Northumbria. Bede is invariably paraded as a model Benedictine. For example, in the collection of essays published to mark the centenary of his death in 1935 it is stated: 'So he stood at the point of new departure – a Benedictine monk in the yet living tradition of Celtic piety, an English student in the rich treasury of Celtic learning, a disciple of Rome inspired by the intellectual passion of Ireland.'[30] But Bede was no more a Benedictine than I am. On the contrary, he himself tells us explicitly, in his *History of the abbots of Wearmouth-Jarrow*, that Benedict Biscop, the founder of the twin house, had compiled his rule

---

29. For the full range of such rules, see Prinz, *Frühes Mönchtum*, p 94 ff.
30. A. Hamilton-Thompson (ed), *Bede, his life, times and writings* (Oxford, 1935), p xiii.

from the best elements of no fewer than seventeen different continental rules which he had encountered in his travels (*ex decem quippe et septem monasteriis quae inter longos meae crebre peregrinationis discursus optima conperi* – from the seventeen monasteries which I found the best during the long travels of my frequent pilgrimage).[31] Benedict had spent two years at Lérins, and shorter periods elsewhere on the continent. He also travelled no fewer than six times to Rome, and brought back with him many treasures, including books. He doubtless brought back a copy of the Benedictine Rule on one of these occasions, but nothing in Bede's *Ecclesiastical History*, or in any other Northumbrian document of the time, allows us to say that St Benedict's was the dominant rule in Northumbria in Biscop's time (notwithstanding his interesting name!).[32]

The same, indeed, can be said for that other notorious Northumbrian prelate, Bishop Wilfrid of York, the *bête noire* of the Irish at the Synod of Whitby in 664, and champion of all things Roman, including (we are told) the Benedictine Rule.[33] But though Wilfrid is credited with having introduced the Rule and the so-called orthodox reckoning of Easter to the churches of northern England, the contemporary author of the memorial verses inscribed on his tomb said no more than that his houses were regulated in accordance with a *regula patrum* ('Rule of the Fathers', genitive plural), not the Rule of St Benedict. In fact, as we know from Wilfrid's own biography, the great champion of Roman ways ruled over a monastic *parochia* (the very

---

31. See Charles Plummer (ed), *Venerabilis Baedae opera historica*, 2 vols (Oxford, 1896) i, pp 374-75 (*Hist. Abb.* §11).

32. And notwithstanding, either, the remark of Wilhelm Levison, *England and the continent in the eighth century* (Oxford, 1946), p 23: 'The Rule of St. Benedict was authoritative in his [Biscop's] two houses, but his institutions were based on the experience of seventeen monasteries which he had visited during his travels'. Bede's citation of the admonition in the Benedictine Rule against appointing close family relations to monastic offices (cap. lxiv, 'De ordinando abbate') in his *Historia abbatum* (§11; Plummer, *Baedae opera*, i, p 375) is not evidence for its dominant position. On the contrary, Biscop's co-abbots and later successors, Eosterwine and Ceolfrid, were both related to him, as is clear from Bede's subsequent narrative in *Hist. abb.* §13 (Plummer, op. cit., i, p 377)

33. 'Wilfrid of York was proud of having first introduced it into Northumbria', Levison, op. cit., p 22, with reference to the *Vita Wilfridi*, cap. xiv (and cf cap xlvii); see Bertram Colgrave (ed & trans), *The Life of Bishop Wilfrid by Eddius Stephanus* (Cambridge, 1927), p 96. 'But it cannot have been followed fully in his monasteries in view of what Eddius tells us about the way Wilfrid controlled the abbatial succession and the nature of his will', as remarked by Eric John, 'The social and political problems of the early English Church', in Joan Thirsk (ed), *Land, church, and people: Essays presented to H. P. R. Finberg* (Reading, 1970), pp 39-63, at pp 54-55. Elsewhere (p 42) John remarks that 'Eddius is a barefaced liar who cannot be trusted in the simplest matters of fact'.

term his biographer uses!) in a distinctively Irish fashion.[34] He was certainly not a Benedictine.

And what of the Irish connection? Columbanus's *Regula monastica* (monastic rule) and *Regula coenobialis* (cenobitic rule) may be the earliest Irish monastic rules to survive, but we know there were others, some of them older than his. In the case of Bangor (Co Down), Columbanus' last-known monastery in Ireland before his departure for the continent, the author of the *Vita Comgalli*, the Life of Columbanus' mentor, states that Comgall had pangs of conscience on his deathbed because his rule had been so harsh.[35] Though now lost, the regime at Bangor can no doubt be reconstructed on the basis of Columbanus' rule for his foundations in Burgundy. The unremittingly severe existence of his monks made no concessions to the frailties of body and soul: 'Let him come weary to bed and sleep walking, and let him be forced to rise while his sleep is not yet finished.'[36] It was perhaps the bleak austerity of Columbanus' monasteries that drove continental clerics to soften the hardship of his Rules by reference to Benedict's more humane prescripts.

The Hiberno-Latin poem on the abbots of Bangor in the seventh-century *Antiphonary of Bangor* states that Comgall ruled the monastery according to a catholic rule (*rexit sanctam ecclesiam / catholicam per regulam* – he ruled the holy church according to a catholic rule), a rule that was *stricta, sancta, sedula*.[37] (strict, holy, unremitting). Although it no longer survives, Comgall's rule was in existence still in the ninth century, when it was catalogued as *regula abbatis Comgelli* (the rule of Abbot Comgall), together with a *regula fratrum Hibernensium* (Rule of the Irish Brethren), in the library of Fulda, alongside another *regula abbatis Columbi cellae*, a Rule of Colum Cille of Iona, now also sadly lost.[38] The ninth-century library catalogues of St Gallen and Reichenau list the rule of Columbanus as well as a *regula Hybernensium fratrum* (rule of the Irish Brethren) and a *regula monachorum Hybernensium* (rule of the Irish monks), in addition to many others of Gallican or eastern origin.[39] Proliferation of rules was thus the norm, in fact, in the Irish church, as it was also in the Gallican church.

---

34. (*Vita Wilfridi*, cap 47); for commentary, see Ó Cróinín, *Early medieval Ireland*, p 164.
35. Charles Plummer (ed), *Vitae sanctorum Hiberniae*, 2 vols (Oxford, 1910), ii, p 21.
36. *Regula monachorum* §10; Walker, *Sancti Columbani opera*, p 140.
37. F. E. Warren (ed), *The Antiphonary of Bangor*, 2 vols. Henry Bradshaw Society Publications, iv & x (London, 1893, 1895), x, p 28.
38. For the Fulda evidence, see Paul Lehmann, 'Fuldaer Studien' in *Sitzungsberichte der Bayerischen Akademie der Wissenschaften*, philos.-philol. Kl., 1925, iii (München, 1925), pp 1-53, at pp 51-52.
39. Prinz, *Frühes Mönchtum*, p 290 & n 112.

It was that prince of Benedictine scholars, the great Jean Mabillon, who first suggested in the seventeenth century that the dissemination of the Rule of St Benedict in the west was the direct result of the personal contacts that came into existence between Columbanus and Gregory the Great.[40] The suggestion is an intriguing one, but does it stand up? Certainly, Columbanus addressed at least one of his surviving letters to Gregory (*Ep.* 1, c 600), in the course of which he referred explicitly to four of Gregory's known works. Thus he remarks:

> I have read your book containing the pastoral rule, brief in style, pregnant in doctrine, replete with sacred lore. I confess that the work is sweeter than honey to the needy. Wherefore in my thirst I beg you, for Christ's sake, to bestow on me your tracts, which, as I have heard, you have compiled with wonderful skill upon Ezekiel. I have read six books of Jerome on him; but he did not expound even the half. But if you see fit, send me something from your lectures delivered in the city; I mean the final expositions of the book. Send too the Song of Songs from that passage in which it says 'I will go to the mountain of myrrh and to the hill of frankincense', right up to the end. Treat it, I pray, either with others' comments or with your own in brief. And in order to expound all the obscurity of Zachariah, open up his secrets, so that in this a blind westerner may render thanks to you. My demands are pressing, my inquiries large, who knows it not? But you too have large resources, since you know well that from a small stock less must be lent and from a great one more.[41]

It is worth pointing out in passing that Gregory's sermons on Ezekiel were preached first in Rome in the autumn of 593, but not published until 601. However, Columbanus's words give the impression almost of a man who had heard them spoken (though we know that cannot be). Certainly, he seems to be uncommonly well informed about Gregory's literary activities, and the public sermons that lay behind several of them.

But did Columbanus receive the *Regula Benedicti* from Gregory? He did not ask for it, and there seems to be no trace of it in his own rules. (Neither, for that matter, is there any trace of the *Dialogues* in Columbanus's extant writings.) We have no direct evidence that Gregory ever replied to Columbanus's letter, but Gregory in one of his own epistles (datable to 594) does state that he sent a copy of his *Regula pastoralis* to an individual in Gaul

---

40. Jean Mabillon, *Annales Ordinis Sancti Benedicti*, i (Paris, 1668), Praef., p xxxi (cited Prinz, *Frühes Mönchtum*, p 645 n 37).
41. Walker, *Sancti Columbani opera*, p 11.

by name of Columbus *Codicem vero regulae pastoralis domno Columbo pres-*
bytero transmittendum per horum portitores direximus[42] (in fact I arranged for
a copy of the pastoral rule to be sent to the priest Columbus via couriers of
theirs). In a later letter (dated Oct 600) addressed to abbot Chonosus of
Lérins, he recommends to his correspondent *filium nostrum Columbum pres-*
byterum (our son, the presbyter Columbus). The two are undoubtedly identical, but there is no proof that our Columbanus is intended in either of these
references, and it must be judged unlikely in the circumstances (since
Columbanus was neither in Rome nor in Etruria, and does not appear to
have had any contact with Lérins).

As a matter of fact, there is no evidence at all that Gregory the Great was
associated, either directly or indirectly, with the early dissemination of the
Benedictine Rule.[43] On the contrary, the German scholar Kassius Hallinger
showed decisively as long ago as 1957 that Gregory himself was no
Benedictine, and that his own monastery of St Andrew in Rome was not
administered in accordance with the rule.[44] The same, needless to remark,
applies to those monks of St Andrew's sent by Gregory as missionaries to
Canterbury in 597, who cannot, therefore, have been the instruments of its
introduction to England – even if the oldest surviving manuscript of the Rule
is written in English uncials of the late seventh century (c 700).[45]

There is no evidence, either, that the Rule was known in Spain in
Gregory's time, though he was personally acquainted with the great Bishop
Isidore of Seville († 636), and even more so with his brother Leander, who
preceded Isidore in that office. We are driven back to the fact that the
Benedictine Rule first makes its appearance in Irish circles associated with

42. Dag Norberg (ed), *S. Gregorii Magni opera: Registrum epistularum libri I-VII, VIII-XIV.*
Corpus Christianorum Series Latina [CCSL], cxl, cxlA (Turnhout, 1982), i, p 285 (Book V.
17); Paul Ewald & Ludwig Hartmann (eds), *Gregorii I papae Registrum epistolarum, libri I-VII,*
VIII-XIV, MGH Epist., i (Hannover, 1897, 1899), i, p 299. The letter was addressed to
Bishop Venantius of Luna (in Etruria); see Prinz, *Frühes Mönchtum*, p 75 and n 168.
43. Robert Markus, *Gregory the Great and his world* (Cambridge, 1997), p 97, has stated: 'It
may well be the case that when in the seventh century the notion of a written Rule gained
ground – along with Benedict's *Rule* (often associated with others, notably that of
Columbanus) – in Gaul and in England, that it was at least in part because of the praise
heaped upon it by Gregory in the *Dialogues*'. In my view, the argument would have more force
if transferred to the period after 750.
44. Kassius Hallinger, 'Papst Gregor der Große und der heilige Benedikt', *Studia Anselmiana*,
42 (1957), pp 231-319, esp p 259 ff. A supposed weakness in Hallinger's case, when he argued
that Gregory did not know the Rule, was countered by Markus, but the citation of the Rule
claimed in evidence against Hallinger is, in fact, in the Commentary on I Kings, now elimi-
nated from the canon of Gregory's writings; see Markus, op. cit., p 69 n 6, and above, footnote n 19.
45. See E.A. Lowe, CLA, ii, No 240, and footnote n 19 above.

Columbanus's monastic foundations in Burgundy and Italy, and those of his followers and disciples. Which prompts me to make an alternative suggestion of my own about the route which it might have travelled.

We know that in the year 628 Pope Honorius I addressed a letter to a group of southern Irish clerics 'exhorting them not to think that their small number, on the farthermost edges of the earth, was wiser than the ancient and modern churches of Christ throughout the world, and not to celebrate a different Easter, contrary to the paschal cycles and synodical decrees of the bishops of the whole world'.[46] The Venerable Bede, who in his famous *Ecclesiastical History* uniquely preserved the text of this letter, remarked that those southern Irish churches had 'long since' on the admonition of the Apostolic See, 'learned to observe Easter in accordance with canonical custom'.

This was the opening salvo in a papal campaign to bring the British and Irish churches into line on this most serious matter of authority. Is it a coincidence that on June 11 in that same year, Pope Honorius also wrote to the abbot of Columbanus' monastery at Bobbio, granting to that house *inter alia* a papal exemption from episcopal control by the Bishop of Tortona? Honorius is known to have been a champion of Gregorian-style organisation.[47] Is it not possible that he sent the community at Bobbio a copy of the Benedictine Rule? The papal privilege granted the monastery in 643 by Pope Theodore I described the monks of Bobbio at that time as living *sub regula sancte memorie Benedicti vel reverentissimi Columbani*[48] (under the rule of Benedict of holy memory and of the most revered Columbanus). It is noteworthy also that the only other pope known to have communicated with the Irish in Ireland around that time, John IV, likewise granted papal privileges of exemption to the Columban house of Luxeuil in 641 and 643.[49] If the

46. 'Misit … Honorius litteras etiam genti Scottorum … sollerter exhortans, ne paucitatem suam in extremis terrae finibus constitutam, sapientiorem antiquis siue modernis, quae per orbem erant, Christi ecclesiis aestimarent; neue contra paschales computos et decreta synodalium totius orbis pontificum aliud pascha celebrarent'; cited by Bede in his *Historia Ecclesiastica gentis Anglorum*, ii. 19; Plummer, *Baedae opera*, i, p 122.
4.7 See Eric John, 'Social and political problems of the early English church' in Joan Thirsk (ed), *Land, church, and people; Essays presented to H. P. R. Finberg* (Reading, 1970), pp 39-63, esp pp 55-56.
48. Carlo Cipolla, *Codice diplomatico del monasterio di san Colombano di Bobbio*, i (Rome, 1918), p 109 f.; cited Prinz, *Frühes Mönchtum*, p 146 n. 130
49. See Eugen Ewig, 'Bemerkungen zu zwei merowingischen Bischofsprivilegien und einem Papstprivileg des 7. Jahrhunderts für merowingische Klöster', in Arno Borst (ed), *Mönchtum, Episkopat und Adel*. Vorträge und Forschungen, xx (Darmstadt, 1974), pp 215-49, esp p 232 ff. The authenticity of the 643 exemption privilege has been thoroughly vindicated by Ewig.

Benedictine Rule first took hold at Bobbio, then what is more natural than that it should have been further disseminated by those monasteries affiliated to Bobbio, namely Luxeuil and its dependencies? The personal links between the abbots of both those houses are amply documented; their links in turn with the Frankish and Burgundian aristocracy are equally well established. Perhaps this was the route whereby the *Regula Benedicti* made its way from Rome to the Irish monasteries in Francia, and the reason why it appears in those foundations always and everywhere in combination with the Rule of Columbanus. I toss this theory up to glitter for a moment in the sunlight, before falling on the dust-heap of idle fancy.

Why did the Benedictine Rule emerge after 800 as the dominant monastic rule in the west? The answer must be, I think, because it was championed by the Carolingians as part of their general campaign to reform the churches in the Frankish kingdoms and in Italy. It may even be possible to identify a particular individual who played a vital part in this process: Paul the Deacon, a Lombard from Friuli, who had trained at the court of Pavia in grammar and theology, and who has been described as the only Carolingian historian of real stature.[50] In 774 he entered the monastery of Monte Cassino and there composed a substantial commentary on the *Regula Benedicti*. His brother was carried off as a prisoner by Frankish armies following Charlemagne's annexation of the Lombard kingdom. Paul composed a poem, which he addressed to Charlemagne, begging forgiveness for his brother and so impressed the Frankish king when he presented it in person that he offered him a position at his palace school in Aachen. The stay that Paul probably imagined would be brief lasted in fact several years, but he eventually returned to Monte Cassino in 787. He maintained his contacts with the Carolingian court, however, and at Charlemagne's request he compiled a homiliary and perhaps also a sacramentary for official use in the Frankish kingdom.

Just as he did in the case of the Dionysio-Hadrianic collection of canon law (in 774), so too Charlemagne and his collaborators may have looked on the *Regula Benedicti* as an appropriate model rule because it was perceived as being the work of Benedict *abbas Romensis*, 'abbot of Rome', an archaic usage which is found in the earliest attestation of the rule in the west, at Altaripa.[51]

50. See J.-M. Wallace-Hadrill, *The Frankish Church* (Oxford, 1983), p 200 ff.

51. Prinz, *Frühes Mönchtum*, p 268. It was precisely this archaic-looking title that convinced Traube of the authenticity of the Altaripa citation. See further Joachim Wollasch, 'Benedictus abbas Romensis. Das römische Element in der frühen benediktinischen Tradition', in N. Kamp & J. Wollasch (eds), *Tradition als historische Kraft* (Berlin & New York, 1982), pp 119-37. In Irish usage, *abbas Romensis* meant the Pope.

Charlemagne wrote to the abbot of Monte Cassino in 787 (that same year in which Paul returned there from Aachen), requesting an authentic copy of the original Rule, just as previously (again through the agency of Paul) he had written to Pope Hadrian requesting a copy of the sacramentary ascribed to Gregory the Great.[52] In their relentless drive for uniformity of practice in every aspect of the religious life, from the design and layout of the standard monastery (reflected in the famous 'Plan of St Gall') to the regulation of its everyday activities, the Carolingians successfully imposed a single monastic rule on the west. The fact that they chose the Benedictine Rule for that purpose was almost certainly an accident.

52. Wallace-Hadrill, *Frankish Church*, pp 212-13.

CHAPTER TWO

Irish Benedictine Monasteries on the Continent

Dagmar Ó Riain-Raedel

'If these mute stones could speak…', we might well know more about the presence of Benedictine monks in twelfth-century Ireland. Cormac's Chapel, which was consecrated in the year 1134 in the presence of its founder, Cormac Mac Carthaig (Mac Carthy), king of Munster, may hold the clue to a better understanding of Irish ecclesiastical affairs at the time. Indeed, from 1101 when, during a synod held there, Muirchertach Ua Briain (O'Brien) donated the Rock of Cashel, ancient seat of the kings of Munster, to the religious of Ireland, the site became inextricably linked with the reforming movement. Ten years after the donation, at the synod of Ráith Bresail in 1111, Cashel was chosen, together with Armagh, as an archiepiscopal see, thus paving the way for a new diocesan structure, which was finalised at the synod of Kells/Mellifont in 1152, when two further archbishoprics, Tuam and Dublin, were added.

Fig 1: Cashel
© Department of the Environment, Heritage and Local Government

It was during the first half of the twelfth century, when Cashel's ecclesiastical pre-eminence was most evident, that Cormac's Chapel was built on the Rock, thus restoring some of the prestige of the ancient seat of the Meic Carthaig, Eoganacht kings of Munster. Cormac's undertaking can truly be regarded as revolutionary; nowhere in Ireland had there been up to then such

PRINCIPAL IRISH CENTRES
IN EUROPE
Columban Foundations
Schottenklöster

a magnificent building. Indeed, it still stands as one of the most intriguing buildings of the Irish Middle Ages.

Yet there are no references in Irish sources to the method of its construction, to where its inspiration came from, nor, indeed, to its purpose. Happily, however, the scarcity of Irish records can be supplemented to a certain degree by written sources compiled at the

Fig 2: Cashel, Cormac's Chapel, Tympanum. ©Department of the Environment, Heritage and Local Government

monastery of Regensburg in Bavaria, the so-called Schottenkloster dedicated to St James. In a thirteenth-century text, the *Libellus de fundacione ecclesie Consecrati Petri* (The book of the foundation of the church consecrated to St Peter), which draws on earlier material, we hear of fund-raising expeditions to Ireland by the abbots of the Irish Benedictine monastery in Regensburg. According to this text, one expedition was led by abbot Dyonisius, also written Dirmicius, some time after 1127, which included two learned Irish noblemen, Isaac and Gervasius, and two others, evidently Germans but allegedly fluent in Irish, Conrad the carpenter, and Enul.[1] Ever since J. Lynch published extracts from this text in his *Cambrensis Eversus* of 1848, from a copy made at Regensburg by the seventeenth-century Irish Jesuit, Stephen White, speculation has been rife as to whether a German *carpentarius* might have helped with the construction of Cormac's Chapel.[2] This theory was expanded upon by Aubrey Gwynn in his contribution on Cashel to the 'Medieval Religious Houses' of Ireland, where he proposed that the delegation had been sent with the purpose of helping in the building of Cormac's Chapel, 'for a new monastery, dedicated to St James …'. Quoting Dom Gerard MacGinty of Glenstal, who thought that a German involvement in the building process would explain its 'Teutonic' character, Gwynn went on to claim that a Benedictine priory dependent on Regensburg was established on the Rock, and that it seemed now 'quite clear that Cormac's Chapel was the chapel of the Benedictine monks.'[3]

1. P. A. Breatnach, *Die Regensburger Schottenlegende - Libellus de fundacione ecclesie Consecrati Petri. Untersuchung und Textausgabe* (Munich, 1977), pp 238-40.
2. J. Lynch, *Cambrensis Eversus* (Dublin, 1850), vol. ii, pp 394-97.
3. Aubrey Gwynn and R. N. Hadcock, *Medieval Religious Houses: Ireland* (London, 1970), pp 104-5 (Hereafter cited as Gwynn & Hadcock, *MRH*).

If such a Schottenkloster ever existed at Cashel, we must assume that it was established there in the course of the expansion of the Schottenklöster during the twelfth century from the motherhouse in Regensburg. It is appropriate, therefore, that consideration first be given here to the early history of the Congregation.

The Irish peregrinatio to the Continent

Long before the foundation of the Schottenklöster, Irish connections with Benedictine monasteries in Germany had been commonplace.[4] All during the centuries of the Irish *peregrinatio* abroad, pilgrims had been in the habit of visiting Benedictine houses. Among those most visited were St Gallen, which traced its beginnings to Columbanus' disciple Gallus, Echternach, which was founded by Willibrord some time after his arrival on the continent from the Irish monastery of Rathmelsigi, or Salzburg, where the Irish bishop Virgilius had administered the diocese from the monastery of St Peter in the latter part of the eighth century. The names of the visiting Irish pilgrims were written into documents preserved in the libraries of several famous abbeys on the continent. Furthermore, Irish manuscripts preserved in the same libraries bear witness to the presence there of Irishmen, who evidently had found employment locally. Although it is probable that some of these pilgrims were professed as Benedictine monks, we have no early information to that effect. Relevant sources first become available in the decades leading up to the end of the first millennium.

The Irish Benedictine monasteries at Cologne

During the tenth and eleventh centuries, in what Leo Weisgerber identified as the third phase of Irish emigration abroad, Irishmen were to be found in a number of Benedictine monasteries in Lotharingia, which then comprised the ecclesiastical provinces of Trier and Cologne. For example, Irish clerics were appointed to the abbacies of Waulsort in the Ardennes, as well as of two episcopal foundations, St Félix (also known as St Clément) and St Symphorien, at Metz.[5] In their latter capacity, they were supported by suc-

---

4. On the Irish *peregrini* abroad, see J. F. Kenney, *The sources for the early history of Ireland. An introduction and guide: I ecclesiastical* (New York, 1929, [reprint Dublin, 1979]); Felim Ó Briain, 'The expansion of Irish Christianity to 1200' in *Irish Historical Studies* 3 (1943), pp 241-266, 4 (1944), pp 131-163; Ludwig Bieler, *Irland, Wegbereiter des Mittelalters* (Olten, 1961) (Engl. translation, *Ireland, harbinger of the Middle Ages*, Oxford, 1966).

5 Leo Weisgerber, 'Eine Irenwelle an Maas, Mosel und Rhein in ottonischer Zeit?' in J. Knobloch and R. Schützeichel (eds), *Leo Weisgerber Rhenania Germano-Celtica* (Bonn, 1969), pp 359-377.

cessive bishops of Metz, who were themselves ardent promoters of the Gorze reform movement then establishing itself in Lotharingia. Within this reform, the Irish played a vital role, and, to a certain degree, maintained a separate identity.[6] Now part of a powerful reform lobby, firmly rooted in the Benedictine rule, the pilgrim Irish received high praise for their asceticism, holy lives, and organisational skills.[7] Moreover, since their episcopal patrons tended to be well connected to the ruling families of Lotharingia, the Irish found themselves assigned a role in the promotion of the newly-emerging Ottonian dynasty. As in the preceding centuries, when Irishmen had occupied important positions at the schools and courts of Carolingian kings and emperors,[8] they now became involved in the *Kirchenpolitik* of Otto the Great. Moreover, in the Rhineland they established a base in *Colonia sacra* (Holy Cologne) in the late tenth century which was to last for more than a hundred years.[9]

Fig 3: Silhouette of Cologne, showing Groß St Martin (left) and cathedral.

6. This had been the case at the eighth-century *monasterium Scotorum* at Honau, near Straßburg; I. Eberl, 'Das Iren-Kloster Honau und seine Regel' in H. Löwe (ed.), *Die Iren und Europe im früheren Mittelalter* (2 vols, Stuttgart, 1982), pp 219-38.
7. J. M. Picard, 'The cult of Columba in Lotharingia (9th-11th centuries): the manuscript evidence' in J. Carey, M. Herbert, P. Ó Riain (eds), *Studies in Irish hagiography: saints and scholars* (Dublin, 2001), pp 221-36, at p 230. See also David Dumville, 'St Cathróe of Metz and the hagiography of exoticism' in ibid., pp 172-88; J. Semmler, 'Iren in der lothringischen Klosterreform' in H. Löwe (ed.), *Die Iren und Europa im früheren Mittelalter* (Stuttgart, 1982), pp 941-57.
8. In the middle part of the eighth century, Virgilius of Salzburg may have been instrumental in the introduction of the anointing ceremony of Pippin as king of the Franks, while in the early ninth century, Dicuil composed treatises on astronomy and geography (*Liber de mensura orbis terrae*) for the emperor, Louis the Pious; M. Enright, *Iona, Tara and Soissons: the origin of the royal anointing ritual* (Berlin / New York, 1985); Kenney, *Sources,* pp 546-8.
9. Semmler, 'Iren in der lothringischen Klosterreform', pp 941-957; Dumville, 'Cathróe of Metz', pp 172-188.

The presence of Irish monks in Cologne, then part of Lower Lotharingia, where they controlled the Benedictine abbey of Groß St Martin from c 975 to the latter part of the eleventh century, and that of St Pantaleon from 1019 to 1042, may have been initially due to the influence of their compatriots in Upper Lotharingia.[10] We can of course discount the claim of the Regensburg *Libellus* that Charlemagne had constructed a monastery dedicated to St Martin in Cologne for Irish monks.[11] Nevertheless, imperial patronage may well have been a deciding factor at Cologne, where the very influential Archbishop Bruno († 965), brother of Emperor Otto I, had had, according to his Life, the Irishman Israel amongst his teachers.[12] Bishop Israel, who was closely connected with Upper Lotharingia, and, especially with Trier, where he seems to have ended his days, enjoyed a high reputation for scholarship. The sizable number of still extant works attributed to Israel[13] prompted Carl Selmer to suggest that he may have been the author of the *Navigatio Brendani* (The Voyage of Brendan), which is first attested in Lotharingian manuscripts, but this theory has not received univocal support.[14] Nevertheless, it may have been due to Israel's influence that, within a decade of Bruno's

---

10. J. H. Kessel, *Antiquitates S. Martini maioris Coloniensis* (Cologne, 1862); P. Opladen, *Groß St. Martin. Geschichte einer stadtkölnischen Abtei* (Düsseldorf, 1854); H. J. Kracht, *Geschichte der Benediktinerabtei St. Pantaleon in Köln 965-1250* (Siegburg, 1975).

11. According to the *Libellus*, Charlemagne had already constructed the monastery of Burscheid for them, next to his headquarters in Aachen: *et alios duxit secum versus Coloniam et ibi claustrum edificavit eis in honore sancti Martini et ibi constituit reliquos fratres in honore debito*; Breatnach, *Libellus*, p 191.

12. On Bruno see W. Neuss, *Das Bistum Köln von den Anfängen bis zum Ende des 12. Jahrhunderts* (2nd ed., Cologne, 1972), pp 102-3; H. Müller, 'Die Kölner Erzbischöfe von Bruno I. bis Hermann II. (953-1056)' in A. von Euw and P. Schreiner (eds), *Kaiserin Theophanu: Begegnung des Ostens und Westens um die Wende des ersten Jahrtausends* (Cologne, 1991), vol i, pp 15-32; O. Engels, 'Ruotgers Vita Brunonis' ibid, pp 33-46; L. Vones, 'Erzbischof Brun von Köln und seine 'Schule'. Einige kritische Betrachtungen' in H. Vollrath and S. Weinfurter (eds), *Köln: Stadt und Bistum in Kirche und Reich des Mittelalters. Festschrift für Odilo Engels zum 65. Geburtstag* (Kölner Historische Abhandlungen 39) (Cologne, 1993), pp 125-38.

13. On the question of Israel's nationality, see C. Jeudy, 'Israël le grammairien et la tradition manuscrite du commentaire de Remi d'Auxerre à l' <Ars minor > de Donat' in *Studi Medievali* 18 (1977), pp 185-205. Israel is called 'scotigena' in Ruotger's Life of Bruno: *Vita Brunonis*, Monumenta Germaniae Historica [MGH] Scriptores [SS] iv, pp 252-75 and I. Schmale-Ott, *Ruotgers Lebensbeschreibung des Erzbischofs Bruno*, Monumenta Germaniae Historica [MGH] Scriptores Rerum Germanicarum [SRG] ns [nova series] 10 (Weimar 1951): p 8; On Israel's connection with Trier see R. Reiche, 'Iren in Trier', *Rheinische Vierteljahresblätter* 40 (1976), pp 1-17.

14. Carl Selmer, 'Israel, ein unbekannter Schotte des 10. Jahrhunderts'in *Studien und Mitteilungen zur Geschichte des Benediktinerordens* (henceforth cited as *StudMittOSB*) 62 (1949-1950), pp 69-86; idem, 'Die Herkunft und Frühgeschichte der Nauigatio Sancti

death, Irish monks were introduced into his newly-founded monastery of Groß St Martin.[15] Plans to this effect may already have been in place before Bruno's death which were then finalised by his successor Everger who, according to the chronicler Marianus Scottus († 1082/3), endowed the Irish with the monastery *in sempiternum* (in perpetuity).[16] Marianus also provides a list of the abbots of the monastery, beginning at 975 with Mimborinus and continuing until the later part of the eleventh century. Abbot Elias, who succeeded in 1019, also held the abbacy of the monastery of St Pantaleon, the burial place of Archbishop Bruno and of his

Fig 4: Cologne, St Pantaleon

Byzantine sister-in-law, Theophanu, wife of Otto. Elias is one of the few Irish emigrés of this period to be mentioned in Irish sources, which identify him as Ailill of Mucknoe in Co Monaghan. This man is described in the *Annals of the Four Masters* for 1042 as the head of the monks of the Gaeidhil in Cologne. In addition, the *Annals of Ulster* record the deaths in Cologne of Donnchad, abbot of Dunshaughlin and brother of the king of Southern

Brendani' in *StudMitt OSB* 67 (1956), pp 5-17; Carl Selmer, *Navigatio Sancti Brendani Abbatis from early Latin manuscripts* (Notre Dame 1959, [repr. Dublin 1989]), pp xxviii-xxxi. For different views see G. Orlandi, *Navigatio sancti Brendani* (Milan, 1969), pp 131-60, David Dumville, 'Two approaches to the dating of < Nauigatio Sancti Brendani>' in *Studi Medievali* XXIX, 1 (1988), pp 87-102 and Michael Lapidge, 'Israel the Grammarian in Anglo-Saxon England' in H. J. Westra (ed.), *From Athens to Chartres: Neoplatonism and Medieval thought: studies in honour of Edouard Jeauneau* (Leiden, 1992), pp 97-114.

15. On the two monasteries see R. Haacke, *Die Benediktinerklöster in Nordrhein-Westfalen* (Germania Benedictina, vol viii) (St Ottilien, 1980), pp 376-89, 390-405; J. H. Kessel, *Antiquitates S. Martini maioris Coloniensis* (Köln, 1862); P. Opladen, *Groß St. Martin. Geschichte einer stadtkölnischen Abtei* (Düsseldorf, 1854); H. J. Kracht, *Geschichte der Benediktinerabtei St. Pantaleon zu Köln 965-1250* (Siegburg, 1975); C. Koch, *Kölns Romanische Kirchen. Architektur und Liturgie im Hochmittelalter* (Regensburg, 2000), pp 81-7; H. Flachenecker, *Schottenklöster Irische Benediktinerkonvente im hochmittelalterlichen Deutschland* (QFGG, NF 18) (Paderborn-Munich-Vienna-Zurich, 1995), pp 48-9.

16. G. Waitz (ed), *Mariani Scotti Chronicon*, MGH SS v (1844), pp 481-564. Reference at p 555.

Brega in 1027, and of Braen, king of Leinster, in 1052. It thus seems that the Cologne monasteries had special affiliations to the general area of Leinster and Brega. This evidence can be refined further.

Raghnall Ó Floinn has recently shown that an impressive number of the relics kept in Dublin's Christ Church Cathedral were brought from Cologne at the beginning of the eleventh century. These relics are enumerated in a list that now forms part of a mid-thirteenth century martyrology in Trinity College Dublin MS 576.[17] Ó Floinn has argued that the relics were acquired by Dúnán (Donatus), first bishop of Dublin († 1074), with a view to using them as foundation relics for his new cathedral.[18] The acquisition appears to have been made possible by the inclusion of Cologne in the itinerary of a pilgrimage to Rome undertaken in 1028 by Sitriuc, king of Dublin, in the company of a large retinue, including Flannacán Ua Cellaig, king of Brega. Sitriuc's pilgrimage may have been inspired by that of his English counterpart Cnut two years earlier, who is known to have visited Cologne on the way.[19] Considering the nature of the relics, five of bishops, three of apostles, one of a pope and one of a king, these were probably chosen deliberately to 'emphasise apostolic succession and therewith the legitimacy of the episcopacy of Dublin's first bishop'. The Cologne background of the relics prompted Ó Floinn to wonder whether Dúnán had, in fact, previously been a monk at the monastery of Groß St Martin, a suggestion made all the more plausible by the documented Leinster and Brega associations of the abbacy of Elias.

The close association with Cologne cathedral is shown particularly in the personal friendship which bound Elias with Archbishop Heribert, founder of the Benedictine monastery of Deutz, situated directly across the Rhine from Groß St Martin.[20] Heribert, who had summoned the Irish abbot to his deathbed, was venerated as a saint soon after his death in 1021, which would

17. A further relic list is included in the late fifteenth-century 'Book of Obits' which forms part of the same manuscript; J. C. Crosthwaite, (ed) and J. H. Todd (intr), *The Book of Obits and Martyrology of the Cathedral Church of the Holy Trinity, commonly called Christ Church, Dublin* (Dublin, 1844). For a discussion of the martyrology relic list see R. Ó Floinn, 'The foundation relics of Christ Church Cathedral' in D. Bracken, J. Hawkes, P. Helmuth, D. Ó Riain-Raedel (eds), *Peregrinatio – pilgrimage in the Medieval World* (forthcoming).
18. For Dúnán see Aubrey Gwynn, 'The first bishops of Dublin' in Howard Clarke (ed), *Medieval Dublin: the living city*' (Dublin, 1990), pp 37-61: 37-40; H. B. Clarke, 'Conversion, Church and Cathedral: the diocese of Dublin to 1152' in J. Kelly and D. Keogh (eds), *History of the Catholic diocese of Dublin* (Dublin, 2000), pp 19-50: 38-40.
19. M. Hare, 'Cnut and Lotharingia: two notes' in *Anglo-Saxon England*, 29 (2000), pp 261-78.
20. H. Müller, *Heribert, Kanzler Ottos III und Erzbischof von Köln* (Cologne, 1977), pp 17-8, 80-1, 246-52.

explain why one of the Christ Church relics is described as *De uestimento Herberti, Coloniensis episcopi* (from a vestment of Heribert, bishop of Cologne). Elias was, therefore, a significant figure in the Cologne of his time, which is of course borne out by his selection as abbot of St Pantaleon, an event that left him holding both abbacies simultaneously. St Pantaleon, burial place of Bruno and Theophanu, held a special place of reverence within a city which could justifiably call itself *Colonia sacra*. Given his standing in Cologne, it seems plausible enough that he would have been given access to the riches of the cathedral treasury, and presented with relics destined to become the foundation relics of Christ Church Cathedral in Dublin.

The martyrology containing the Christ Church relic list had also attracted the attention of Pádraig Ó Riain, who studied the text in the course of his research into the Irish martyrological tradition.[21] He has shown that the primary layer of entries in the text, which is a recension of the ninth-century martyrology of Ado of Vienne, received a large number of additions in Cologne in the early eleventh century. Furthermore, he identified an even earlier set of additions made in the Upper Lotharingian city of Metz, consisting mainly of bishops' feasts. As has been seen above, Metz too had a strong Irish presence, and about the year 1000 the bulk of the martyria of the local bishops were kept within the city's two Irish monasteries, St Clément and St Symphorien. It would seem, therefore, that Irish connections played a role in the transmission of the source text of the martyrology from Metz to Cologne, along a route which had previously been travelled by one of the most important relics acquired for Cologne Cathedral, that of the Staff of St Peter. Originally part of the Trier Cathedral treasure, this was kept at Metz until brought to Cologne by Archbishop Bruno, where it was later joined by the chains of St Peter which had been secured in Rome. These two relics in particular testify to Bruno's efforts to transform Cologne into a second Rome. Bruno's passion for collecting relics was remarked on by his biographer Ruotger who provides a list of gifts made by the archbishop to various Cologne churches. The Christ Church document supplies a new witness for the cults of the saints which Bruno had brought to Cologne, some of which – such as parts of the staff and chains of St Peter – found later their way to Dublin. Ó Floinn drew attention to the preamble to the Christ Church list

---

21. Pádraig Ó Riain, 'Dublin's oldest book? A list of saints 'made in Germany' in Seán Duffy (ed), *Medieval Dublin V* (Dublin 2004); idem, 'Das Martyrologium der Kölner Klöster Groß St Martin und St Pantaleon und St Symphorian zu Metz aus dem frühen 11. Jahrhundert: Textzeugen aus Irland und Dänemark' in *Archiv für Liturgiewissenschaft* (2005, forthcoming); idem, *The Irish martyrological tradition* (forthcoming).

which recorded the translation of the relics from the casket where they had been placed by Dúnán into a new shrine by his successor Gregory (Gréne, † 1162), fifth bishop and first archbishop of Dublin.[22] The new-found interest of Gréne in the relics indicates a recent upsurge in liturgy in the second part of the twelfth century, and this is corroborated by a spate of new entries in the martyrology. Since no entries had been previously added after the Cologne source had come to Dublin, the martyrology seems to have been considered a relic in its own right. Moreover, since the translation of the relics seems to have taken place in the aftermath of the elevation of Dublin to an archiepiscopal see at the Synod of Kells/Mellifont in 1152, the specific character of both relics and martyrology may have been perceived as being particularly relevant to the time. The Synod of Kells had underlined the introduction of a diocesan system which put the Irish church firmly under the control of the papacy. The symbols of St Peter, in conjunction with the other relics originating in the 'second Rome' which Cologne claimed to be, would certainly have conveyed a strong message.

The outline of the history of the Cologne foundations was, as we have seen, chronicled by Marianus Scotus, who at one stage had been a member of the community there.[23] Marianus, alias Máelbrigte, a monk of the monastery of Bangor in Co Down, had been sent into exile by his abbot for what he himself considered to be a minor misdemeanour. Arriving at Cologne in 1052, he spent two years there before travelling on to Fulda and Würzburg, where he visited the grave of his compatriot Killian. From there he went on to end his days in the year 1082/3 as an *inclusus* in the monastery dedicated to St Martin at Mainz. His chronicle, one of the first universal histories, is still extant, partly in autograph form, in the Vatican Library. In line with the Irish annalistic tradition, Marianus chronicled contemporary events, adding episodes from his own life. Unfortunately, while he provided some of the succession dates of the abbots of Groß St Martin, he did not add any details about his own sojourn there. Nevertheless, the visit to Cologne equipped him with the necessary means to move on to other German Benedictine houses, travelling from monastery to monastery, with little heed to the concept of *stabilitas*. His composition of a world chronicle, while walled up in a cell both at Fulda and at Mainz, shows us that Irishmen, for-

22. *Reliquie sanctorum, que a tempore Donati, primi Dublinie ciuitatis episcopi, usque ad tempus Gregorii eiusdem urbis episcopi, in quadam capsa latuerunt, in uno cum eadem capsa posite sunt scrinio, scilicet …*, Ó Floinn, 'Foundation relics'.
23. B. Mac Carthaigh, *The Codex Palatino-Vaticanus* 830 (Royal Irish Academy, Todd Lectures Sr. III) (Dublin, 1892); MGH SS v (1884), pp 481-564; Kenney, *Sources*, pp 614-6.

merly noted for their learning and manuscript-writing abilities, still had little difficulty in procuring hospitality and employment wherever they chose to travel.

The establishment of the 'Schottenklöster'

The early history of the Schottenklöster is reflected in the career of another Marianus Scotus, this time bearing the native name of Muiredach mac Robartaig (Mac Groarty).[24] Of an Ulster family who were hereditary keepers of the *Cathach*, Ireland's oldest surviving manuscript, Muiredach arrived on the continent, together with a number of companions, named Johannes, Clemens and Candidus, around the year 1068.[25] According to the late twelfth-century account of his life, the *Vita Mariani*, and according to the *Libellus de fundacione*, this group, while on pilgrimage to Rome, first stopped over at the monastery of Burscheid near Aachen, and then at the city of Bamberg in Franconia. Here they were encouraged by Bishop Otto (1102-1139), who admired their ascetic and prayerful life, to take on monastic life under the Benedictine rule. It was at Bamberg, in the Benedictine abbey dedicated to St Michael, that they were instructed both in German and in the Benedictine

24. On Muiredach Mac Robartaig see William Reeves, 'Marianus Scotus of Ratisbon' in *Proceedings of the Royal Irish Academy* 1, Ser. 7 (1860), pp 290-301 and Mark Dilworth, 'Marianus Scotus: scribe and monastic founder' in *Scottish Gaelic Studies,* 10 (1965), pp 125-48. His Life has been edited in *Acta Sanctorum [AASS] Februarius tomus ii* (repr. Bruxelles, 1966) and in P. Hauck, *Die Vita Mariani. Überlieferung und Text,* Magisterarbeit in der Philosophischen Fakultät III (Geschichte, Gesellschaft und Geographie) der Universität Regensburg (Regensburg, n.d.). I wish to thank Petra Hauck for providing me with a copy. The history of the Schottenklöster has been dealt with by W. Wattenbach, 'Die Congregation der Schottenklöster in Deutschland' in *Zeitschrift für christl. Archaeologie und Kunst* 1 (1856), pp. 21-30, 49-58; translated and annotated by William Reeves, 'The Irish monasteries in Germany' in *The Ulster Journal of Archaeology* 7 (1859), pp 227-47, 295-314; D. A. Binchy, *Die irischen Klöster in Regensburg* (Ph.D. dissertation, Munich, 1923); idem, 'The Irish Benedictine congregation in Medieval Germany' in *Studies* 18 (1929), pp 194-210; Aubrey Gwynn, 'Ireland and Würzburg in the Middle Ages' in *Irish Ecclesiastical Record* 78 (1953), pp 401-11; idem, 'Some notes on the history of the Irish Scottish Benedictine monasteries in Germany' in *The Innes Review* 5 (1954), pp 5-27; idem, 'The continuity of the Irish tradition at Würzburg' in *Herbipolis Iubilans. Würzburger Diözesangeschichtsblätter* 14/15 (1952), pp 37-82; P. Mai, 'Das Schottenkloster St Jakob zu Regensburg im Wandel der Zeiten' in idem (ed.), *100 Jahre Priesterseminar in St. Jakob zu Regensburg* (Regensburg, 1972), pp 5-36. L. Hammermayer, 'Die irischen Benediktiner-"Schottenklöster" in Deutschland und ihr institutioneller Zusammenschluss vom 12.-16. Jahrhundert' in *StudMitt OSB* 87 (1976), pp 249-338; Breatnach, *Libellus;* idem, 'The origins of the Irish monastic tradition at Ratisbon (Regensburg)' in *Celtica* xiii (1980), pp 58-77. The most recent, and comprehensive, study is H. Flachenecker, *Schottenklöster.*

25. The Bavarian chronicler Aventinus († 1534) transcribed the colophon of an autograph copy containing a commentary on the psalms, written by Marianus and preserved in the

rule. The phrase, *a sancto Abbate S. Michaelis praefatum habitum S. Benedicti susceperunt* (They received from the holy abbot of St Michael the said habit of St Benedict), as the *vita* describes it, may, in fact, indicate that the author viewed this complete subjugation under an abbot and a rule as a new form of *peregrinatio*, a complete relinquishment of all ties to family and homeland.[26] The author of the *Vita Mariani*, writing more than a century after the event and, following him, the author of the *Libellus*, depart here from the facts. Although it is quite feasible that Marianus would have stopped over at Bamberg, lying, as it does, en route to Regensburg, we have no corroborative evidence from Bamberg itself. More importantly, Otto did not succeed to the bishopric until 1102, some thirty years after Marianus' supposed visit there. Otto, however, became greatly involved in the establishment of Benedictine monasteries within the diocese of Regensburg, amongst them those at Biburg and Prüfening. Both of these monasteries had close connections with the Irish at Regensburg, Biburg constituting one of the members of a *Gebetsverbrüderung*, or union of prayer, which also included the monastery of St George in Prüfening in the vicinity of Regensburg. Home to a powerful cult of Otto, which commenced with the composition of his Life c 1140-6 and culminated in his beatification in 1189, Prüfening's famous scriptorium co-operated with that of the Schottenklöster and other Regensburg monasteries in the compilation of the *Magnum Legendarium Austriacum*, a legendary which contains some 580 saints' Lives, including a sizeable number of Irish ones. Moreover, Prüfening may also have been influential in the architectural style of St James.[27] Therefore it is understandable that the Irish historiographers at Regensburg should have wanted to establish a connection between

Benedictine convent of Niedermünster at Regensburg. In this, Marianus described the year 1074 as the seventh year of his pilgrimage. The codex is not known to have survived: J. Riezler (ed.), *Johannes Turmair's genannt Aventinus Sämmtliche Werke* (6 vols, Munich, 1884), vol 5, p 11; Hauck, *Vita Mariani*, pp 64-5. The *vita* mentions two companions only, Johannes and Candidus, while the *Libellus* counts six: Machantinus, Murchertachus, Clemens, Gervasius, Ysaac and Donatus (Breatnach, *Libellus*, p 201). Most of these are commemorated in the necrology, but they may have arrived at Regensburg after the death of Marianus. The testimony of the *vita* seems reliable; Candidus is said to have died on pilgrimage to Jerusalem and Johannes became an *inclusus* at the abbey of Göttweig in Austria. He is documented in the *vita* of the monastery's founder, Altmannus: W. Wattenbach (ed), *Vita Altmanni*, MGH SS xii (Hannover, 1856), pp 240-1; Breatnach, *Libellus*, p 49; Flachenecker, *Schottenklöster*, pp 69-76. Gervasius and Ysaac may have been part of the first fund-raising delegation to Ireland.

26. Hauck, *Die Vita Mariani*, p 99; *AASS Februarius tomus ii*, pp 361-72. Reference at p 366. This observation has been made by Flachenecker, *Schottenklöster*, pp 60-1.

27. Dagmar Ó Riain-Raedel, 'Das Nekrolog der irischen Schottenklöster. Edition der Handschrift Vat. lat. 10 100 mit einer Untersuchung der hagiographischen und liturgischen Handschriften der Schottenklöster' in *Beiträge zur Geschichte des Bistums Regensburg* 26

the beginnings of their foundation and Bishop Otto.[28] In due course, Marianus and his companions decided to resume their pilgrimage to Regensburg in order to pray at the tombs of the allegedly Irish saints Erhard and Albert.[29] Here they were persuaded to remain after receiving an offer of employment as scribes from the abbesses of the two royal convents of the Ober- and Niedermünster, where they lived as *inclusi*.[30] According to tradition, an Irish *inclusus* of the name Muirchertach (also Mercherdach) had already lived at the Obermünster and it was he who persuaded Marianus to remain in Regensburg.[31] In return for the hospitality of the abbess of Obermünster, *reverenda matre peregrinorum* (the reverend mother of pilgrims), Marianus busied himself with the production of manuscripts.[32]

In 1075, Marianus and his companions were presented by the abbess Willa of Obermünster with a small church called Weihsanktpeter and some adjoin-

---

(Regensburg, 1992), pp 1-119; eadem, 'The travels of Irish manuscripts: from the Continent to Ireland', pp 52-67. On Prüfening see: A. Kern, 'Magnum Legendarium Austriacum' in *Die österreichische Nationalbibliothek: Festschrift für Josef Bick* (Vienna, 1948), pp 429-34; H-G. Schmitz, *Kloster Prüfening im 12. Jahrhundert* (Munich, 1975); The twelfth-century Prüfening codex (Munich, Bayerische Staatsbibliothek clm 13080) of a part-autograph copy of patristic texts by Marianus (Scottish National Library, Rat. 1) shows that manuscripts were exchanged between the two abbeys. The latter codex was brought to Fort Augustus in Scotland when the Scots, who had taken over the Schottenkloster in the early sixteenth century, left in 1862; A. Forbes, 'Account of a manuscript of the eleventh century by Marianus of Ratisbon' in *Proceedings of the Royal Society of Antiquaries of Scotland* 6 (1864/5), pp 33-41; Hauck, *Die Vita Mariani*, p 64. The many glosses have been edited by Mark Dilworth, 'Marianus Scotus: scribe and monastic founder', pp 125-48.

28. In addition, the association with Otto's reformed foundation Prüfening near Regensburg, can be traced in the literature and architecture of the Schottenkloster. Nevertheless, as the necrology shows, the Schottenkloster also maintained close links with the conservative monastery of St Emmeram in Regensburg, which also accepted the Hirsau convention in 1143. Regensburg's involvement in the reform and its stand in the Investiture controversy is discussed by C. Märtl, 'Regensburg in den geistigen Auseinandersetzungen des Investiturstreits' in *Deutsches Archiv* 42 (1986), pp 145-91.

29. Breatnach, *Libellus,* p 202. Neither Bamberg nor Regensburg lay on the customary route to Rome.

30. On the *inclusi* see O. Doerr, *Das Institut der Inklusen in Süddeutschland* (Münster, 1934).

31. Muirchertach (Mercherdach) is known only from the *Vita Mariani*. He may well have been one of the 'companions' of Marianus, mentioned by the author of the *Libellus*. His obits are given both in the necrology of the Obermünster: F. L. Baumann (ed.), *MGH Necrologia Germaniae* 3: Dioceses Brixinensis, Frisingensis, Ratisbonensis (Berlin, 1995), p 342, and the Schottenkloster necrology: 3 August, Murchertachus inclusus monacus; Ó Riain-Raedel, 'Das Nekrolog', p 70; Flachenecker, *Schottenklöster*, pp 72-4. His thirteenth-century epitaph, which describes him as a pilgrim, is still extant. It may have formed part of a chapel dedicated to him at the spot where his *inclusorium* at Obermünster had stood; H. Graf von Walderdorff, 'St Mercherdach und St Marian und die Anfänge der Schottenklöster zu Regensburg' in *Verhandlungen des historischen Vereins der Oberpfalz* 34 (1879), pp 187-232.

32. Hauck, *Die Vita Mariani*, p 100.

ing property.[33] The date is confirmed by a marginal entry in a codex written by Marianus, now in Scotland, and also in a privilege issued by Henry IV in 1089.[34] The descriptions of the *Vita* and the *Libellus* differ in regard to the early years of the pilgrims in Regensburg. The former source claims that Marianus was the first abbot, followed by seven others, but since Weihsanktpeter was dependent on Obermünster, it could not have had abbots, only priors. The *Libellus* paints a different picture, describing how the monks lived as *inclusi*, in cells surrounding the church. Not long after the move to Weihsanktpeter, Marianus died; the last entry by him in his codex is dated to 13 July 1080. The necrology of the congregation dates his death to 23 April, presumably of the following year, 1081.

The monastery of St James at Regensburg

It soon became necessary to construct a new monastery, dedicated to the patron of all pilgrims, St James.[35] During his sojourn at Regensburg in 1089/90, Henry IV is known to have taken the community of Weihsanktpeter under his protection, but contemporary letters by Irish monks to the king of Bohemia, Wratislaw II, already spoke of the *fraternitas sub levi iugo Christi infra ecclesiam sancti Iacobi militans* (the brotherhood fighting under the light yoke of Christ, within the church of St James). In these letters, the

33. The *Vita Mariani* gives the name of the Obermünster abbess as Hemma, probably, in an attempt to project the Irish presence at Regensburg further into the past and to associate the monks with influential persons. The name is reminiscent of Queen Hemma († 876), wife of Louis the German, whose cult was cultivated at Regensburg during the twelfth century: F. Fuchs, 'Das Grab der Königin Hemma († 876) zu Emmeram in Regensburg' in F. Karg (ed), *Regensburg and Ostbayern. Max Piendl zum Gedächtnis* (Kallmünz, 1991), pp 1-12. The charters have been catalogued by G. A. Renz, 'Beiträge zur Geschichte der Schottenabtei St Jakob und des Priorates Weih St Peter (OSB) in Regensburg' in *StudMitt OSB* 16 (1895), pp.64-84, 250-259, 418-425, 574-581; 17 (1896), pp 29-40, 229-239, 416-426, 629-639; 18 (1897), pp 79-86, 263-274. Renz's transcripts do not contain some 92 documents removed by Bishop James Gillis to Fort Augustus in Scotland in 1848, and now, for the most part, deposited in the Scottish Catholic Archives in Edinburgh. These are in two sections, SK 1 (Monastic documents 1177-1509) and SK 2 (Miscellaneous documents). Some transcripts can be consulted in Th. Ried, *Historische Nachrichten von dem im Jahre 1552 demolierten Schotten-Kloster Weyh Sanct Peter zu Regensburg aus Archival-Urkunden verfaßt von Thomas Ried* (Regensburg, 1813).
34. Edinburgh, Scottish National Library Rat. 1, fol. 141r: *Anno Domini millesimo octogesimo tertio me autem peregrinationis pene septimo et huis habitationis ab Scottis octavo, regnante quarto Henrico. Miseri Iohannis requiescat in pace amen.* 1083 was the eighth year of the Irish presence at Weihsanktpeter. It is not certain whether the scribe was identical with the inclusus of Göttweig.
35. The *Libellus* claims that pilgrims who had left Ireland to evangelise the whole world heard about the fame of Weihsanktpeter and that some seventy of them travelled to Regensburg from Africa, Europe and Asia: Breatnach, *Libellus*, p 235.

Ratispone peregrini assured the Bohemian king of their intercession in the form of perennial prayer, fasting and alms-giving, while, at the same time, asking for a contribution towards their impoverished community.[36]

Fig 5: Regensburg, St James, northern elevation. *Photograph Diarmuid Ó Riain*

It is quite astonishing to observe how these Irish Benedictines were already successfully integrated into their surroundings within some two decades of their arrival at Regensburg. The *Vita Mariani* and the *Libellus*, both of which draw on written material, elaborate on these early years of the congregation, by naming the benefactors and donors who contributed to the purchase of the site, and by stressing the enthusiastic co-operation of the Regenburg citizens. However, these texts are also careful to point out that the community itself provided towards the costs. For example, a brother Mauritius, who was dispatched to Kiev in the company of Regensburg merchants, returned richly endowed. In addition, successful fund-raising delegations were sent to Ireland. Although both texts date to a much later period, *Vita* and *Libellus* are at pains to portray a comprehensive picture of the circumstances of the foundation. Moreover, much of what they have to say can be verified from privileges that still survive or are known from later copies. These show that the monastery in Regensburg enjoyed the protection of kings, emperors and popes, and that it was also supported by local bishops, aristocracy and burghers. For example, the 1112 charter provided by Henry V, which refers to a church named after St James, includes a list of benefactors in addition to guarantees concerning the monastery's exemption from all secular interference. Similarly, a no longer extant privilege by Pope Calixtus (1119-1124), known from the confirmation of his successors, placed the community under the protection of the Holy See. All protectors were gratefully remembered in the liturgical documents of

---

36. C. Erdmann and N. Fickermann, *Briefsammlungen der Zeit Heinrichs IV.* (MGH Briefe der deutschen Kaiserzeit 5) (Weimar, 1950 [repr Munich, 1977]), pp 392-5.

the monastery.[37] Clearly, the spiritual care of the monastery's benefactors, and also of those with whom its community had formed a union of prayer, was deemed to be paramount in importance. Manifest also in these documents is the community's concern for the surrounding faithful, as well as for the wider *familia sancti Jacobi* (household of St James). For example, a parish church, dedicated to St Nicholas, is recorded as having served the local community.[38]

Work on the construction of the Regensburg church, already perhaps begun by 1089/90, appears to have been concluded by 1111, when it was dedicated to St James and St Gertrude.[39] Following a further consecration in the year 1120,[40] St James became the mother-house for a series of new foundations throughout southern Germany. Expansion started in the 1130s under the abbacy of Christianus Mac Carthaig who, as his name suggests, was a member of the royal family of Desmond and probably a kinsman of Cormac's.[41] By this stage, the composition of the personnel of the Schottenklöster had changed from an initial Ulster background to a near-exclusive Munster one, a development which is also noted in the *Vita Mariani*.[42] Monks from Munster continued to play a major part in the activities of the houses during the abbacy at Regensburg of Gregorius (c 1153/56-

37. Many benefactors are remembered in a separate necrology, styled *Tentamen primum Necrologii Monastici seu libri mortuorum confratrum etc. complectentis, inceptum 1722.* Unusually for a necrology, this document also enters the years of death of each person, most of which are now unverifiable. Nevertheless, it contains all of the names of the 1112 charter. The manuscript is in the Diocesan Archives at Regensburg, without signature. On these and other benefactors see also Flachenecker, *Schottenklöster*, pp 88-91, 98-109.

38. The church or chapel of St Nicholas was situated on the north side of the St James and functioned as a parish church and burial place for the extended monastic family. The building was demolished in 1560; Flachenecker, *Schottenklöster*, pp 110-1.

39. The *Tentamen primum* refers to a consecration of the monastery already in 1111: *Hartwicus Episcopus Ratisbonensis, qui plura beneficia nobis praestitit et anno 1111 nostrum templum in honorem S. Jacobi apostoli et S. Gertrudis virginis suis sumptibus consecravit.* The entry is for 30 November, with the year 1125 added in the margin. Bishop Hartwig of Regensburg, who died in 1126, is commemorated in the necrology at 2 March.

40. The historiographer, Andreas von Regensburg, recorded the following: *Anno domini 1120 consecratum est monasterium S. Iacobi Ratispone a venerabili Hartwico*; G. Leidinger (ed.), *Andreas von Regensburg, Chronica pontificum et imperatorum Romanorum* (Munich, 1903, [repr. 1969]), p 55.

41. *Tunc fratres habito tractatu de modo eleccionis, invocata sancti spiritus gracia unanimiter velut ex uno ore elegerunt abbatem nomine Christianum, nobilem virum quoad examen humanum, Makicarthige, licet in genere valde nobilis nobilior moribus et religione...*: Breatnach, *Libellus*, p 254. According to the *Vita Mariani*, Christianus received the abbacy in person from Pope Innocent II (1130-1143) at Rome, a claim which cannot be substantiated in any papal documents; Hauck, *Die Vita Mariani*, pp 110-11.

42. Hauck, *Die Vita Mariani*, p 106.

1185/94) who proved a worthy successor to Christianus. It was during his incumbency that a collection of Irish, and mainly Munster, saints' Lives found its way into the voluminous *Magnum Legendarium Austriacum*. Besides a Life of the founder, Marianus, this collection contains a Life of St Patrick in fragmentary form, composed by the same author. This man was also responsible for the refashioning of the Lives of two County Clare saints, Flannán of Killaloe and Mochuille of Tulla.[43] Significantly, the portrayal of kingship in these texts, as reflected, for example, by the 'sainting' of Flannán's father, Tairdelbach, royal ancestor of the Uí Bhriain, owes much to fashions then current in German treatments of the subject. The immediate inspiration may have been the canonisation in 1165 of Charlemagne, the alleged founder of Weihsanktpeter. The decision to introduce saints into the Dál Cais line of kings could have been taken at a meeting thought to have taken place between abbot Gregorius and Muirchertach Ua Briain at Lismore in 1166.[44] Gregorius appears to have been a partisan of the Uí Bhriain, much in the same way as his predecessor, Christianus, had championed the Meic Carthaig. Not surprisingly, therefore, a significant proportion of the clerical dignitaries commemorated in the late twelfth-century entries of the necrology concern natives of the northern part of Munster. Before his arrival in Germany, and subsequent profession as a Benedictine, Gregorius is said to have been a member of the Augustinian order.[45] As we shall see, his Augustinian background could well be the key to determining a possible place of origin for him and for others of the Irish contingent in Regensburg.

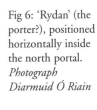

Fig 6: 'Rydan' (the porter?), positioned horizontally inside the north portal. *Photograph Diarmuid Ó Riain*

Gregorius' achievement in building the church at Regensburg, said to have been made possible by funds received from Muirchertach Ua Briain in 1166, equalled, if not surpassed, the achievement of his predecessor, Christianus. Moreover, as far as the fabric of the church is concerned, his design is still intact today. Retaining the two towers of the previous construction, he rebuilt the church to include the

43. Ó Riain-Raedel, 'Patrician documents in Medieval Germany', pp 712-24; eadem, 'The travels of Irish manuscripts', pp 52-67.
44. Dagmar Ó Riain-Raedel, 'German influence on Munster Church and kings in the twelfth century' in A. Smyth, (ed), *Seanchas: studies in early and medieval Irish archaeology, history and literature in honour of Francis J. Byrne* (Dublin, 2000), pp 323-30; see also D. Ó Corráin, 'Foreign connections and domestic politics: Killaloe and the Uí Bhriain in twelfth-century hagiography' in D. Whitelock, R. McKitterick, D. Dumville (eds), *Ireland in early medieval Europe* (Cambridge, 1982), pp 213-31.
45. Breatnach, *Libellus*, p 255.

famous northern portal, (fig 7) together with the cloister and auxiliary buildings, which included a viaduct.[46] Moreover, Gregorius continued the expansion of the congregation in Southern Germany, which his predecessor had
begun.

St James at Würzburg

Christianus' first foundations outside Regensburg, at Würzburg in Franconia
and at Erfurt in Thuringia, were both dedicated to St James.[47]

The church in Würzburg was founded c 1138 with the express intention
of catering for the numerous Irish pilgrims to the tomb of St Killian, who
was reputed to have been martyred in the year 689.[48] According to its (still
extant) forged foundation charter, the building of the church was first proposed at a meeting between abbot Christianus and Bishop Embricho at
Mainz. The *Libellus*, which places the event in the time of Gregorius, has a
different account. According to this, Macarius, a *vir nobilis* (a noble man) of
Ireland, who was sub-prior during the abbacy of Gregorius, had expressed the

46. M. Stocker, *Die Schottenkirche St. Jakob in Regensburg. Skulptur und stilistisches Umfeld*
(Regensburg, 2001).
47. The expansion of the Schottenklöster is covered extensively by Hammermayer, 'Die
irischen Benediktiner-Schottenklöster' and Flachenecker, *Schottenklöster.*
48. Vat lat 10100 contains, in addition to the 'official' necrology, a separate Würzburg Book
of the Dead, which mentions the year 1140 as the date of the establishment: Ó Riain-Raedel,
'Das Nekrolog', p 52.

Fig 8: Würzburg,
St James. *Photograph
Diarmuid Ó Riain*

wish to return to Ireland with three companions. On their way, they visited
the tomb of St Killian, where the saint appeared in a vision and asked
Macarius to stay at Würzburg: *Ego sum Kylianus, compatria tuus, qui martyrii
palmam merui habere in terra ista pro Iesu Christi amore, et sic Deus voluit, ut
expectarem diem resurreccionis mee in terra ista, sicut te oportet facere* (I am
Killian, your compatriot, who earned the martyr's palm for the love of Jesus
Christ in this land, and as God wishes that I await the day of my resurrection in this land, so it is also proper for you to do). Killian then also appeared
to bishop Embricho, alerting him to the presence of Macarius and his companions.[49] In this way the Irish monks of the monastery could build on local
reverence for Killian, patron of the cathedral, as well as on the protection of
bishop Embricho (1127-1146) who is credited with the establishment of the
monastery and its consecration in 1140. According to the early sixteenth-
century historian, Johannes Trithemius, himself an abbot of St James for
some years, Embricho chose Macarius, who had come from Ireland to
Würzburg as *peregrinus et exul* (a pilgrim and exile), as the first abbot of the

49. Breatnach, *Libellus*, pp 263-74.

newly-founded monastery.[50] Moreover, when at a dinner function in the company of Embricho, Macarius allegedly performed a miracle by changing the wine in his glass into water (so as not to break his own abstinence but at the same time so as not to appear impolite), the greatly impressed bishop endowed the monastery lavishly and exhorted others to do the same. Embricho's commitment to the success of the monastery is attested elsewhere. According to a sixteenth-century Spanish document, the bishop presented relics of St James, which he had brought back from a pilgrimage to the saint's shrine at Santiago de Compostela, to the newly-established Schottenkloster in 1138.[51] Embricho may also have instituted the custom by which the body of each bishop would spend the first night after his death in the Schottenkloster, again underlining the close connection between the Irish community and the episcopal see at Würzburg.

Before the foundation of the local Schottenkloster, there had been an Irish presence at Würzburg in the person of David Scotus, leader of the cathedral school and official chronicler of Henry V, whom he accompanied on his expedition to Rome to receive the title of emperor from Pope Paschalis in 1111. Although David's chronicle has been lost, extracts from it have been incorporated into William of Malmesbury's chronicle, as well as the Regensburg *Kaiserchronik* and the chronicle of Ekkehard of Aura.[52] An Irish colony at Würzburg previous to the foundation of the Schottenklöster is also indicated by a claim that Irish monks were employed at the episcopal chancery. This again bears witness to the high degree of service that the Irish were deemed capable of delivering.[53] As at Regensburg the Irish monks in Würzburg were instrumental in setting up unions of prayers and confraternities with their lay and clerical neighbours. Later, when the mother house in

50. Johannes Trithemius, *Breve fundationis monasterii S. Jacobi Ordinis S. Benedicti* in J. P. Ludewig, *Geschichtsschreiber von dem Bischofftihum Wirtzburg* (Frankfurt, 1713), pp 993-1003; Flachenecker, *Schottenklöster*, pp 166-7. Trithemius was interested in stressing the independence of St James, Würzburg from the house at Regensburg.

51. Nothing else is known of this pilgrimage, but the date and other details of the document can be verified from other sources; P. Plötz, '1 Roer de corpore S. Jacobi Apostoli' in *Würzburger Diözesangeschichtsblätter* 40 (1978), pp 95-103.

52. W. Stubbs (ed.), *William of Malmesbury, Gesta regum Anglorum* v, Rer. Brit. Medii Aevi SS 2 (1857), pp 420-26; See also R. Bauerreiß, 'Ein Quellenverzeichnis der Schriften Aventins', *StudMitt OSB* 50 (1932), pp 315-35 and I. Schmale-Ott, 'Die Rezension C der Weltchronik Ekkehards', in *Deutsches Archiv* 12 (1956), pp 363-87; eadem, 'Untersuchungen zu Ekkehard von Aura und zur Kaiserchronik', ZschrfbayerLandesgesch 34 (1971), pp 403-61 and F-J, Schmale and I. Schmale-Ott, *Frutolfs and Ekkehards Chroniken und die anonyme Kaiserchronik* (Darmstadt, 1972), pp 254-5.

53. P. Johanek, *Die Frühzeit der Siegelurkunde im Bistum Würzburg* (Würzburg, 1969), pp 262, 277.

Regensburg, and also some of the other foundations, were experiencing a steady decline, St James in Würzburg had a new lease of life under Abbot Philip (1343-1361) whose west Cork connections will be explored below. He managed not only to obtain confirmation of all imperial and papal privileges but also to raise funds and reform the spirit of the monastery as a whole. Chosen as imperial chaplain, he maintained scholarly and friendly relations with many of his contemporaries. He may also may have taken over responsibility for the houses at Konstanz and Memmingen, as well as for the priory at Ross Carbery.[54]

St James in Erfurt

Sharing its dedication to St James, the patron of pilgrims, with the houses in Regensburg and Würzburg, the foundation at Erfurt in Thuringia, the most northerly of the Schottenklöster, is also one of the earliest. Surprisingly, neither the *Vita Mariani*, nor the *Libellus*, include Erfurt in their accounts, a distinction shared with the foundation dedicated to St James at Konstanz. Its early history has therefore to be gleaned from external sources, some of which put the

Fig 9: Erfurt, St James

foundation date as early as the eleventh century. The first charter evidence becomes available in 1193, but both the architecture of the Romanesque church, which is dated to the middle of the twelfth century, and the identity of some of the benefactors point to a foundation date in line with the houses of Würzburg and Nürnberg. In Erfurt too, an episcopal sponsor, in the person of archbishop Arnold of Mainz († 1160), seems to have favoured the Irish 'who had come with their pilgrims' staff from the end of the world'.[55] References to contributions by local noble families strengthen the view that the Erfurt community quickly became an integral part of the emerging township, while at the same time maintaining a good relationship with other monastic institutions.[56]

---

54. Hochholzer, 'Iren und "Schotten"', pp 336-7.
55. Flachenecker, *Schottenklöster*, pp 153-64: 157.
56. A novel explanation for the arrival of the Irish at Erfurt was given by the seventeenth-

St Aegidius at Nürnberg

In contrast to Würzburg and Erfurt, where the foundation of the Irish monasteries had been initiated by local bishops, the monastery dedicated to St Aegidius (Giles) at Nürnberg was a royal foundation. It was founded about 1140 by King Conrad III (1138-1152) and his wife Gertrud, who chose the first abbot, Carus, as their royal chaplain, a position also filled by his successor, Declanus.[57] According to the Life of Marianus, Conrad presented an already existing royal chapel to Carus, who had previously been prior of the Würzburg community, with the wish that all the monks should be of the *gens Scotorum* (the race of the Scoti). The duty of the community was to pray both for the immunity of the empire and the protection of the emperor himself. Declanus, then, allegedly *capellanus* to both Conrad and emperor Frederick I (1155-1190), began with the extension of the monastery and the building of a church.[58] According to Flachenecker, both king and emperor were anxious to extend their control over the important town of Nürnberg, relying on the help of the Irish community to strengthen their position in a territory which did not possess an episcopal see.[59] Close proximity to the castle underlines the role of the Irish monastery, the first to be built within the town, which was to be upheld by a succession of royal benefactions. In return, the monks arranged to have the founders of the house included in the necrology of the *Schottenkongregation*, thus guaranteeing prayers for them in perpetuity. A privilege granted in 1225 by King Henry VII, similar to that issued to the mother-house at Regensburg about the same time, assured the status of the house in Nürnberg. In addition, the *Vita Mariani*, which can be augmented by reference to later chronicles, is a valuable source for the early history of this filiation. Although silent on the foundation in Nürnberg, the *Libellus* clearly had in mind to report on it. It reports, for example, that King Conrad, having learned of the fame of Abbot Macarius and his Irish companions during a visit to the palace of Würzburg, spontaneously decided to erect a monastery for them himself.[60] Unfortunately, the text of the *Libellus* breaks off at that point.

---

century local historian, Zacharias Hogel, in his *Chroniken von der Stadt Erfurth*. According to this, Charlemagne entered into an agreement with the king of Ireland in 790, in the process asking to have Irish scholars sent to him, who went on to found the first university in Europe, at Paris, in 791. It was allegedly the reputation of their compatriots that prompted the Erfurt citizens to found a monastery for them in 1036; Flachenecker, *Schottenklöster*, p 159.

57 Flachenecker, *Schottenklöster*, pp 180-197.
58 Hauck, *Die Vita Mariani*, pp 119-20.
59 Flachenecker, *Schottenklöster*, pp 180-81.
60 Breatnach, *Libellus*, pp 273-4.

St James at Konstanz

Neither the Life of Marianus nor the *Libellus* refer to the foundation of the Konstanz Schottenkloster which is generally believed to have taken place in the year 1142.[61] Although charter evidence does not become available until the year 1220, a number of later chronicles report the involvement of King Conrad III, this time in co-operation with his trusted ally, Bishop Hermann (1138-1165). Indeed, a number of sixteenth-century chroniclers refer to earlier Irish foundations at Konstanz, one of them allegedly by St Fridolin of Säckingen in the sixth century. Although this tradition was taken over by the Scottish historian Marianus Brockie, who claimed to have used a now lost copy of *Annales monasterii Scotorum Ratisbonae* (The annals of the monastery of the Scoti of Ratisbon), there is not much else in the way of evidence of an Irish presence at Konstanz.[62] The monastery, whose *libertates et immunitates* (liberties and immunities) were confirmed in a lengthy charter by Pope Innocent in 1245, seems never to have developed into a thriving community. Still, the fact that the founding abbot Macrobius is also stated to have been archdeacon to the Bishop of Konstanz again points to close co-operation between the Irish community and the local episcopal authorities. The house in Konstanz was among those later taken over by Scottish monks whose occupancy was, however, of short duration as the buildings were demolished in 1530 for military reasons.

St Mary's in Vienna

A policy of close association with ruling dynasties, as shown by the histories of the houses in Nürnberg and Konstanz, is also evidenced by the circumstances of the foundation of St Mary's at Vienna, the only Schottenkloster which still remains a Benedictine monastery.[63] Here the Irish monks were installed by Henry

Fig 10: Vienna, St Mary's. *Photograph Diarmuid Ó Riain*

61. Flachenecker, *Schottenklöster*, pp 198-205.

62. Brockie's *Monasticon* is preserved in an autograph copy in the Scottish Catholic Archives SK 9 at Edinburgh and is quoted here after Flachenecker, p 200.

63. On the Schottenstift in Vienna see Dagmar Ó Riain-Raedel, 'Ireland and Austria in the middle ages: the role of the Irish monks in Austria', in P. Leifer and E. Sagarra (eds), *Austro-Irish Links through the centuries* (Vienna, 2002), pp 7-40; Flachenecker, Schottenklöster, pp 214-36.

Jasomirgott, who, as duke of Bavaria in his capital of Regensburg, had already been impressed by the *simplicitas* of the Irish, a term that is used in the foundation charter of 1161.[64] When the newly-founded duchy of Austria was offered to Henry, he planned to involve the Irish monks in the setting up of an independent diocese at Vienna. Although these plans did not materialise, the Schottenstift, which the duke chose as his place of burial, nevertheless remained closely connected with the ruling dynasty. The new foundation was staffed by a delegation from Regensburg, led by its first abbot, Sanctinus († 1169), who, living up to the meaning of his name, is credited with having enjoyed supernatural capabilities. According to the *Vita Mariani*, Sanctinus saw in a vision a richly-leafed tree reaching from earth to heaven along which dove-like birds both ascended and descended. The brethren interpreted this as a replica of Jacob's ladder along which angels climbed in order to negotiate between divine matters and human intentions.

At Vienna, as at Würzburg, the Irish became involved in the administration of the chancery, this time a ducal one, as is certified by still extant charters. The close connection with the ruling house is further illustrated by the monastery's physical proximity to the palace, in much the same way as at Nürnberg. The monastic scriptorium also produced annals recording the history of the fledgling duchy, together with a full-scale chronicle, now lost but known from extracts in other works.[65] In spite of their full integration into local society, the Irish monks in Vienna never forgot their native land, and this is borne out by entries in their annals relating to events in Ireland, which are of great interest. From these, one can again see how the monks' allegiance mostly lay with Munster factions, especially with the Mac Carthaig and Ua Briain kings. The much-endowed Vienna filiation, which produced an extensive series of charters and other documents, was the location of a famous, still surviving, school. Moreover, as can be deducted from a large number of surviving medieval musical fragments, this contained a *schola cantorum*. The musical notations, discovered when the bindings and fly-leaves of later codices were examined, turned out to be the oldest surviving musical scores

---

64. *Solos eligimus scottos, eo quod et nostra experientia et religiosorum potissimum relatione, noverimus laudabilem eorundem simplicitate*, E. Hauswirth, *Urkunden der Benediktiner-Abtei Unserer Lieben Frau zu den Schotten in Wien vom Jahre 1158 bis 1418* (Wien, 1859) (*Fontes rerum Austriacarum*, II, vol. 18), No 4. The original charter is kept in the monastic archive.

65. Dagmar Ó Riain-Raedel, 'Twelfth-and thirteenth century Irish annals in Vienna' in *Peritia* 2 (1983) pp 127-36. Cölestin Rapf, *Das Schottenstift* (Wiener Geschichtsbücher 13), (Vienna/Hamburg, 1974); idem, 'Die Bibliothek der Benediktinerabtei Unserer Lieben Frau zu den Schotten in Wien' in J. G. Plante (ed), *Translatio Studi:. manuscript and library studies honoring Oliver L. Kapsner* (Collegeville, Minnesota, 1973), pp 4-36.

in Vienna, otherwise famous as the city of music. Some of them even date to earlier than the mid-twelfth century, which means that they were probably brought to Vienna from Regensburg or possibly even from Ireland.[66]

The high intellectual and cultural standing of the Schottenstift is reflected by the role successive abbots played in the early history of the university at Vienna, which was founded in 1365. Abbot Clemens (1349-1372) was a witness to the charter of the university provided by Duke Rudolf IV, and his successor Donaldus (1380-1392), who was elected rector of the university, was instrumental in the creation of a faculty of theology. The last known Irish abbot of the Schottenstift, Thomas III, acted as conservator of the university before he was obliged to relinquish the monastery in 1418.[67]

Holy Cross at Eichstätt

Although little information survives about the Schottenkloster at Eichstätt, we can glean some details of its early history from the short account of the *Vita Mariani*, which places its foundation in the years 1158/66. The benefactor in this case was Walbrun, *canonicus* of Eichstätt cathedral, who is said to have endowed the foundation from his own funds. The motive for the donation possibly underlies the dedication of the house to the Holy Cross, which may reflect Walbrun's participation in the crusade that left Regensburg in the year 1147. The church not only housed a particle of the True Cross, it also contained an exact, and still extant, copy of the sepulchre of Christ, the inspiration for which must have been brought back from

Fig 11: Eichstätt, Holy Cross, Holy Sepulchre. *Photograph Diarmuid Ó Riain*

---

66. M. Czernin, 'Fragments of liturgical chant from medieval Irish monasteries in continental Europe' in *Early Music,* xxvii (2000), pp 217-24; Dagmar Ó Riain-Raedel, 'Ireland's oldest music manuscript?' in *History Ireland,* 5/3 (1995), pp 11-13. László Mezey, 'Fragmentenforschung im Schottenstift 1982-1983' in *Codices manuscripti* 10 (1984), pp 60-71. Some of the fragments are described in *Musik im mittelalterlichen Wien* (Vienna, 1987), pp 21-6, 48-53, 59.
67. Ó Riain-Raedel, 'Irish Monks in Austria', pp 37, 39-40.

Jerusalem by Walbrun. That Holy Cross was mainly intended to serve as a pilgrims' hospice, while functioning also as a leper hospital, is confirmed by charters which refer to a *domus hospitalis* and *hospitium*. The pilgrims came there either to venerate the replica of the Holy Sepulchre or to the shrine of Willibald, Anglo-Saxon founder-saint of the diocese, who had himself been a pilgrim to the Holy Land. The concourse of pilgrims there is confirmed by a number of indulgences issued both by successive bishops of the diocese and also by Pope Innocent IV. However, the initial patronage which it received does not seem to have sustained the Schottenkloster for long, and its line of abbots ended at the beginning of the fourteenth century.[68]

St Nicholas at Memmingen

Personal concerns were again to the fore in the story of the foundation of the church of St Nicholas at Memmingen. Following the death of his only surviving son during the siege of Rome by Emperor Frederick I, and after his own second pilgrimage to the Holy Land, Duke Welf II founded the monastery some time after 1176. He may also have wished to emulate the establishment of the Schottenkloster at Vienna by his old rival, Duke Henry of Austria. The foundation at Memmingen receives no mention in the *Vita Mariani* which was probably written shortly before it took place. Instead, there is a lengthy passage appended to the *Libellus*, which seems so different from the previous text that it may have been composed by a different author. As in the case of Konstanz, abbot Macarius of Würzburg fame, is described here as the inspiration for the foundation by Duke Welf of the Memmingen Schottenkloster. The exemplary piety of the Irish monks, which is also mentioned in the foundation charter of Vienna, is confirmed by a charter issued by Emperor Frederick I in 1181 which refers to their *pauperum Christi vota et humilium preces* (devotions and prayers of Christ's poor and humble).[69] As in Nürnberg, Eichstätt and Vienna, the foundation of the Schottenklöster coincided with the emergence of the town of Memmingen as a *civitas*, which was strategically located at a junction of important trade routes. Its role as a hospice and place of burial for both guests and strangers is described as one of the privileges awarded to it by the bishop of Augsburg in 1181. Emperor Frederick's charter of the same year, followed by that of Pope Urban III in 1186, placed the monastery *sub Beati Petri et nostra protectione* (under our protection and that of the blessed Peter). However, the initial success of the

68. Flachenecker, *Schottenklöster*, pp 205-13; idem, 'Das ehemalige Schottenkloster Heiligkreuz in Eichstätt' in *Schönere Heimat* 81 pp 87-9.
69. Breatnach, *Libellus*, pp 275-310; 65-71; Flachenecker, *Schottenklöster*, pp 236-43.

monastery could not be sustained, and a gradual decline became noticeable in the course of the thirteenth century. By the year 1400 the monastery seems to have ceased to exist.[70]

St John the Evangelist in Kelheim

Founded about a century after the initial expansion, this priory was the last of the filiations of St James of Regensburg. It was built by Duke Otto II of Bavaria for the salvation of the soul of his father, Ludwig I, at the spot where the latter was murdered in 1231. As elsewhere, the decision to staff the church with Irish monks is attributed to their piety. Here, too, the monks played their part in the emergence of the town of Kelheim which, because of its strategic location, was frequently home to the new Wittelsbach dukes of Bavaria. The Schottenkloster, which

Fig 12: Kelheim, St John the Evangelist. *Photograph Diarmuid Ó Riain*

also pursued a charitable function as hospital and hospice, was the first monastery within the town. The monastery remained closely connected to Duke Otto, and the necrology of the Congregation dutifully listed the days on which the community was obliged to pray for the salvation of the souls of the Wittelsbach line.[71] The foundation ceased to exist in the course of the fourteenth century.

* * *

In many ways, the history of the Irish foundations in Germany and Austria reveals a similar pattern. Once established, the mother house at Regensburg was instrumental in providing staff for the new foundations. In most cases, we hear of the esteem in which the Irish monks were held, with recurrent references to their piety and strict religious observance. Although normally founded by kings and dukes with the support of local bishops, charters of protection were also regularly obtained from successive emperors and popes. In return, the monks actively supported their benefactors, both lay and clerical, by contributing to their chanceries and scriptoria. Moreover, they helped

70. Flachenecker, *Schottenklöster*, p 241.
71. Ó Riain-Raedel, 'Das Nekrolog', pp 57, 59, 69, 73, 77.

to promote the political aims of their lay founders, by contributing to the development of their towns. Fully integrated into their new environments, the Irish monks co-operated with the neighbouring German religious houses and joined into fraternities with them. They also maintained, at least in the mother house and in the bigger filiations, productive scriptoria, which exchanged texts and ideas with their neighbours.

These neighbourly relationships of the founding years were to come under severe pressure during the following centuries. Weakened by internal difficulties and by lack of suitable recruits from Ireland, the monasteries came more and more under the scrutiny of local clerical hierarchies. While some houses, such as the Schottenstift at Vienna, became German communities in the early fifteenth century, the monasteries at Regensburg, Würzburg, Erfurt and Konstanz, were subjected to a different fate. Taking advantage of the confusion caused by the name, and with papal sanction, Scotsmen took over the monasteries from 1515 onwards, claiming that the *monasteria Scotorum* had, in fact, been founded by their forebears. While it may be regrettable that none of the Schottenklöster remained in Irish hands, we may be thankful to the Scots for preserving documents which shed light on the early history of the congregation. In order to strengthen their own claims to these houses, the Scots engaged in considerable scribal activity, in the process copying and re-editing earlier texts. In the case of the mother-house at Regensburg, the Scottish phase lasted until 1862, when the monastery became the new local diocesan seminary. The few surviving monks left for the newly-founded Benedictine house of Fort Augustus in Scotland, taking with them a number of manuscripts (including an autographed copy of Marianus) and a large part of the library.[72]

The products of the scriptorium at Regensburg
Included in the output of the Regensburg scriptorium are the two sources already referred to above, the Life of Marianus, which was written nearly a century after his death, and the foundation chronicle, entitled *Libellus de fundacione ecclesiae Consecrati Petri*.[73] To these can be added the necrology of the

---

72. The latter phases of the congregation have been discussed by Mark Dilworth, 'Two necrologies of Scottish Benedictine abbeys in Germany' in *The Innes Review* 9 (1958), pp 173-203; idem, 'Scottish Benedictines at Würzburg: a supplement to the necrology' in *The Innes Review* 15 (1964), pp 171-181; idem, 'The first Scottish monks in Ratisbon' in *The Innes Review* 16 (1965), pp 180-198; idem, *The Scots in Franconia: a century of monastic life* (Edinburgh-London, 1974).
73. Vita Mariani, *AASS Februarius tomus ii*, pp 361-72; P. Hauck *Die Vita Mariani. Überlieferung und Text*, Breatnach, *Libellus*.

congregation, which contains some 1000 entries concerning members of the community, as well as the names of members of befriended monasteries and lay benefactors in Ireland and Germany. The text, which was begun about the middle of the twelfth century, but which only survives in a seventeenth-century Würzburg copy now in the Vatican Library, provides a comprehensive picture of the multifaceted make-up of the Schottenklöster.[74]

From an Irish viewpoint, we can deduce from the composition of the necrology, which gratefully recognises the patronage of the two southern royal families, the Uí Bhriain of Thomond and the Meic Carthaig of Desmond, that Munster was the homeland of the majority of the monks. Likewise, the bishops of such Munster dioceses as Limerick, Inis Cathaig, Roscrea, Kilfenora, Killaloe, Waterford and Lismore, and Cork are commemorated here. A Munster bias is also visible in other literary products of the Schottenkloster, for example, in the twelfth-century Würzburg calendar, and in some later calendars from Regensburg, which commemorate predominantly Munster saints.[75] A number of Irish saints' Lives found entry through the Schottenkloster into a voluminous legendary, which because of its manuscript distribution in Benedictine and Cistercian monasteries of Austria, is called *Magnum Legendarium Austriacum*. First written down in the last two decades of the twelfth century, the legendary drew on a collection of *vitae* brought together at a number of Regensburg monasteries in the preceding years, with the Schottenkloster contributing its own share. Apart from the Lives of the three national saints, Patrick, Brigid and Colum Cille, we find here *vitae* of *peregrini* on the continent, such as Gallus, Killian and Fursey, together with biographies of local Irish saints of predominantly Munster provenance, such as Senán of Inis Cathaig, Ita of Killeedy, Flannán of Killaloe and Mochuille of Tulla, all of whom were connected with churches in counties Limerick and Clare. Other literary products of the Schottenklöster confirm the Munster bias of the congregation. Thus, the Life of Albert, reputedly first Archbishop of Cashel and a pilgrim to Regensburg, where he found his last resting place, was written about the middle of the twelfth century, as was Brother Marcus' *Visio Tnugdali*, an account of a vision

---

74. Dagmar Ó Riain-Raedel, 'Das Nekrolog'; eadem, 'Irish kings and bishops in the memoria of the German Schottenklöster' in P. Ní Chatháin and M. Richter (eds), *Irland und Europa* (Stuttgart, 1984), pp 390-404.

75. For an edition of the Würzburg calendar see: A Dold, 'Wessobrunner Kalendarblätter irischen Ursprungs', ArchZschr 58 (1962), pp 11-33; the Regensburg calendars are in Ms 8, Ms 22 and Ms 40 of the Diözesanarchiv. Other calendars and martyrologies, surviving in manuscripts traceable to a number of Bavarian monasteries, show evidence of having used Irish exemplars, Ó Riain-Raedel, 'Das Nekrolog', pp 41-4.

of heaven and hell, allegedly seen by a knight of Cashel named Tnugdal (Tundal) in the army of Cormac Mac Carthaig.[76] Both texts not only address themselves to a Regensburg audience but also include episodes reflective of contemporary Irish politics. In both cases, the fortunes of the Desmond kings of Munster are of special relevance; Albert seems to have been a Germanised form of the name of the native saint Ailbe, patron of Emly, the ancestral church of the Meic Carthaig, and by providing the saint with metropolitan status at Cashel, by right the royal seat of the Eoganacht kings of Munster, it is implied that the Rock should be restored to the Meic Carthaig. This theory finds support in an episode of the *Libellus* which relates how abbot Christianus Mac Carthaig, on a fund-raising trip to Ireland, was unanimously elected Archbishop of Cashel on the death of the incumbent, only to be deprived of the honour by his own sudden death. No vacancy is known for Cashel at this time and it may well be that this episode again serves to underline the ancestral rights of the Meic Carthaig within the structures of the church in Munster.

As it happens, Christianus would not have been the first Benedictine Archbishop of Cashel, since Malchus (Máel Isú Ua hAinmire), bishop of Waterford, and previously monk of the Benedictine abbey of Winchester, had been chosen as the first archbishop at the synod of Ráith Bresail in 1111. Although his Winchester connections are well known, Malchus must also have had some connection with the Schottenkloster, substantial enough to merit the inclusion of his name in the official necrology.[77]

Brother Marcus's account of Tnugdal's vision of paradise makes an explicit reference to Cormac Mac Carthaig, describing him as receiving a procession of monks and pilgrims while seated on a throne of gold in a splendid house, reminiscent of the wise and just King Solomon of the Old Testament. Cormac was not the only lay person encountered by Tnugdal *in campo letitie* (on the plain of joy). The knight was also brought face to face with Donnchad Mac Carthaig, brother and successor of the more famous Cormac, as well as with Conchobhar Ua Briain.[78] Although both of these inveterate enemies are known to have led violent lives, they are said to have

---

76. A. Wagner, *Visio Tnugdali. Lateinisch und Altdeutsch* (Erlangen, 1882) has now been superseded by a new edition of the text in: B. Pfeil, *Die 'Vision des Tnugdalus' Albers von Windberg'. Literatur- und Frömmigkeitsgeschichte im ausgehenden 12. Jahrhundert* (Frankfurt am Main, 1999). See also H. Spilling, *Die Visio Tnugdali. Eigenart und Sonderstellung in der mittelalterlichen Visionsliteratur bis zum Ende des 12. Jahrhunderts* (Munich, 1975) and J. M. Picard and Y. de Pontfarcy, *The vision of Tnugdal* (Dublin, 1989).
77. Ó Riain-Raedel, 'Das Nekrolog', pp 64, 90; eadem, 'Irish kings and bishops', p 395.
78. Pfeil, *Die 'Vision.des Tnugdalus'*, p 43-44, 'De Danacho et Conchober regibus'.

repented before their deaths, Conchobhar becoming a monk, and Donnchad giving all that he had to the poor. One can only surmise that the recipients of the largesse must have included the Schottenkloster monks, those *pauperes Christi et peregrini* (the poor of Christ and pilgrims) who are alleged to have formed part of the thanksgiving procession to Cormac's throne.[79] The gratitude of the Schottenkloster to Conchobhar is also implied by his place in the necrology, where he is commemorated as *Conchubur rex Mummensis frater noster* (Conchobhar king of Munster, our brother).[80]

In a separate chapter of the *Visio*, it is revealed to Tnugdal that all builders and defenders of churches are assured of favourable treatment, including reception into religious confraternities. Elsewhere in the *campus letitie* (plain of joy), Tnugdal is said to have encountered a large number of bishops in the company of St Patrick, amongst them four that he knew, namely St Malachy of Armagh and his brother Christianus, Bishop of Louth, Celsus or Cellach, Archbishop of Armagh, who was buried at Lismore in 1129, and Nehemias Ua Muirchertaig, Bishop of Cloyne († 1149). All of these were supporters of the twelfth-century reform movement and strove, as is exemplified by the case of St Malachy, to establish churches and give alms to the poor.[81] St Malachy is singled out in the text as the founder of fifty-four congregations of monks, canons and nuns. In the previous chapter, Tnugdal is said have encountered St Ruadán, who reminded him that he was his patron, so that Tnugdal owed him burial rights. Although no other evidence exists for a connection with Lorrha, reference to this saint of Eoganacht stock again reflects the author's concern for the Meic Carthaig.[82] It may also not be without significance that Lorrha had adopted the Augustinian rule around 1140, while still maintaining its dedication to St Ruadán.[83]

By thus describing the people that he had encountered in paradise, and by enumerating the ways in which his readers could aspire to reach this place themselves, Marcus cleverly put forward a scheme of things that otherwise found its counterpart in the necrology. Those who merited a place in the

79. Ibid., pp 44-46, 'De Cormacho rege'.
80. Vat lat 10100, fol. 22v; 20 March: Ó Riain-Raedel, 'Das Nekrolog', p 62; eadem, 'Irish kings and bishops', p 399.
81. Op. cit., 55-56: '*De sancto Patricio et quattuor sibi notis episcopis*'. Bishop Nehemias, alias Giolla na Naomh Ó Muircheartaigh, may have been a monk at the Schottenkloster in Würzburg before his elevation to the bishopric at Cloyne. Nehemias is named as *Nemias episcopus et monachus nostre congregationis* in a Calendar fragment from Würzburg; Ó Riain-Raedel, 'Irish kings and bishops', pp 392-3.
82. Picard & de Pontfarcy, *The vision of Tnugdal*, pp 30-32.
83 Gwynn & Hadcock, *MRH*, p 185.

necrology, through their virtuous lives, as in the case of monks and nuns, or by providing donations and protection, as could be done by lay and clerical patrons, could be assured the prayers of the community. It may be no accident, therefore, that both the *visio* and the necrology were commenced at the same time.[84] The message they contained was a universal one, comprehensible to all who read them. Why the abbess of the Bavarian convent to which Marcus dedicated his work should have been interested in the fates of Irish bishops and kings has often been asked. The answer to this lies in the necrology.

Irish nuns at Regensburg

A number of the females listed in the necrology of the Niedermünster, whose patron, the above-mentioned St Erhard, was an Irishman, are again commemorated in the Schottenkloster necrology, which identifies them as Irish by using the epithet *scotigena*. As the Niedermünster only admitted ladies of aristocratic background, we may conclude that these Irish nuns belonged to the nobility of Munster.[85] There are no indications as to which convent in Ireland they came from, or when and how they were admitted into the Benedictine order. Although convents of nuns are among the foundations ascribed by Marcus to St Malachy, none is otherwise known from south Munster. Instead, we know of a number of houses founded by the Uí Bhriain within their territory of Thomond, all of which seem to have followed the Augustinian rule. In this case, it may be pertinent that abbot Gregorius of Regensburg is also said to have been an Augustinian canon before he joined the Benedictines at Regensburg.[86] It was he who organised the third fundraising mission to Ireland, meeting there Muirchertach Ua Briain, alias 'Dún na Sciath' († 1168), who provided him with enough money to extend the Regensburg monastery. A number of Augustinian convents were founded by the Uí Bhriain during the latter part of the twelfth century and these were probably the mother houses of the Regensburg nuns. Amongst them were a convent dedicated to St John the Baptist at Killone, Co Clare, which was founded on lands belonging to the Augustinian abbey of Clare, and another one dedicated to St Peter in Limerick, by then the centre of the Uí Bhriain kingdom. Both convents first come to notice during the reign of Domnall

---

84. A. Angenendt, 'Theologie und Liturgie der mittelalterlichen Toten-Memoria' in K. Schmid and J. Wollasch (ed), *Memoria* (Munich, 1984), pp 79-199.
85. To the names of *Beatrix monacha scotigena* (7 Jul) and *Gertrudis monacha scotigena* (19 Aug) can be added *Brechta Schottin* in an entry for 1126 in a Niedermünster text; Ó Riain-Raedel, 'Das Nekrolog', pp 29-30.
86. Breathnach, *Libellus*, p 255.

Fig 13:
Killone Abbey,
Co Clare. *Photograph
Diarmuid Ó Riain*

Ua Briain († 1194), who is credited with their foundation, and the only two recorded abbesses of Killone belonged to the Uí Bhriain. One of these, Sláine, was the daughter of Donnchad Cairbreach Ua Briain († 1242), who is commemorated in the necrology together with his wife (presumably Sláine's mother), *Sabba comitissa soror nostra* (Countess Sabba, our sister).[87] St Peter's became a cell of Killone some time after 1189 and was known as 'Monaster ne Callow Duffe' or Black Abbey, presumably after the habits of its nuns.[88] The same title was borne by the convent of St Catherine de O'Conyl at Shanagolden, Co Limerick. It has been suggested that the Latin Life of St Ita was written at Shanagolden in an attempt to furnish the new convent with an 'ancient history'.[89] With the Latin Life of St Senán, which may have been composed at Clare Abbey, this found its way via Regensburg into the *Magnum Legendarium Austriacum*.[90]

We may infer, then, that the origins of the Irish nuns at Regensburg are most likely to be sought in the area now covered by north Limerick and Clare, a region which also figures prominently in Schottenkloster documents of the second part of the twelfth century.

---

87. Ó Riain-Raedel, 'Das Nekrolog', pp 91-2.
88. Gwynn & Hadcock, *MRH*, pp 309, 321-2. Gwynn described the order at St Peter's as Augustinian Black nuns, thus allowing for the fact that a number of Augustinian convents may have followed a Benedictine rule in the early stages of their establishment. For Clare Abbey and Killone see A. Gwynn and D. F. Gleeson, *A history of the Diocese of Killaloe* (Dublin, 1962), pp 200-8.
89. P. Ó Riain, personal communication.
90. Ó Riain-Raedel, 'Das Nekrolog', p 36-7

FILIATIONS OF THE SCHOTTENKLÖSTER IN IRELAND

The priory of St Mary's at Ross Carbery (Ros Ailithir, Ross), Co Cork

The prosperity of the Schottenklöster obviously depended on a sufficient supply of recruits from the homeland and it is probably for this reason that dependencies were established in Ireland. That there must have been at least two of these, is known from letters issued by Pope Innocent IV in 1248. In his first communication the Pope authorised the abbot of St James at Regensburg, who had been worried about a possible lack of discipline, to send a visitation to the priories in Ireland. The second letter entitled the abbot to send a prior to Ireland to accept the vows of novices who were not able to undertake the long and dangerous journey to Germany.[91] As far as physical evidence is concerned, however, we know of only one priory in Ireland, that dedicated to St Mary at Ross Carbery in west Cork, whose dependency on Regensburg, and later on Würzburg, was maintained until the sixteenth century.[92] One of the most important churches of Corca Laoighdhe, a territory which now corresponds roughly to the extent of the diocese of Ross, Ross Carbery was elevated to the status of an episcopal see at the Synod of Kells in 1152. The foundation date of St Mary's is not known, but the traditional date of 1218 rests on a misunderstanding. In an anonymous article in the *Edinburgh Review* of 1864, Bishop Forbes suggested that the priory was founded by Nehemias Scotus, an erstwhile monk of Würzburg and later Bishop of Ross.[93] The date of the Ross Carbery foundation was chosen by later writers, following Forbes, on the grounds that a prior named Nehemias appeared in Würzburg sources in 1218. However, the founder named Nehemias may have been the Bishop of Cloyne who died in 1149. At any rate, Regensburg is named as the *ecclesia matrix* (mother church) in papal documents, and the priory was governed from Würzburg only from the fourteenth century onwards. The reason for the change-over may have been that there was a strong Ross contingent in Würzburg at that time. The earliest surviving document of the Ross priory is a declaration of obedience by the prior to Abbot Philip, one of the most successful abbots of Würzburg, who himself had strong west Cork connections. In a document preserved in

---

91. Maurice Sheehy, *Pontificia Hibernica* (2 vols, Dublin, 1965), ii, pp 146-8: ...*monachi monasterium seu prioratuum ordinis sancti Benedicti in Ibernia tuo monasterio (St James / Regensburg) subiectum.*
92. The history of the priory has been pieced together by J. Coombes, 'The Benedictine Priory of Ross' in *Journal of the Cork Historical and Archaelogical Society* 73 (1968), pp 152-60. See also Ó Riain-Raedel, 'Das Nekrolog', pp 22-4 and Flachenecker, *Schottenklöster*, pp 282-7.
93. 'Scottish religious houses abroad' in *Edinburgh Review* CXVX (1864), pp 168-203.

Würzburg University Library (Ms. M. ch. f 260), Philip's mother is named *'Gerwalde dicta Ingerdesteyl'* (probably Dirbhail inghean (Uí) Dhrisceóil), the daughter of Domhnall Ó Driscéil, a family closely connected with Ross. Similarly, Philip's own name, reproduced as 'Irhinger', points to the family of Uí Ingerdail, later Uí Urdail (Harrington), likewise widespread in West Cork. The O'Driscoll family supplied a number of priors to St Mary's and one of them, Odo, succeeded in 1490 to the local see, following a lengthy dispute between his family and the Uí hAodha (O'Heas), who, like the Uí hAirt, also provided priors to St Mary's. Their fortunes also reflect the link between Ross and Germany. For example, Guilielmus (Ó hAirt), *prior Rossensis*, died in Germany *in itinere ad Curiam Romanam* (on his way to the Roman curia) in 1450. Shortly before this, in 1442, a certain Benedict Mac Namyn, monk of Ross and of St James in Würzburg, had been elected abbot of the mother-house at Regensburg. A further west Cork connection is borne out by an entry in the necrology for 10 February, which reads: *Pie memorie Donatus Wagarij et Donaldus glas Wagrij duces qui fuerunt ex Hibernia scotorum, armatam manum et mediam aquilam insigniis gerents* (Donatus Wagarij and Donaldus glas Wagarij of holy memory, rulers who were from Ireland of the scotti, bearing as insignia a mailed hand and half eagle'). It would be most interesting to know which battle Donnchad and Domnall Glas Mac Carthaig, lords of Carbery, both of whom lived in the fourteenth century, had fought under the imperial banner of the Regensburg Schottenkloster.[94] In 1648, when attempts were made at Ross Carbery to revive the priory, the German affiliation was still well remembered, with 'the monastery of St James next to the river Main, in the diocese of Würzburg' named as the mother-house.[95]

A priory of St Mary's at Cashel, Co Tipperary?

The comparatively well-recorded history of the priory at Ross Carbery makes the lack of documentation concerning other Irish dependencies all the more conspicuous. Ever since the seventeenth-century Jesuit, Stephen White, drew attention to the *Libellus*, Cashel has been linked with the Schottenklöster. The possibility that Irish monks with German experience could have helped with the building of Cormac's Chapel, which would go a long way towards explaining its 'exotic' character, has proved very attractive. However, although to suggest that the chapel could have been the church of a

---

94. Ó Riain-Raedel, 'Das Nekrolog', p 59; eadem, 'Irish kings and bishops', pp 397-8.
95. G. Renz, 'Beiträge zur Geschichte der Schottenabtei St Jakob und des Priorats Weih-St Peter in Regensburg', *StudMitt OSB* 18 (1897), pp 79-87: 80.

Benedictine monastery dedicated to St James is not warranted by any source, we have some, admittedly circumstantial, local evidence for a foundation at Cashel. Archbishop David Mac Carwill († 1289) is said to have seen in a dream that the 'Black monks' (ie. Benedictines) of the Cashel 'abbey', were plotting to cut off his head, whereupon he decided to replace them with Cistercian monks. Subsequently, having taken the Cistercian habit, Mac Carwill is supposed to have founded the Cistercian monastery of Hore Abbey at the foot of the Rock of Cashel, colonising it with monks from Mellifont, and annexing to it possessions of the Benedictine monastery and of the Leper Hospital of St Nicholas.[96] There is some supporting evidence for this somewhat bloodthirsty story. One year after Mac Carwill's death in 1289, King Edward I confirmed to the abbot and convent of the Cistercian monastery of the 'Lower Rock of Cashel' the assignment made to them of the lands and possessions 'formerly held by the religious of the houses of the Upper Rock', which they had previously surrendered to the archbishop.[97] On this evidence, Archbishop Mac Carwill could well have suppressed the religious of the Rock in order to further his own new foundation at Hore Abbey. Some slight supporting evidence is also provided by the Regensburg necrology, which commemorates on 23 January *Petrus presbyter et monachus Sanctae Mariae Casseli* (Peter, priest and monk of St Mary's in Cashel). The (later?) Hore Abbey was also dedicated to St Mary, but this could have been inherited from its Benedictine predecessor.[98]

If a Benedictine monastery ever existed on the Rock, it is not known to have survived and only archaeological excavations could tell us more. Considering that recent excavations have yielded the foundations of no fewer than three previous churches on the Rock, an extension of the area of research would surely lead to more.[99] Without any doubt, Cashel was the most important place in Ireland as far as the monks of the Schottenklöster were concerned. Particularly in the decades leading up to the middle of the twelfth century, the Regensburg scriptorium expended much energy in promoting Cashel, which is described in the *Vita Albarti* as 'metropolitan city, royal town of Ireland' and in the *Visio Tnugdali*, as 'famous metropolis'.[100]

96. Gwynn & Hadcock, *MRH*, pp 104-5.
97. H. S. Sweetman, *Calendar of documents relating to Ireland* (London, 1875-6), vol. iii, p 346.
98. On Hore Abbey see Gwynn & Hadcock, *MRH*, p 129.
99. B. Hodkinson, 'Excavations at Cormac's Chapel, Cashel, 1992-1993: a preliminary statement' in *Tipperary Historical Journal* (1994), pp 167-74. I am grateful to the author for supplying me with his full, yet unpublished, report.
100. *Vita Albarti Archiepiscopi Casellensis*, MGH SS rer. Merov. vi, pp 21-3: 22; Pfeil, *Die 'Vision des Tnugdalus'*, * 4.

Moreover, additional material in the Middle High German translation of the *Visio Tnugdali* by Alber von Windberg, which drew the well-known episode of Patrick's piercing of the king of Munster's foot from a now lost Life of St Patrick, provided a new version of the tale of the banishment of snakes from Ireland. In this version, in atonement for the injury received at Cashel, the king is said to have been granted his request that the snakes, which up to then had plagued his land, be banished. Usually connected with Croagh Patrick in the West of Ireland, the credit given here to the king of Munster at Cashel for causing the banishment of the snakes, i.e. paganism, from Ireland, no doubt derives from the author's wish to promote Munster and its chief place.

This was exactly the time when the Congregation under the abbacy of Christianus Mac Carthaig had begun its expansion in southern Germany, which increased the need for recruiting houses in Ireland. It was also the time when Cormac Mac Carthaig's foundation of a church at Cashel expressed in architectural terms the traditional right of his dynasty to a presence on the Rock, a right which had effectively been usurped by Muircheartach Ua Briain in 1101. Moreover, the Rock's high status is further indicated by a genealogical tract preserved in the *Book of Lecan* which makes the point that the king of Munster was to be chosen in the same way as the German emperor, and proclaimed king at 'Cormac's great church'.[101] Given the emphasis placed on Cashel, especially in their early documents, it would be indeed surprising if the monks of the Schottenklöster had not striven to place one of their daughter houses there.

Further possible locations in Ireland?
The papal letters of 1248 to the abbot of St James at Regensburg do not mention any specific places. However, when the fortunes of the Schottenkloster at Memmingen had deteriorated so far in the fourteenth century that it could be described as *monasterium desolatum* (deserted monastery) efforts were made to raise funds through the supply of indulgences to possible benefactors. Six archbishops and twenty bishops are said to have consented to issue these in honour of Sts Mary, Nicholas, Erhard and Oswald. Likewise, these indulgences could be purchased in some fifty Benedictine abbeys *in Hybernia et in Allemania* (in Ireland and in Germany).[102]

---

101. Lec. 181 V c 21 = RIA Stowe C. I. 2, 44; F. J. Byrne, *Irish Kings and High-Kings* (London, 1973), p 191.
102. It may be of significance that Memmingen, just as Rosscarbery, seems later to have been administered from Würzburg; Flachenecker, *Schottenklöster*, pp 236–43; idem, 'Das mittelalterliche Schottenkloster St Nikolaus zu Memmingen', pp 188, 193.

How many of the fifty were Irish, or where they were located, is unknown. With the abbacy of Christianus' successor in Regensburg, Gregorius, the focus of the community in Regensburg shifted to Thomond, and Cashel seems to have played no further role in the literature of the Schottenklöster. Thus, while the necrology continues to commemorate Uí Briain kings and bishops of Thomond, as well as Mac Carthaig kings and bishops of Cork, of the twelfth and thirteenth-centuries, no further mention is made of archbishops of Cashel. Judging by the necrology, then, the dioceses most likely to have hosted a dependency are Limerick, Killaloe, Lismore, Cork and Cloyne.[103]

Holy Cross Abbey emerges as one of the main contenders for the role of a dependency of Regensburg in Ireland. Its dedication to 'St Mary, St Benedict and the Holy Cross', echoes the emergence of the cult of the Holy Cross, which the Schottenklöster of the same period recognised in their 'Heilig Kreuz' foundation in Eichstätt.[104] Lismore, where Cormac Mac Carthaig had reputedly founded twelve churches in the early twelfth century, is another case in point. Certainly, this monastery received its share of attention from a number of Schottenklöster texts. For example, saints Erhard and Albert are said to have heard the exhortation of its bishop to leave Ireland in pursuit of pilgrimage: *Si vis perfectus esse, vade, vende omnia que habes et da pauperibus et veni sequere me et habebis thesaurum in cello* (if you wish to be perfect, go, sell everything you have and give it to the poor and come follow me and you will have treasure in heaven).[105] Similarly, the *Vita Flannani*, which was reworked in Regensburg by the author of the *Vita Mariani* during the sixties and seventies of the twelfth century, contains a number of references to Lismore. Indeed, at one point, it expresses the fear that Lismore might displace Killaloe as the *paterna urbs* ('parental town') of the Uí Bhriain.[106]

---

103. Other relevant material is contained in some twelfth-century royal charters, which, as M-T. Flanagan has shown, depend, not on Anglo-Norman influence as previously thought, but on German imperial usage. The charter given by Diarmaid Mac Carthaig to the monks of Gill Abbey of Cork, confirming the benefactions of his father Cormac, is styled after charters issued by emperor Friedrich Barbarossa, a generous patron of the Schottenklöster. Furthermore, the charter given by Domnall Ua Briain to Holy Cross Abbey, Co. Tipperary between 1168 and 1185, shows in its contents and style influence of both papal and Imperial German chancery: M-T. Flanagan, 'The context and use of the Latin charter in twelfth-century Ireland' in H. Pryce (ed.), *Literacy in medieval Celtic societies* (Cambridge, 1996), pp. 115-32.
104. Flachenecker, 'Das ehemalige Schottenkloster Heiligkreuz in Eichstätt', pp 87-9; idem, *Schottenklöster*, pp 205-13.
105. *Vita Albarti*, MGHG rer. Merov. vi, p 22.
106. D. Ó Corráin, 'Foreign connections and domestic politics: Killaloe and the Uí Bhriain in twelfth-century hagiography', p 229.

Given the achievements of the Schottenklöster in Germany, it is difficult to explain why there is so little trace of significant Benedictine activity in twelfth-century Ireland. Apart from the dependency in Rosscarbery, known from later sources, and the bare possibility of the existence of others, there is relatively little to show of a *Hibernia Benedictina*. The traces that it has left are discussed below by Colmán Ó Clabaigh.

All in all, although the evidence of Benedictine activity in Ireland is relatively meagre, Cashel may still hold the key. With the original twelfth-century fabric of Cormac's Chapel still largely intact, the manner of its construction, its sculpture and wall paintings have still much to divulge.[107] The place lauded by the monks of the Schottenklöster as *celebris locus qui dicitur Caselle, que est civitas metropolis, urbs Hybernie regis* (famous place which is called Cashel, metropolitan city, town of the king of Ireland),[108] or as *metropolis … precellentissima* (pre-eminent metropolis), may yet prove to have been part of the tangled web of Irish Benedictine history.[109]

---

107. For a discussion of these questions see the papers in D. Bracken and D. Ó Riain-Raedel (eds), *Reform and renewal: Ireland and Europe in the twelfth century* (Dublin, forthcoming); See also R. Stalley, 'Solving a mystery at Cashel: the Romanesque painting in Cormac's Chapel' in *Irish Arts Review* 18 (2002), pp 25-9 and T. O'Keeffe, *Romanesque Ireland: architecture and ideology in the twelfth century* (Dublin, 2003).

108. Vita Albarti, MGHG rer. Merov. VI, p 22. A similar description is provided by the author of the *Libellus*: '*civitas regie, sedis regum Hyberniae*', '*archiepiscopatus Cassilensis regie sedis*'; Breatnach, *Libellus*, p 256.

109. Pfeil, *Die 'Vision des Tnugdalus'*, p *5. I wish to acknowledge the assistance received from the Royal Irish Academy and the Max Planck Institut für Geschichte, Göttingen, in the preparation of this article.

CHAPTER THREE

Early Irish Monastic Arts and the Architecture of the Benedictines in Ireland

Peter Harbison

The Benedictine monastery founded in the early 1180s in the beautiful valley of Fore in Co Westmeath (Fig 1) was dedicated to two saints of very different origins – Taurin and Fechin. St Taurin was the patron saint of the mother house at Evreux in Normandy, which had been granted the churches of Fore and other endowments by the Norman baron Hugh de Lacy. Gwynn

Fig 1: Fore, Co Westmeath. St Fechin's monastery with the Benedictine priory of Sts Taurin and Fechin in the background

and Hadcock point out that the new foundation was described by Gerald of Wales as a priory cell of a Norman monastery in Meath.[1] In contrast, St Fechin was a native Irish saint, a Sligo man who succumbed to the Yellow Plague in the 660s.[2] He founded other monasteries at Ballisodare in his native county, Cong in Co Mayo and on Omey Island off the Connemara coast in Co Galway which, in turn, may have been the mother house for Ardoilean, or High Island.[3] Fore may be the only instance of a late medieval

1. Aubrey Gwynn and R. N. Hadcock, *Medieval religious houses, Ireland* (London, 1970), p 106, (henceforth cited as Gwynn & Hadcock, *MRH*).
2. J. F Kenney, *The sources for the early history of Ireland: I, Ecclesiastical* (New York, 1929), pp 458-9.
3. J. White Marshall and G. D. Rourke, *High Island: an Irish monastery in the Atlantic* (Dublin, 2000).

monastic house dedicated jointly to a Norman and an Irish saint, perhaps a diplomatic move to ensure continuity with the earlier Irish foundation, which looks down on the Benedictine ruins from a terraced location on the lower slopes of the hills that rise gently on either side of the valley floor. A possible further link between these earlier and later medieval monasteries is the small figure carved on the chancel arch (Fig 2) that was added around 1200 to the church of St Fechin's old monastery, presumably after the arrival of the new community from Normandy. Harold Leask interprets it as a monk which, if a Benedictine, would make it into the earliest known representation of a member of the Order in Ireland.[4] But, it should be said that the vertical folds on the figure's overgarment would not fit in comfortably with the Benedictine habit - leaving the figure's nature and identity preferably an open question.

This church, to which the chancel was added, was a simple rectangle with a few narrow windows and a massive trabeate doorway with inclined jambs and a lintel famously bearing a cross in circle carved in relief upon it (Fig 3) – one of the few instances known in early Irish church architecture where a cross in stone was placed over the entrance. This feature alone is not sufficient for us to be able to date the church, which is unlikely to be earlier than the tenth century, and no later than the twelfth.

In the churchyard behind it is an undecorated High Cross[5] of uncertain vintage, which is a product of the early monastery, and one which reminds us of the marvellous art and craftsmanship that emanated from such early foundations, not just in stone but also in metalwork and manuscripts as well. One only has to look at the High Crosses of Moone, Monasterboice, Kells and Clonmacnois to realise what sculptural masterpieces were carved in order to deliver the message of the Bible to monk and layperson alike, each one varying the choice of Old and New Testament subjects represented, according to the story or dogma to be taught, and to explain – as at Moone – how the Lord saved the good in time of danger. These crosses are among the greatest stone testimonies to the artistic activities of those old Irish monasteries, some of which may have started in the time of St Patrick, but which did not really begin to flourish until the sixth century, under the leadership of saints like Finnian of Clonard, Ciarán of Clonmacnois, Brendan of Clonfert, as well as Columba (Colum Cille) and Columbanus. It was these latter two who

Fig 2: Fore, St Fechin's church, figure on chancel arch. © Department of the Environment, Heritage and Local Government

Fig 3: Fore, St Fechin's church, cross-inscribed lintel. © Department of the Environment, Heritage and Local Government

4. Harold Leask, *Fore, Co Westmeath* (Dublin, 1938), p 6.
5. Peter Harbison, *The High Crosses of Ireland* (3 vols, Bonn, 1992) vol i, p 90, and vol ii, figure 289.

started the *peregrini* movement, where monks – in a form of white martyr-dom – left their native land forever (though Columba did probably return on occasions) in order to mortify the flesh while simultaneously preaching the word of God. These monasteries gained an international reputation as seats of learning, where students could come from abroad to obtain free schooling, and where biblical exegesis was to reach a very high standard, respected throughout central and north-western Europe. Their physical surroundings were often modest – probably meagre huts of wood, and churches of the same material, many of which are unlikely to have been very much larger than an extensive modern living room. Adomnán's *Life of St Columba*, writ-ten in the late seventh century, gives us some idea of the daily lives of the monks, which frequently otherwise have to be pieced together from saints' lives written centuries after the lifetimes of their subjects.

One astonishing feature of early Irish Christianity is how the people adopted the new religion through a language not their own, which they would have had to learn *ab initio*. But they took to it like ducks to water and, though they did write short lyrical verses in Old Irish in the margins of their manuscripts, it was Latin that they used for their most important religious codices, even developing their own style of lettering that evolved from Late Antique models. Among the more renowned illuminated manuscripts, the oldest is the copy of the Psalter known as the *Cathach* ('the Battler') of St Columba, written around 600 and, thus, probably not long before the life-time of St Fechin. The most famous one is, of course, the *Book of Kells* of around 800, now in the Library of Trinity College, Dublin, which also houses the century-older *Book of Durrow* which is one of the most important artistic documents to survive anywhere in Europe from the time of its production – both manuscripts illuminated in a scriptorium or scriptoria within the family of Columban monasteries known as the *paruchia Columbae*, be it in Ireland or Scotland. The *Book of Kells* in particular shows clear borrowings from met-alwork and enamel decoration produced in monastic workshops, of which the Ardagh Chalice and the contents of the Derrynaflan hoard are among the finest examples.

Production in all three branches – sculpture, illumination and metalwork – seems to have slackened off during the tenth century, but surviving shrines for books such as the *Soiscél Molaise* show that metalwork, at least, revived again during the eleventh. But the opening of the following century was to see the beginnings of the end of many of the old Irish monasteries that had produced such great works of art and craftsmanship – ushered in by the Synod of Cashel in 1101. Here, church reform initiated decades earlier by

Pope Gregory VII first came up against the old Irish monasteries, which were inimical to the reformers. Rome disapproved of Irish lay abbots living in matrimony or concubinage, managing what amounted, in today's terms, to business corporations, and ensuring to some extent 'jobs for the boys' – usually, though probably not always, related by blood. Above all, these monasteries were not subservient to local bishops, a painful thorn in Rome's side, which wanted a church with bishops in control who were to be responsible to the central papacy. The seed sown at Cashel in 1101 matured a decade later at the Synod of Ráith Bresail. There, the papal legate, Gille (Gilbert), Bishop of Limerick, was an influential figure, laying down the guidelines by arguing in a document that the monasteries should be responsible to bishops who, in turn, made obeisance to the Pope.[6] Ráith Bresail saw the setting up of bishoprics throughout the country under two archbishoprics – Armagh and Cashel – which were to be extended to the present four by the addition of Dublin and Tuam at the Synod of Kells/Mellifont in 1152.

The old monasteries saw themselves as keepers of ancient Irish traditions and lore, both pagan and Christian,[7] and they did what they could to record as much of it as possible before the Reformers sapped their life-blood dry, to such an extent that most of the older monasteries had gone out of existence by around 1200, except for those which had been taken over and revitalised by the Augustinian Canons. Of all the continental religious orders that came to Ireland during the course of the twelfth and thirteenth centuries, the Augustinian Canons and the Franciscan Friars were the principal ones who could lay claim to having helped to preserve the old Irish culture, whereas others, particularly the Cistercians, set their sights much more on reform and the revitalisation of religious life.

But, as Dagmar Ó Riain-Raedel and Colmán Ó Clabaigh demonstrate, the Benedictines were also linked to the twelfth-century reform movement through their extensive continental and English contacts, the Rock of Cashel being perhaps the most impressive, if controversial, symbol of those links. Gwynn and Hadcock[8] outline in brief how two Irish monks, along with Conrad a carpenter and another man named William, were sent from Ratisbon/Regensburg in Germany to found a Benedictine priory at Cashel,

6. John Fleming (ed.) *Gille of Limerick* (Dublin, 2002).
7. Peter Harbison, 'Church reform and Irish monastic culture in the twelfth century' in *Journal of the Galway Archaeological and Historical Society,* 52 (2000), pp 2-12; idem, 'The otherness of Irish art in the twelfth century' in Colum Hourihane (ed) *From Ireland coming: Irish art from the Early Christian to the late Gothic period in its European context* (Princeton, 2001), pp 103-20.
8. Gwynn & Hadcock, *MRH,* pp 104-5.

Fig 4: Cashel, Cormac's
Chapel © Department
of the Environment,
Heritage and Local
Government

where the cousin of one of the monks was Cormac Mac Carthaigh (Mac Carthy), king of Desmond, who was building, or about to build, Cormac's Chapel at the time. Named after the king, this chapel (Fig 4) may not be the largest or the tallest building on the Rock, but it certainly is the most remarkable,[9] and was taken by Gwynn[10] to be 'a symbol of the reforming movement'. Constructed of a warm sandstone that was also used to roof it, it is one of the first and most exotic of all the Romanesque churches of Ireland – a unique structure consecrated with great pomp and circumstance in 1134. It 'seems quite clear that Cormac's Chapel was the chapel of the Benedictine monks' say Gwynn and Hadcock, who quote the suggestion of the late Dom Gerard MacGinty of Glenstal that Conrad and William were German monks with experience in building which, again in Gwynn and Hadcock's words, 'would explain the Teutonic character of the architecture of Cormac's Chapel'.

Gwynn and Hadcock's identification of Cormac's Chapel as the priory of the Benedictines who came from Bavaria has been challenged recently, and not without justification, by Roger Stalley in a talk given at a conference in Cashel in 2001, the text of which he has kindly let me study in advance of publication.[11] He argues that what has been taken as particularly Germanic in Cormac's Chapel, such as the two towers, are features found from Italy to England, so that they need not be seen as having necessarily come from Germany, and he has long argued that Cormac's Chapel is much more influenced by West of England design and decoration than by anything specifi-

9. A. Hill, *Ancient Irish architecture: a monograph of Cormac's Chapel, Cashel, Co Tipperary* (Cork, 1874).
10. Aubrey Gwynn, *The Irish Church in the eleventh and twelfth centuries* ed Gerard O'Brien (Dublin, 1992), p 214.
11. Roger Stalley, 'Architecture and ideology: the architecture and decoration of Cormac's chapel at Cashel', conference paper delivered at Reform and renewal: Ireland and Europe in the twelfth century, Cashel, October 2001.

cally Teutonic.[12] The apparent lack of any known domestic buildings associated with the chapel would, he thinks, argue against it having been built for the Benedictine community. Instead, he tends more towards the idea of its having been built as a political statement by Cormac Mac Carthaigh, who wanted to make Ireland aware that he was the first of his family to be the undisputed king of Munster since his traditional family power-base had been taken over a century and a half earlier by the Uí Bhriain (O'Briens), whom he had now finally succeeded in ousting. In a word, Cormac's Chapel should be seen as a symbol more of political change than church reform, one that was erected in haste perhaps in preparation for some specific occasion, or to look imposing as a kind of Chapel Royal. But if the Benedictines did not occupy Cormac's Chapel, where did they function on the Rock of Cashel? The question is best left open, due to lack of formal evidence, but a large question mark certainly has to be placed over their having been the inspirers of the chapel's architecture.

Even if the grounds are not strong enough for associating Cormac's Chapel with the church reform movement initiated at Cashel by his arch-rivals, the Uí Bhriain, it can be said that what the reforming continental orders did achieve with spectacular success was the introduction of a new monastic architecture with an orderly plan integrating church and community buildings into a single rectangular complex of stone. The results must have appeared vast and impressive in scale to those accustomed to the contemporary native churches like the present nave of St Fechin's church at Fore – which was presumably once surrounded by a number of small, individual domestic buildings made of wood. The newly-introduced scheme envisaged a large church with transepts, and often aisles to the nave, standing on one side of an open-air rectangular cloister-garth which was flanked on the other three sides by Chapter House, refectory, kitchen, stores and dormitory buildings. This is the layout seen in the 'classic' Cistercian houses of Mellifont, Jerpoint and Holy Cross among others,[13] and followed with variations by orders such as the Dominicans[14] and Franciscans.[15]

But this was also the plan used by the Benedictines at Fore[16] when the

12. Idem, 'Three Irish buildings with West Country origins' in N. Coldstream and P. Draper (eds) *Medieval art and architecture at Wells and Glastonbury* (London, 1981), pp 62-71.

13. Roger Stalley, *The Cistercian monasteries of Ireland* (London/New Haven), 1987.

14. Patrick Conlan, 'Irish Dominican medieval architecture' in M. Timoney (ed) *A celebration of Sligo: First essays for Sligo field club* (Sligo, 2002), pp 215-28.

15. Canice Mooney OFM, 'Franciscan architecture in Pre-Reformation Ireland' in *Journal of the Royal Society of Antiquaries of Ireland* 85, pp 133-73; 86, pp 125-69; 87, pp 1-38 and pp 103-24.

16. Leask, *Fore.*

Norman monks started building in the valley around 1200, and the scheme
was retained when the monastery was considerably rebuilt in the fifteenth
century (Figs 5-6). The rectangular and aisle-less church stands on the north
side of the cloister garth and, except for the western end, it is the major part
of the monastery which survives from the first phase of Benedictine building
at Fore – characterised by the trio of windows in the east wall, the central one
taller than the other two but all being now shorter than they were originally
because of blocking at the bottom. The eastern wall of the cloister also
belongs to the early phase of construction, but the main difference between
the earlier and later plan was that the early refectory lay further to the south
than its fifteenth-century successor, and only survives as little more than
foundations outside the main building complex.

Otherwise, most of the structures around the cloister – as well as the
attractive cloister-arcade itself – date to the fifteenth century, as does the
tower guarding the western end of the church. Even though Fore had its difficulties with various English kings during the Anglo-French wars because it
was regarded as an 'alien' French foundation, we may assume that it was not
until the fifteenth century that Fore took on the appearance of a fortified
monastery, not only with the aforementioned tower at the western end of the
church, but also with the unexpectedly massive one above the sacristy, providing living quarters but also a refuge in times of danger. The reason for
making Fore a fortress was that the monastery lay near the western extremity
of the Pale, that movable and largely imaginary boundary guarding the area
where English writ ran in Ireland and separating it from the land further west
where the Irish dominated. Gaelic raids on Fore by the Ó Fearghail

Fig 6: Fore Priory, from the west, in a drawing attributed to George Petrie, the present whereabouts of which are unknown. Photograph courtesy of Triarc, Trinity College, Dublin.

(O'Farrell) and Ó Raghaillaigh (O'Reilly) in 1423 and 1428 respectively may have prompted the erection of these towers, possibly by Prior William Anglond who is known to have built castles on the monastery's lands to keep the 'enemies' at bay. But, as Rory Masterson pointed out in his recent case-history of the monastery, Fore was not just a place where the monks spent their lives in peaceful prayer and contemplation.[17] They were part of the political and land-owning scene – hence the need for fortification – supporting the government in Dublin and being, as it were, a pre-Reformation version of 'Castle Catholics'. The last prior of the monastery was a Nugent, who surrendered it under duress to Henry VIII in 1539 – and doubtless, not without regret because, in the following year, it was found to consist not only of 'certain castles or towers with other stone buildings in sufficient repair … very necessary for defence against attacks of the wild Irish upon the king's subjects' but also 2000 acres of land and much else besides.[18]

At around the same time that Hugh de Lacy was establishing the monks at Fore, his northern counterpart, John de Courcy, was settling other Benedictines at Downpatrick in County Down. He allegedly replaced some earlier Canons there, and brought in monks from Chester to create a priory,

---

17. Rory Masterson, 'The alien priory of Fore, Co Westmeath, in the middle ages' in *Archivium Hibernicum*, 53 (1999), pp 73-79; Idem., 'The Church and the Anglo-Norman colonisation of Ireland: a case study of the priory of Fore' in *Ríocht na Midhe* xi (2000), pp 58-70; Idem, 'The early Anglo-Norman colonisation of Fore, Co Westmeath' in *Ríocht na Midhe* xiii (2002), pp 44-60. I am grateful to Colmán Ó Clabaigh for drawing my attention to these articles.
18. Gwynn & Hadcock, *MRH*, p 106.

on the site where – according to Gerald of Wales – he miraculously discovered the remains of Sts Patrick, Brigid and Colum Cille (or Columba) in what can only be described as a massive public relations ruse. The priory continued to exist until the Reformation, but during the first two decades of the thirteenth century it was so damaged in the wars of John de Courcy that the monks had to request Henry III to find them habitation in England while their church was being rebuilt. It suffered further under Edward the Bruce and his army in 1315-16, and was burned in 1538 by the Lord Deputy, Leonard Grey – a deed which contributed to his beheading in the Tower of London three years later.

A drawing said to be by, or after, Charles Lilly, the architect who restored the cathedral between 1789 and 1812, has been taken by Fred Rankin to be the most accurate depiction of the cathedral before Lilly himself started work. It shows the building from the north-east, with stout buttresses flanking the broad east window (perhaps a fifteenth-century insertion), and a northern arcade of five arches separating the side-aisle from the main body of the church.[19] A string course is hinted at over the arcade, above which there are small clerestory windows placed above each arch. Other late-eighteenth or early-nineteenth century illustrations seen from a similar angle and also reproduced by Rankin mark the string course more clearly, and show the clerestory windows varying in size but invariably above the arches of the arcade.[20]

In 1986, Nick Brannon took what he described as 'a once-in-a-lifetime opportunity' to strip the walls above the arcade, and uncovered evidence for the string course which had been crudely chopped off prior to modern plastering – thus vindicating the accuracy of the old drawings in this respect. But, more dramatically, he discovered above it 'four surviving features which have been interpreted as windows, apertures in the walls outlined in dressed sandstone and infilled with later brickwork or stone' which, to his surprise, were placed over the arcade piers, rather than over the arcade arches as they are today and as they were in all the early drawings assembled by Rankin. This led Brannon to conclude that there were two building stages of the medieval Benedictine church – the first (presumably thirteenth century) with the windows over the piers, as represented by what he found under the plaster, and

---

19. J. F. Rankin, 'The round tower of Down' in *Down Survey 1997, the Yearbook of the Down County Museum*, pp 23-28, at pp 23-4.
20. Ibid. See also J. F. Rankin, 'Down Cathedral ruins – a newly discovered painting' in *Down Survey 2000, the Yearbook of the Down County Museum*, pp 78-80.

Fig 7: Downpatrick
Cathedral. © National
Library of Ireland

the second (which he took to be late medieval) as seen in the Lilly and other
drawings.[21]

However, an eighteenth-century drawing which I came across recently in
the National Library in Dublin suggests that only the first of Brannon's two
stages need be considered medieval, as its details correspond to what he
found in the medieval fabric rather than to what can be seen in the early illustrations published by Rankin. The drawing (Fig 7), preserved in what is
known as the Grose volume in the National Library (with the accession number 1976 TX 86), has no title and has, therefore, hitherto remained unidentified and unrecognised, but there can be no doubt that it represents
Downpatrick Cathedral, though seen directly from the north, rather than
from the north-east as in the other early illustrations. We can recognise the
vanished Round Tower on the extreme left, and the ruined cathedral shell
occupying the centre of the picture. The external wall is a rag-bag of openings, secondary or built up, but above it the tops of the five heavily-moulded
arcade arches are clearly visible. About five stone courses above them comes
the string course, marked clearly as standing out from the wall, and – above
it again – come four openings placed above the arcade piers as Brannon
found them. Three are pointed, that on the extreme right having bifurcating
tracery, and the other two apparently blocked up. The fourth opening, on the
extreme left, has vertical sides linked on top by a slightly rounded arch.

---

21. Nick Brannon, 'Recent discoveries at Down Cathedral and Quoile castle: an interim
report' in *Lecale Miscellany*, 5 (1987), pp 3-9.

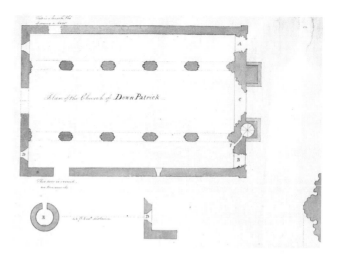

The Grose album gets its name because a number of drawings in the volume were seemingly prepared for use in Grose's *Antiquities of Ireland*, the first engravings for which were done in 1791. The Downpatrick drawing was not one of those finally selected for engraving in the two Grose volumes but, though undated, it is likely to be no later than 1791 – and may well be a copy of an earlier original. It is sadly unsigned, but it is difficult not to see this view or elevation as the companion to a plan of the cathedral which I also discovered in the National Library – with the accession number 2122 TX (102) in the Prints and Drawings Department – and which was subsequently published twice by Rankin.[22] The plan (Fig 8)was part of the collection of the antiquary Austin Cooper (1759-1830), which included material that he had acquired from the estate of William Burton Conyngham (1733-1796). The plan of the cathedral was drawn by Cooper himself in October 1799, but the letters GB in the bottom left-hand corner shows that he was copying an original by the Huguenot artist Gabriel Beranger (1729-1817). The original is now, sadly, lost, but it is likely to have been in the Burton Conyngham collection to start with, as Beranger was heavily involved in collecting and making drawings for Burton Conyngham in the years around 1779 to 1781. Many, though by no means all, of the drawings in the Grose album in the National Library – including the view of Downpatrick Cathedral – are likely to be copies of originals formerly in the Burton Conyngham collection, as the attributions of those engraved in Grose's *Antiquities* attest. It would not be unreasonable to suppose, therefore, that the plan – and probably also the

---

22. J. F. Rankin, *Down Cathedral: The Church of Saint Patrick of Down* (Belfast, 1997), p 39 and idem., 'Round Tower of Down', p 27.

view – of Downpatrick were the products of an expedition undertaken by Beranger for Burton Conyngham at some date unknown and unrecorded, though quite likely in the period 1779-81. The view of Downpatrick in the National Library is, however, not in the style of Beranger, and should be seen as a copy of an original by some artist, as yet unidentified, who may have accompanied Beranger to Downpatrick – the anonymous artist doing the elevational view and Beranger the plan, just as Bigari and Beranger had done in Connacht in the summer of 1779.[23] If my hunch be correct, the original of the copy reproduced here (Fig 7) may have been drawn about a decade or so before Lilly's picture (which can be no earlier than 1789), and is, therefore, likely to be the only known drawing showing the cathedral in its medieval state before Lilly started his work of restoration. Because the Lilly drawing and its followers show the clerestory windows above the arches, and not above the piers as in the drawing reproduced here (and as found by Brannon in the medieval fabric beneath the plaster), it would seem that the placing of the clerestory windows above the arches, as Lilly drew them, represents not the medieval state of the cathedral but the way in which Lilly wanted to reconstruct the building, thereby making Brannon's second medieval phase superfluous.

We may take it that the medieval part of the present cathedral is the result of the re-building that took place in 1220 and later, and it may have replaced an earlier cruciform church which excavations by Nick Brannon uncovered within its walls.[24] There is as yet no supporting evidence for the suggestion by Waterman that the medieval building now forming the core of the cathedral was once the choir of a much larger church extending further to the west.[25] But the source of the inspiration for the medieval church (Fig 7) has never been the subject of any major investigation, and might make a good topic for a small thesis. Like Cormac's Chapel, Down Cathedral is something of an exotic that does not fit into any obvious Irish context. With monks coming from Chester in the 1180s, and their successors seeking succour in England while their ravaged church was being rebuilt (or replaced), it would be only natural to look to somewhere in England for its model, but influence from Chester's mother house at Le Bec in Normandy should not be ruled

---

23. Peter Harbison, '*Our treasure of antiquities': Beranger and Bigari's antiquarian sketching tour of Connacht in 1779* (Bray, 2002).
24. Bannon, op.cit.
25. D. M. Waterman, 'Downpatrick Cathedral' in *An archaeological survey of County Down* (Belfast, 1966), pp 266-72.

out, as shown by comparison with an engraving of 1677 illustrated in Fred Rankin's definitive monograph on the cathedral.[26]

It has been presumed that domestic buildings of the monks would have been attached to the medieval church, though what they looked like or how they linked in with the church has never been established. The nineteenth-century Phillips plan of their layout reproduced by Rankin may be taken as illusory,[27] but a Time Team programme for Channel 4 television in 1997 – in which I participated – carried out an excavation on the site of the modern tennis courts in an effort to shed further light on the matter.[28] But the remains of the structure which was tentatively identified as a rubbish chute (rather than the even less attractive alternative of garderobes or lavatories) did little to add to our scant knowledge of the finer aspects of life that the medieval Benedictines left behind them in Ireland.[29]

These finer aspects may have included two manuscripts illustrated and discussed in some detail by Fred Rankin in his book on the cathedral. One is a twelfth-century Gradual (Ms Rawlinson C 892 in the Bodleian Library in Oxford), and the other the so-called Rosslyn Missal of the later thirteenth century, now in the National Library of Scotland in Edinburgh, for both of which reasonable grounds – though no absolute proofs – exist that they were used in Downpatrick by the Benedictines.[30] I have also been made aware of a claim by Canon Power that a combined ciborium and chalice in three parts, and made of silver and bone, was traditionally associated with the Benedictine priory of St John the Evangelist in Waterford city, some of the walls of which he described. But the connection of the liturgical vessel with this house of the Order must remain an open question.[31]

This brief overview of the architecture of the medieval Benedictines in Ireland shows that the churches at Fore and Downpatrick are very different in style and, even if Cormac's Chapel were to be proven to have been Benedictine, it would only serve to demonstrate that the variety would have been even greater. What is quite clear is that there is nothing that can be characterised as typical Benedictine architecture in Ireland – or indeed anywhere else in Europe either.

26. Rankin, *Down Cathedral*, p 22.
27. Ibid., p 100
28. T. Taylor, 'Downpatrick, Co Down' in *Time Team 98, the site reports* (London, 1998), pp 47-51.
29. Rankin, *Down Cathedral*, p 49
30. Ibid., pp 60-62. But see Colmán Ó Clabaigh's article below, p 87
31. Patrick Power, 'The priory, church and hospital of St John the Evangelist, Waterford' in *Journal of the Waterford and South-East of Ireland Archaeological Society*, 2, (1896) pp 81-97, at p 97. I am grateful to Colmán Ó Clabaigh for drawing this article to my attention.

Given the foreign inspiration of the buildings erected by the medieval Benedictines in Ireland, it may be said that their modern counterparts would seem to have been following in their footsteps. Richard Hurley suggested that the church built at Glenstal in 1951-56 by Dom Sebastian Braun (who came from Maredsous Abbey in Belgium), owed something to a movement a century ago which turned away from neo-Gothic towards a stronger neo-Romanesque design.[32] But we must keep in mind the strong possibility that the architect may have borrowed ideas from his native Belgium, reverberating echoes of medieval churches such as that of St Hadelin at Celles,[33] with its unadorned nave arcade having simple chamfered capitals and tall clerestory windows above (without intervening string course), a raised choir, flat wooden ceiling, a large proscenium arch with another slightly lower one behind it – and with an apse which Fr Sebastian had planned for Glenstal,[34] but which was never built. However, even without it, the new church must have made Glenstal's Belgian monks feel very much at home, and provides their Irish successors with a dignified ambience for their daily glorification of God.

---

32. R. Hurley, *Irish Church architecture in the era of Vatican II* (Dublin, 2001), pp 27-28.
33. A. Courtens, *Romanische Kunst in Belgien*, (Vienna/Munich, 1969), pl 27.
34. Hurley, *Irish Church architecture*, p 27.

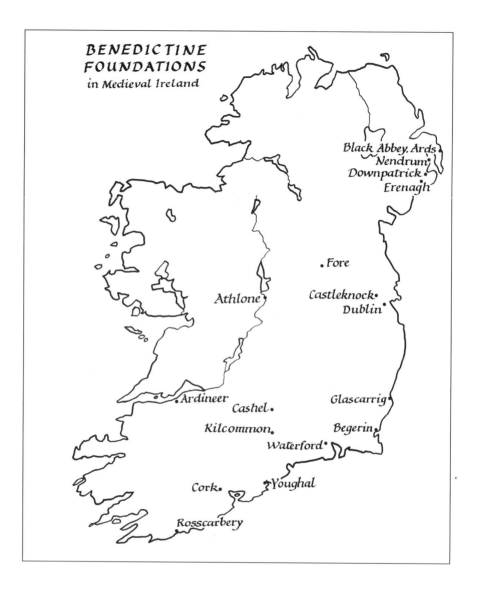

BENEDICTINE
FOUNDATIONS
in Medieval Ireland

Black Abbey, Ards
Nendrum
Downpatrick
Erenagh

. Fore

Castleknock.
Dublin

Athlone

Ardineer   Cashel .   Glascarrig

Kilcommon.   Begerin

Waterford .

Cork .   Youghal

Rosscarbery

CHAPTER FOUR

The Benedictines in Medieval and Early Modern Ireland

Colmán Ó Clabaigh OSB

Hibernia Benedictina?

The late Fr Bernard O'Dea of Glenstal took a great deal of pride in his status as the first native Benedictine monk to be professed in Ireland since the Reformation. This, however, did not prevent him recounting an incident which occurred while studying as a young monk in Belgium in the late 1930s. While visiting the abbey of Mont César in Louvain he was introduced to a distinguished member of the English Benedictine Congregation. On hearing his provenance, the English monk exclaimed, 'An Irish Benedictine? Impossible! Irishmen are temperamentally unsuited to Benedictine life, our hallmark is "moderation" and our motto is "peace".' In this he was giving a somewhat extreme expression to a widespread, and indeed lingering, perception that the Irish temperament, with its perceived predilection for the romantic, the harshly ascetic, and the extreme, was at variance with the more moderate monastic programme outlined in the Rule of St Benedict. That this is not entirely true for Irish monks and nuns on the continent has already been demonstrated by Dáibhí Ó Cróinín and Dagmar Ó Riain-Raedel. What this essay proposes to examine is the extent to which it is not entirely true for medieval Ireland.

It will proceed by first presenting the evidence for the circulation of the Rule of St Benedict and awareness of his cult in Ireland before the eleventh and twelfth centuries. The evidence for contact with monasteries of Black Monks in England and elsewhere will also be examined. These contacts played a significant role in the development of the twelfth-century reform movement in the Irish church, and a small number of Benedictine monasteries was established in consequence. The impact of the Anglo-Norman invasion and the role of English and Norman monasteries as agents of colonisation will then be examined. The later medieval experience will be explored by examining the individual houses and the survey concludes with an analysis of the impact of the Dissolution campaign on those monasteries that survived into the sixteenth century.

While making allowance for local circumstances, certain broad patterns emerge. After an initial period of expansion and consolidation in the twelfth and early thirteenth centuries, the foundations shared in the general fate of the Anglo-Norman colony, experiencing decline, uncertainty and hardship in the wake of the resurgence of Gaelic Ireland and the upheavals of the fourteenth century. Surviving evidence suggests that the internal affairs of the houses, particularly those in Gaelic or border areas, followed the pattern of better documented orders like the Cistercians and Augustinian Canons. In some cases, community living, maintenance of hospitality, and the celebration of the Divine Office had lapsed by the fourteenth and fifteenth centuries. The observance of celibacy also seems to have been somewhat sporadic, with a number of monasteries coming under the control of hereditary clerical dynasties.

It is perhaps appropriate to enter the *caveat* that this picture of Benedictine life in medieval Ireland owes much to the character of the surviving sources which are largely of a legal or punitive nature. The Irish material in official sources like the Patent, Close, Justiciary and Exchequer rolls, is almost exclusively administrative. The material contained in papal and episcopal archives generally relates to ecclesiastical court cases involving Irish monks and nuns, which, though interesting and informative, is rarely edifying. A number of references to the Irish properties of English monasteries in the chartularies and administrative records of the mother houses shed incidental light on Irish affairs, but this too is fragmentary and sporadic, as are the entries in the Gaelic and Anglo-Irish annals. Nothing of a literary or theological nature survives to give an insight into the intellectual culture of Irish houses similar to that given above by Dagmar Ó Riain-Raedel for the *Schottenklöster*, or by Martin Heale for comparable foundations in England.[1] Very little survives to illustrate their material or artistic culture. Indeed, there is practically nothing to convey any sense of what ordinary monastic life, with its daily round of liturgy and prayer, work and study, was like for the Black Monks and Nuns of medieval Ireland. Yet the simple fact of the survival of these communities over several centuries provides evidence for at least a modicum of vitality.

The Rule and Cult of St Benedict in Medieval Ireland
While, as Dáibhí Ó Cróinín has demonstrated, Irish monasteries on the continent played a seminal role in the transmission of both the Rule and the cult of St Benedict, the extent to which this tradition was known in Ireland is less

---

1. Martin Heale, 'Books and learning in the dependent priories of the monasteries of medieval England' in C. M. Barron and J. Stra (eds) *The Church and learning in later medieval society: essays in honour of R. B. Dobson* (Donnington, 2002), pp 64-79.

well documented. A number of early references indicate however that the Rule was known and respected as an authoritative guide for the monastic life. The earliest and most extensive borrowing occurs in a text known as the *Bigotian Penitential*, which dates to the late seventh or eighth century. Its preface includes a lengthy quotation from chapter four of the Rule of Benedict, dealing with the tools of good works.[2] While the purely Irish character of this work is disputed,[3] it does draw on the mid seventh-century *Penitential of Cummian* and in turn is drawn on by the early ninth-century *Old Irish Penitential* indicating that it was at least known in Ireland even if it received its final form elsewhere.

The eighth-century collection of Irish ecclesiastical legislation known as the *Collectio Canonum Hibernensis* includes a chapter *De monachis* dealing with the monastic life. Citing an apocryphal letter from St Jerome to St Benedict, it enumerates the four different types of monks in terms that derive directly from the first chapter of the Rule of Benedict. The chapter also shows Benedictine influence in nominating the cenobites, 'soldiering under a rule and an abbot', as the 'best kind of monk'.[4]

In his edition of the *Voyage of St Brendan*, Carl Selmer draws attention to a number of references and allusions in the text which indicate knowledge of the Benedictine tradition.[5] In the second chapter, before embarking on his voyage, St Brendan summons fourteen of the brethren for counsel in a manner reminiscent of the Rule of Benedict's injunction to the abbot to seek advice before making important decisions.[6] In chapter twelve, during the visit to the island monastery of St Ailbe, the abbot's suggestion to Brendan that they return to the refectory while it is still light and references to the office of Compline are also thought to indicate familiarity with Benedictine practice. It is possible however, as Michaela Zelzer argues, that, while the text preserves a genuine account of an early Irish sea voyage, the Benedictine ref-

---

2. Ludwig Bieler, *The Irish penitentials* (Dublin, 1963), pp 198-239. Quotation at pp 210-12.

3. Ibid., p 10. But see also J. F. Kenney, *The sources for the early history of Ireland: I ecclesiastical* (New York, 1929), p 241, where he argues for an Irish provenance. The composite nature of the *Bigotian Penitential* and its complex relationship with the monastic and disciplinary writings of Columbanus are discussed by T. M. Charles-Edwards, 'The Penitential of Columbanus' in *Columbanus: studies on the Latin writings* (Woodbridge, 1997), pp 217-39, particularly pp 226-32. I am grateful to an tOll Dáibhí Ó Cróinín for drawing my attention to this article.

4. Hermann Wasserschleben (ed), *Die irische Kanonensammlung* (Leipzig, 1895), pp 147-52, quotation at p 149.

5. Carl Selmer (ed.) *Navigatio Sancti Brendani Abbatis* (Notre Dame, 1959).

6. Ibid., pp 9-10, 84. I am grateful to Dr Westley Follett for drawing my attention to the above references.

erences are due to the text's recension in a continental monastic setting rather than in an Irish milieu.[7]

The influence of the Rule of St Benedict on the liturgy of the reformed ninth-century Céli Dé monastery at Tallaght in Co Dublin has recently been traced by Westley Follett, who argues that the arrangement of the psalms for the liturgy in Tallaght may have been influenced by the cursus outlined in the Rule.[8] Other liturgical texts from Tallaght provide further evidence for a widespread awareness of St Benedict's cult in certain sections of the early Irish church. The *Martyrology of Tallaght* and the *Martyrology of Óengus*, composed c 830, both commemorate Benedict twice, on March 21st and July 11th, while the former commemorates his disciple St Maur on January 15th.[9] On Iona, as Ó Cróinín has noted, the ninth abbot, St Adomnán, is one of the earliest witnesses to the circulation of the *Dialogues* attributed to St Gregory the Great. The second book of the *Dialogues* was the sole source of information about Benedict during the middle ages, and Adomnán borrowed a number of topoi from this work in his own *Life of Columba*, most memorably the account of how Columba once saw the whole world gathered up into a single ray of light.[10] The *Martyrology of Drummond*, recently assigned an Armagh provenance, and a composition date in the latter half of the twelfth century by Pádraig Ó Riain, combines the liturgical and hagiographical elements in its entry for March 21st:

> *Apud Casinum castrum, natale sancti Benedicti eximi abbatis, cuius vitam, virtutibus et miraculis gloriosam in Dialogorum libris beatus papa Grigorius scripsit.*[11] (At the fortress of Cassino, the birth of the distinguished abbot, St Benedict, of whose glorious life, virtues and miracles the blessed Pope Gregory has written in the Books of the Dialogues.)

Dom Hubert Janssens OSB lists a number of other possible early literary references to the Rule in Irish literature and to monasteries which may have

7. Michaela Zelzer, 'Frühe irische Amerikafahrten und monastische reform: Zur Navigatio sancti Brendani Abbatis' in *Wiener Humanistiche Blatter*, 31 (1989), pp 66-87. See also Dagmar Ó Riain-Raedel, above p 30.
8. Westley Follett, 'The Divine Office and extra-Office vigils among the Culdees of Tallaght' in *Journal of Celtic Studies* v (forthcoming).
9. R. I. Best and H. J. Lawlor, *The martyrology of Tallaght* (Henry Bradshaw Society, London, 1931), pp 8, 25, 28; Whitley Stokes, *On the calendar of Oengus* in *Transactions of the Royal Irish Academy: Irish manuscripts series* (Dublin, 1880) pp lvii, cx. The commemoration of St Maur may be a twelfth-century addition. Professor Pádraig Ó Riain, personal communication.
10. A. O. Anderson and M. O. Anderson (eds and translation) *Adomnan's life of Columba*, (London, 1961), pp 204, 302.
11. Pádraig Ó Riain (ed), *Four Irish martyrologies: Drummond, Turin, Cashel, York* (Henry Bradshaw Society, London, 2002) p 48.

followed it before the twelfth century, but these are fragmentary and uncertain.[12]

Despite these early references, no manuscript of the Rule of St Benedict survives in Ireland before the end of the thirteenth century, when a copy was included in Trinity College Dublin MS 97, a collection of monastic rules and related legislation compiled for the Augustinian Canons of St Thomas' Abbey in Dublin. While it is almost certain that it owes its inclusion in this codex to the proximity of the Cistercian community at St Mary's Abbey on the north bank of the river Liffey, the presence of extensive marginal commentaries on various chapters, and a formula of monastic profession, would repay further investigation.[13]

Unlike the English and continental monasteries, which formed national and reform congregations in the late middle ages, the Black Monks in Ireland remained fragmented, with no central authority to maintain discipline or to keep records. There is some slight evidence that this might have been attempted, or at least envisaged, for the Irish monasteries. In 1336, the reforming pope, and former Cistercian monk, Benedict XII, outlined a comprehensive reform programme for the Benedictines in the bull *Summi Magistri*, more commonly known as the *Benedictina*.[14] Central to this programme was the amalgamation into congregations of monasteries within specified ecclesiastical provinces or geographical territories. These were to meet in chapter triennially and to appoint visitators to ensure that the programme outlined in the bull's thirty-nine chapters was observed. The four ecclesiastical provinces of Ireland were nominated as the basic unit for the Irish 'congregation', but evidence that this was ever put into effect is lacking.[15] Similarly, in 1394, Pope Boniface IX appointed Francis da Cappanago, prior of the Augustinian house of St Martin in Siena, as papal nuncio to Ireland. He was specifically commissioned to

> visit in person and enquire, correct and reform monasteries, priories, provostries and other regular places of Cistercians, Cluniacs, Canons Regular of St Augustine and other non-mendicant orders immediately

---

12. Hubert Janssens de Varebeke, 'The Benedictines in medieval Ireland' in *Proceedings of the Royal Irish Academy*, lxxx, (1950), pp 92-96.

13. Trinity College, Dublin, MS 97, folios 166-78; Marvin L. Colker, *Trinity College Library Dublin, descriptive catalogue of the Medieval and Renaissance Latin manuscripts* (2 vols, Aldershot, 1991), i, p 190.

14.Carolus Cocquelines (ed), *Bullarum privilegorum ac diplomatum Romanorum Pontificum*, Tomus tertius, pars secunda (Rome, 1741), pp 214-40.

15. Ibid., p 216.

subject to the Roman church, which are known to be in no small need thereof.[16]

His powers included the right to impose decisions without right of appeal, but no record of his visitation, or of its effect, survives.

The Benedictines and the Hiberno-Norse sees

The close association between the Hiberno-Norse sees of Waterford, Limerick and particularly Dublin and various English Benedictine monasteries is well established. The recent work of Raghnall Ó Floinn and Pádraig Ó Riain,[17] discussed above by Dagmar Ó Riain-Raedel, has introduced an important new element into the debate and it now appears that the origins of the diocese of Dublin owe much to the involvement of Irish Benedictine monks based, not in England, but in Germany. In his analysis of the relic list of Christ Church, Dublin, Ó Floinn argues that a core group of relics represent the foundation relics of the new cathedral. The presence of several relics of apostles, bishops and popes, he argues, would be particularly appropriate for a newly established diocese. These relics were procured for the cathedral by Dúnán (Donatus), first Bishop of Dublin, and the fact that many of the 'authority' relics, along with others recorded in the Christ Church list, were venerated in Cologne indicates close ecclesiastical contacts with that city. He suggests that the 1028 Roman pilgrimage of King Sitriuc of Dublin may have included *Colonia sacra* (Holy Cologne) on its itinerary and that the relics might have been procured there. He further suggests that Dúnán may have been a monk of one of the two Irish Benedictine houses in the city.[18] It can further be added that the list's relic of St Benedict, described as *sancti patris nostri* (of our Holy Father), also indicates an authority role and filial attachment and suggests that from the outset a Benedictine community may have been established in Christ Church, Dublin.

This German connection notwithstanding, the closest and most sustained contacts between the Hiberno-Norse sees in the eleventh and twelfth centuries were with Benedictine monasteries in England. Here monastic life had undergone a re-invigoration in the tenth and eleventh centuries under the

16. W. H. Bliss and J. A. Twemlow, *Calendar of the entries in the papal registers relating to Great Britain and Ireland; papal letters, vol. iv, AD 1362-1404* (London, 1902), p 289 (henceforth cited as *Cal. pap. letters*).

17. Pádraig Ó Riain, 'Dublin's oldest book? A list of saints 'made in Germany' in Seán Duffy (ed) *Medieval Dublin* V (Dublin, 2003), pp 52-71.

18. I am grateful to Raghnall Ó Floinn for allowing me to read this article in advance of publication.

leadership of outstanding abbots such as Sts Dunstan, Aethelwold and Oswald.[19] Many of the centres of this reform were in the West Country and Severn valley, areas with longstanding Irish associations. As well as claiming to be the burial place of King Arthur, the abbey of Glastonbury in Somerset also claimed to be the birthplace of St Patrick, and Irish pilgrims were frequent visitors to the abbey of Evesham in the late eleventh century.[20]

In particular, the links between Dublin and the church of Canterbury, both with its archbishops and the Benedictine cathedral priory of Christ Church, are recognised as central to the development of the early diocese.[21] Both cathedrals shared the same dedication, to the Holy Trinity, as did the cathedral in Waterford; all three were commonly known as Christ Church. Four of the first five bishops of Dublin made professions of obedience as suffragans of Canterbury and at least three of them were monks of English Benedictine houses. A number of Irishmen are recorded as members of the Canterbury community and the establishment of a community of monks serving Christ Church, Dublin was similar to the arrangement obtaining at a number of English cathedrals, including Canterbury and Worcester. The monks' expulsion from Christ Church, Dublin c 1096 by Bishop Samuel, himself a former monk of St Albans, led to a sharp letter of reprimand from St Anselm.[22]

Dublin links with other English monasteries were also strong. The relics of St Wulfstan (d 1095), monastic reformer and bishop of Worcester, were among those venerated in Dublin, and the Worcester library contained a large number of Irish texts.[23] Bishop Gilla Pátraic (Patrick) of Dublin, formerly a monk of Worcester, was the author of a number of Latin poems and prose pieces, some dedicated to his erstwhile confrères.[24] Close trading links with the west of England are the reason for the dedication of one of Dublin's

---

19. David Knowles, *The monastic order in England* (Cambridge, 1941), pp 31-82; Janet Burton, *Monastic and religious orders in Britain, 1000-1300* (Cambridge, 1994), pp 1-20; Oswald McBride, 'The tenth-century monastic revival' in Daniel Rees (ed), *Monks of England* (London, 1997), pp 65-83.
20. Denis Bethell, 'English monks and Irish reform in the eleventh and twelfth centuries' in T. D. Williams (ed), *Historical Studies VIII* (Dublin, 1971), pp 111-35. Reference at p 116.
21. Howard B. Clarke, 'The diocese of Dublin to 1152', in James Kelly and Dáire Keogh (eds) *A history of the Catholic diocese of Dublin* (Dublin, 2000), pp 19-50, particularly pp 40-50; Martin Holland, 'Dublin and the reform of the Irish church in the eleventh and twelfth centuries' in *Peritia*, 14 (2000), pp 111-60.
22. *S. Anselmi Cantuariensis Archiepiscopi opera omnia*, ed F. S. Schmitt (5 vols, Edinburgh, 1946-1951), iv, pp 191-92.
23. Bethell, 'English monks', pp 116-17.
24. Aubrey Gwynn (ed) *The writings of Bishop Patrick 1074-1084* (Dublin, 1955).

parish churches to St Werburgh, patron saint of Chester, whose relics were enshrined in the Benedictine monastery there. In the late twelfth century the monks of Chester were also granted property in Dublin by William de Mesech.[25]

Nor were these intellectual and cultural influences confined to Dublin. Bishop Gille (Gilbert) of Limerick corresponded with St Anselm[26] and Bishop Malchus (Máel Isú Ua hAinmire) of Waterford, formerly a monk of Winchester, may have followed the Rule of Benedict in the reformed monastery he established at Lismore. These contacts, though significant, were relatively small scale and resulted in few foundations.

The Benedictines and the 12th century reform of the Irish church

These increased contacts inevitably brought the Irish church into contact with reform currents in European ecclesiastical affairs. Pilgrimage to Rome in particular exposed Irish secular and ecclesiastical leaders to the principles of the reform promoted by Pope Gregory VII and various of his successors in the See of Peter. In the late eleventh century a community of Irish monks at Rome established the monastery of Holy Trinity of the Scots on the Palatine hill. While the principal evidence for this community consists of two lists of names surviving in a contemporary manuscript now in the Vatican library, it seems likely that they followed the Benedictine rule.[27] These monks would have provided hospitality to their countrymen on pilgrimage to Rome and were probably recruited from among Irish pilgrims who decided to end their days in retirement there. Like their confrères in the *Schottenklöster*, the community in Rome appears to have had ecclesiastical and royal contacts in Munster and may have acted as a liaison between the reforming Uí Bhriain dynasty and the papacy.[28]

The evidence for Irish Benedictine links with German monasteries and the emergence of the Irish Benedictine Congregation of St James (the *Schottenklöster*) is discussed above by Dagmar Ó Riain-Raedel.

Further evidence for Benedictine influences on the twelfth-century reformers comes from a number of liturgical sources. A recent analysis of the liturgical references in the writings of Bishop Gille of Limerick has led Martin Holland to suggest that he was a Benedictine monk, possibly of St

25. J. T. Tait (ed), *The chartulary or registers of the abbey of St Werburgh, Chester* (2 vols, Manchester, 1920-23[Chetham Society, vols 79 & 82]), ii (vol 82), pp 471-2, no 884.
26. *S. Anselmi opera omnia*, ed. Schmitt, v, pp 374-76.
27. André Wilmart, 'La Trinité des Scots a Rome et les notes du Vat. Lat. 378' in *Revue Bénédictine*, 41 (1929), pp 218-30.
28. Holland, 'Dublin & reform', p 144.

Albans in England.[29] The peculiarities of Bodleian MS Rawlinson C 892, a twelfth-century Irish Gradual, led Derek Turner to suggest that it was produced for an Irish cathedral staffed by Benedictine monks. As Downpatrick was the only cathedral to fulfil these criteria in the twelfth century, he proposed Down as a possible provenance. This has been accepted by subsequent scholars but has recently been challenged on repertorial and liturgical grounds by Frank Lawrence who, while accepting its Benedictine elements, argues for a provenance in a southern cathedral in the vanguard of the twelfth century reform movement.[30]

The Benedictine Archbishops of Canterbury, Lanfranc and St Anselm, took a keen interest in Irish church affairs and a number of their letters to Irish secular and ecclesiastical leaders survive. Under the leadership of reformers like Gille of Limerick, Malchus of Waterford and Malachy (Máel Máedoc Ua Morgair) of Armagh a comprehensive programme of reform was introduced in Ireland. In structural terms it led to the re-establishment of dioceses and a hierarchy. In monastic circles it led to reinvigoration through the introduction of reformed groups from the continent and, while the religious orders most favoured by the reformers were the Cistercians and the Augustinian Canons, a small number of houses, described below, were established for reformed Benedictines.[31]

The priory of Sts Peter and Paul de Innocentia, Athlone

In terms of monastic foundations, Ireland was largely unaffected by the reform movement associated with the great Benedictine abbey of Cluny (founded in 909) in Burgundy and Irish contacts with the reformers on the continent generally do not seem to have been happy ones.[32] By the mid-twelfth century, the abbot of Cluny was an immensely powerful figure, presiding over a network of almost 1,200 priories which, to varying degrees, followed the Cluniac constitutions and acknowledged his authority. The

29. Dr Martin Holland, personal communication.
30. Derek Turner (ed), *The missal of the New Minster, Winchester (Le Havre, Bibliothèque Municipale, MS 330)* (Leighton Buzzard, Henry Bradshaw Society, 1962), appendix p 3; I am grateful to Frank Lawrence for discussing these aspects of his UCD PhD topic 'A paleographical, repertorial and liturgical study of Rawlinson C 892 – a twelfth-century Irish gradual' with me.
31. Aubrey Gwynn and R. Neville Hadcock, *Medieval religious houses: Ireland* (London, 1970) (henceforth cited as Gwynn & Hadcock, *MRH*); Aubrey Gwynn, *The Irish Church in the eleventh and twelfth centuries* ed. Gerard O'Brien (Dublin, 1992); John Watt, *The Church in medieval Ireland* (2nd edn, Dublin, 1998), pp 1-27, 229-36; John Fleming, *Gille of Limerick (c. 1070-1145)* (Dublin, 2001).
32. Gwynn, *Irish church*, pp 1-16.

observances of Cluny, with their emphasis on liturgical prayer, were hugely influential on other reform movements. The monastery's close association with the papacy, symbolised by its direct subjection to papal authority and the frequent dedication of Cluniac monasteries to the apostles Peter and Paul, gave it an unprecedented degree of independence from episcopal super-vision and provided the reforming popes of the eleventh and twelfth cent-uries with a powerful ally in implementing their reform programme. The first Cluniac house in England was established at Lewes in 1077 and eventually forty-one Cluniac houses, of varying status, were established there.

The priory of Sts Peter and Paul *de Innocentia* at Athlone is generally described as Ireland's only Cluniac monastery.[33] While its dedication to the patrons of Cluny is suggestive, the first description of it as a Cluniac found-ation occurs in a 1363 petition to Pope Urban V, and there is no record of any direct relationship with Cluny at any stage in its history. The foundation is attributed to Toirdelbach Ua Conchobair (Turlough O'Connor, d 1156), high king of Ireland, but here again, the source is late and uncertain. An annalistic entry of 1200 suggests that it was already in existence, and the first contem-porary reference occurs in 1214, when King John ordered Archbishop Henry of Dublin to allocate one tenth of the income of the royal castle at Athlone to compensate the monks for the loss of the site on which the castle had been built. Further compensation for losses of lands and the disruption of fishing and milling rights were made in 1216 and 1235.[34] In 1279 the community was granted rights to the lucrative fishing weirs on the Shannon in return for an annual payment. The construction of two mills by royal officials in 1290 interfered with these rights and Prior Gilbert, the first Athlone monk known to us by name, was awarded forty shillings in compensation. The monks were recipients of an annual royal grant of ten marks between 1275 and 1280 and again in 1290.[35]

References to the priory in official sources cease at the end of the thirt-eenth century, but entries in the registers of papal letters shed some light on the monastery's subsequent history. In 1363, Pope Urban V granted the request of Brother Roger, subprior of Athlone, confirming the election of the community's cellarer, Brother William Othomolteys (Ó Tomaltaigh? Tumelty?), as prior of the house. The new prior was also absolved from the

33. Gywnn & Hadcock, *MRH*, pp 110-11; Patrick Conlan OFM, 'The medieval priory of Saints Peter and Paul in Athlone' in Harman Murtagh (ed.), *Irish midland studies; essays in commemoration of N. W. English* (Athlone, 1980), pp 73-83.
34. H. S. Sweetman, *Calendar of documents relating to Ireland,* (5 vols, London, 1875- 86) (henceforth cited as Sweetman, *CDI*) i, nos 507, 693
35. Ibid., ii, nos 1038,1624, 1713, 2360.

canonical impediment of illegitimacy, being the son of a priest. An oblique reference to the internal state of the community may be gleaned from the appellant's assertion that there was 'a notorious lack of fit persons in Ireland of their order'.[36] In a subsequent appeal Prior William added that his father had been both a priest and a religious.[37] Though the religious order is not stated, it is likely that his father was also a monk of Sts Peter and Paul's and that the monastery, like many Irish religious houses and dioceses of the period, was controlled by a group of family members in clerical orders and monastic vows for whom celibacy was not a priority. The suspicion of hereditary succession is strengthened by the fact that when, after forty years in office, Prior William resigned in 1402, he postulated as his successor a monk bearing the same surname, Brother Domhnall Ó Tomaltaigh. The Archbishop of Tuam was ordered to inquire into the circumstances of the case, paying particular attention to any suspicions of simony.[38] As nothing further is heard of Brother Domhnall, and the *Annals of Connacht* record Prior William's death in office in 1410, it seems nothing came of this plan.[39]

In William's successor, Prior Simon Mac Aodhagáin (MacEgan), the community experienced one of the other besetting problems of the medieval Irish church – pluralism. Originally a Knight Hospitaller, Mac Aodhagáin secured appointment as prior of the house of *Fratres Cruciferi* or Crutched Friars at Rindown on the shores of Lough Ree near Athlone in 1409. Though not a priest, he was appointed prior of Sts Peter and Paul by papal authority in 1410, having first secured dispensation from the impediment of illegitimacy, being, like his predecessor, the son of a religious priest and an unmarried woman. The appointment was conditional on his being ordained priest within a year, adopting the Cluniac habit and lifestyle and on his resignation as prior of Rindown. He may not however have gained possession of the priory as, in 1412, the Pisan antipope, John XXIII, appointed Raymond Ó Ceallaigh (O'Kelly), a twenty-two year old monk of Athlone, as prior. Despite his youth, he seems to have been the community's choice all along as they had elected him to succeed William Ó Tomaltaigh in 1410. As such appointments were reserved to the papacy the election was declared void. Ó Ceallaigh was

36. W. H. Bliss, *Calendar of entries in the papal registers relating to Great Britain and Ireland: petitions to the pope, Vol I, AD 1343-1419* (London, 1896), pp 445-46.
37. Ibid., p 460.
38. W. H. Bliss & J. A. Twemlow, *Cal. pap. letters, vol. v, A.D. 1396-1404* (London, 1904), p 572.
39. A. Martin Freeman (ed) *Annála Connacht; the annals of Connacht (A.D. 1224-1544)*, pp 410, 411.

Fig 1: Seal of the Prior
of Sts Peter and Paul,
Athlone
© National Museum of
Ireland.

succeeded shortly afterwards by Magnus Mac Eochadha (MacKehoe). In March 1428 Pope Martin V granted an indulgence to all who visited the priory church on the patronal feastday (June 29th) and contributed to the restoration of the building. Throughout the fifteenth century the prior was frequently deputed to act for the papacy in various ecclesiastical court cases. Unfortunately, the names of the priors are not given in these letters and the next one whose identity is known is Thomas Ocarneayn who was eulogised by the annalists as 'the most eminent man in Connacht for wisdom and learning' on his death in 1455. In 1480 another Ocarneyn, Nemeas, alias Magonl, brought charges against Prior Cornelius Ó Neachtain (O'Naughton). He was accused of keeping a concubine, allowing his monks to wander outside the monastery and letting them keep private property. Normally the accuser would be appointed to the office of the accused if he was found guilty. In this case Ocarneyn was not successful. This indicates either that the charges were false or, equally likely, that he was unable to assert himself in the face of a well established incumbent. Though such accusations are almost formulaic, they do indicate that the standard of monastic observance at Athlone was at a low ebb. The priory appears to have been well endowed with land, tithes and rectories. Unusually, the monks seem to have exercised the cure of souls in some of these parishes themselves. Nothing survives of the monastery buildings, but the prior's attractive bronze seal matrix, dating to the thirteenth century, is preserved in the National Museum of Ireland. It depicts a monk saying Mass beneath a canopy, above which an image of the Virgin and Child is enthroned.

Reformed Benedictine Congregations

While the Cistercians were by far the most widespread and influential of the monastic reform movements of the late eleventh and twelfth centuries, they were by no means the only ones. Two other Benedictine reform congregations, those of Tiron and Savigny, were also active in Ireland. The Order of Tiron was represented by the post invasion foundation at Glasscarrig in Co Wexford, discussed below.

The Order of Savigny originated in 1105 when a group of hermits under the direction of St Vitalis of Mortain retired to the Forest of Savigny in Normandy. This group later developed into a cenobitic community, following the Rule of St Benedict. They were highly esteemed and a number of foundations were made including eleven in England and Wales, one on the Isle of Man and two in Ireland.[40] In 1147, at the instigation of Abbot Serlon

40. Beatrice Poulle, 'Savigny and England' in David Bates and Anne Curry (eds), *England and Normandy in the middle ages* (London, 1994), pp 159-168.

of Savigny, the congregation transferred *en masse* to the Cistercians, retaining certain distinctive practices and rights. This transfer was confirmed by Pope Eugene III in 1148.

Two houses were founded for the order of Savigny in Ireland. The earliest, at Erenagh (Carrig) in the diocese of Down, was founded by Niall Mac Duinn Shléibe (Dunleavy) in 1127, possibly at the instigation of St Malachy. The founding group may have come from Tulketh where the first Savigniac house in England was established in 1124.[41] This community transferred to Furness in Lancashire in 1127 and when the Savigniac houses became Cistercian in 1147, Erenagh was affiliated to Furness. The *Coucher Book of Furness* preserves a number of details concerning the early years of Erenagh, including the identities of the first four abbots and the premonition of the first superior, Abbot Evodius, that the monastery would be destroyed and replaced by a foundation at Inch.[42] The subsequent destruction of the house by John de Courcy during his conquest of Ulster and his foundation of a Cistercian house at Inch in reparation in either 1180 or 1187, was interpreted as the fulfilment of this prophecy.[43]

The second Savigniac foundation in Ireland, St Mary's Abbey near Dublin, was established as a daughter house of Savigny itself in 1139. At the time of the transfer to the Cistercians, the Dublin foundation was affiliated first to Combermere abbey in Cheshire and then, in 1156-7, to Buildwas abbey in Shropshire. Though its Savigniac period was a relatively short one, it was sufficient to inculcate a sense of seniority on the part of the later Cistercian community at St Mary's, who deliberately falsified the chronology of their foundation in order to assert their independence from Mellifont, the first Irish Cistercian foundation.[44]

A number of other Irish houses also began as communities of Black Monks before being aggregated to the Cistercian order by its general chapter. The principal evidence for this pre-existence occurs in the dedication of these houses. Normally Cistercian monasteries invoked the Virgin Mary in their dedications, the additional invocation of St Benedict indicating that the house had originally been Benedictine before adopting the Cistercian reform.[45] In Ireland such joint dedications occur in five cases: Holy Cross,

41. Gwynn & Hadcock, *MRH*, pp 115 & 132.
42. J. C Atkinson, *The Coucher book of Furness abbey* (Manchester, 1886), pp 11-13; William Reeves, *Ecclesiastical antiquities of Down, Connor and Dromore* (Dublin, 1847), pp 232-3.
43. Gwynn & Hadcock, *MRH*, pp 132 & 135.
44. Aubrey Gwynn, 'The origins of St Mary's Abbey, Dublin' in *Journal of the Royal Society of Antiquaries of Ireland*, 79 (1949), pp 110-25.
45. Gwynn & Hadcock, *MRH*, pp 116-17.

Kilcooly, Killenny, Monasterevin and Newry. In the cases of Holy Cross, Kilcooly and Killenny[46] other evidence indicates a Benedictine phase in their early histories and Jerpoint Abbey also seems to have existed for a number of years before becoming Cistercian in 1180.[47] There is a possibility that a Benedictine house existed in Drogheda for a short period in the twelfth century.[48] The most likely scenario is that these foundations had adopted a reformed Benedictine lifestyle from the outset and their transfer to the more centralised and better organised Cistercian reform was a natural progression.

English and Norman monasteries and their Irish lands

The well established links between Ireland and the English church meant that the religious houses of England and Normandy were among the earliest beneficiaries of the Anglo-Norman incursion into Ireland.[49] They were granted large tracts of newly conquered lands as well as tithes and the rights of appointment to benefices in the new lordship. A variety of considerations motivated this patronage. In a religious age the welfare of one's soul and those of one's relatives, patrons and ancestors was an important consideration, as surviving charters demonstrate. The foundation of a monastery added to a baron's prestige in this life and the prayers of its inmates counterbalanced his sins in the next. In old age it offered the possibility of a quiet place of retirement, the added security of death in the monastic habit and an honourable place of burial for the founder and his descendants. More mundanely it helped secure a baron's grip on his newly conquered territories, rendering them more attractive to settlers and colonists and, in theory, bolstering the local economy through a more efficient exploitation of resources. Nor were the monasteries mere passive recipients of baronial largesse; the surviving material clearly indicates the presence of English monks in Ireland actively canvassing support and benefactions for their communities. In all this the Anglo-Norman adventurers in Ireland were in keeping with the pattern established after the conquest of England in 1066 when Norman monasteries were granted lands in England.[50] In time these possessions proved vul-

46. Colmcille Ó Conbhuidhe, *The Cistercian abbeys of Tipperary* (Dublin, 1999), pp 165-69, 279-81.
47. Colmcille Ó Conbhuidhe, 'The origins of Jerpoint Abbey, Co Kilkenny' in *Cîteaux*, 14 (1963), pp 293-306.
48. Aubrey Gwynn, 'A forgotten Abbey of St Mary's, Drogheda' in *Louth Archaeological Society Journal*, xiii, no. 2 (1954), pp 190-99.
49. For the ecclesiastical background to the invasion see Denis Bethell 'English monks' *passim*; Marie-Therese Flanagan, *Irish society, Anglo-Norman settlers, Angevin kingship* (Oxford, 1989), pp 7-55.
50. Donald Matthew, *The Norman monasteries and their English possessions* (Oxford, 1962).

nerable to the ebb and flow of England's relationship with France and a similar pattern can be traced with Norman foundations in Ireland.

In many cases the land granted to the English and Norman monasteries
was already church land and this frequently led to tension with bishops or
existing communities.[51] The Cistercians and Augustinian Canons were more
successful at establishing fully-fledged communities than the Black Monks
and their willingness to exploit the land themselves or, in the case of the
Canons, to establish parishes and supervise pastoral activity, rendered them a
more attractive option for many donors. The Black Monks were generally
content either to let the land to others or to administer it through proctors.
Even when priories were established they tended to be small foundations
dependent on English or Norman mother houses. These small houses have
generally been dismissed as ineffectual and tending towards decadence[52] but
the recent work of Martin Heale on dependent priories in England challenges this interpretation and demonstrates that they were established and
supported primarily because they were religious institutions and should not
be viewed solely as economic units.[53] The material from the Irish dependencies does not allow such full assessments, but does indicate that a sojourn in
Ireland was not viewed with enthusiasm by English monks, though the Irish
estates did occasionally prove useful as places to which incompetent superiors,
recalcitrant subordinates or those with thwarted ambitions could retire to
nurse their wounds.

As the strength of the colony waned the monasteries were occasionally
penalised, like other absentees, for drawing revenues from Ireland without
residing there and contributing to the defence of the colony. Eventually some
of the English houses relinquished the administration of their Irish lands to
representatives in Ireland in return for an annual rent, or surrendered them
altogether. Like their counterparts in England, the Irish revenues of Norman
houses were frequently confiscated in the fourteenth century to help with the
war effort in France. Eventually these foundations either became independent, as at Fore, or passed to local interests, as at St Andrews in Ards.

51. Geraldine Carville, *The occupation of Celtic sites in medieval Ireland by the Canons Regular
of St Augustine and the Cistercians* (Kalamazoo, 1982).
52. For example Knowles, *Monastic order*, p. 136, 'Natural as was the process by which these
houses came into being, their appearance must be pronounced one of the most unfortunate
by-products of the Conquest in England; save for a few of the larger priories, they served no
religious purpose whatever, and were a source of weakness to the house that owned them.'
53. Martin Heale, *The dependent priories of medieval English monasteries* (Woodbridge, 2004),
pp 3-4.

Canterbury Cathedral Priory

The experience of the Benedictine monks of Christ Church cathedral priory, Canterbury, serves to illustrate many of the above points, and the survival of a substantial amount of material relating to Ireland in the cathedral archives makes it possible to trace the relationship in some detail.[54] Granted land and extensive rights of ecclesiastical patronage in Wexford c 1183 by one of the first Norman adventurers, Hervey de Montmorency, their benefactor later entered the community at Canterbury and died with a reputation for holiness.[55] This contrasts starkly with Gerald of Wales' description of him in the *Expugnatio Hibernica* as

> a jealous man, an informer and deceitful, wily, polished and thoroughly false, on whose tongue milk and honey were compounded with poison. He was inconstant and vain with no reliable element in his make up save his unreliability.[56]

Even his decision to grant land to Canterbury and subsequent taking of the habit there did nothing to redeem him for Gerald:

> About that time Hervey de Montmorency chose to follow the monastic life and took himself off to the community at Canterbury. He had previously, as an act of charity, presented it with the church livings of his estates on the coast between Waterford and Wexford. Would that he had laid aside his evil disposition along with his layman's habit, and given up his malevolence along with his profession as a knight![57]

---

54. Some of the Irish material preserved in Canterbury Cathedral archives was published by J. B. Sheppard (ed.) *Literae Cantuarienses: the letter books of the monastery of Christ Church, Canterbury*, (3 vols, Rolls series, London, 1887-89), (hereafter cited as *Lit. Cant.*). Since December 2004 a calendar of all the Irish material may be consulted at www.kentarchives.org.uk. I am grateful to Ms Cressida Annesley, Canterbury Cathedral archives, for advice on this point.

55. The land had first been offered to Walden priory in Essex, but the prior was unable to persuade any of the community to migrate to Ireland and the grant was transferred to Canterbury. See H. G. Richardson, 'Some Norman monastic foundations in Ireland' in J. A. Watt, J. B. Morall and F. X. Martin (eds), *Medieval studies presented to Aubrey Gwynn SJ* (Dublin, 1961), pp 29-32. For the wider context of these grants and monastic involvement in the process of sub-infeudation see Billy Colfer, 'Anglo-Norman settlement in County Wexford' in Kevin Whelan (ed) *Wexford: history and society* (Dublin, 1987) pp 65-101, particularly pp 86-89. Also idem, *Arrogant trespass: Anglo-Norman Wexford 1169-1400* (Enniscorthy, 2002) pp 183-222.

56. A. B. Scott and F. X. Martin (eds) Giraldus Cambrensis, *Expugnatio Hibernica: the conquest of Ireland* (Dublin, 1978), pp 159, 161.

57. Ibid., p. 189.

Fig 2: Canterbury Cathedral Archives, DCc/ChAnt I 242. Agreement between the Prior and Convent of Canterbury and the Bishop of Ferns concerning the Manor of Fethard, 1245. Reproduced with permission of the Dean and Chapter of Canterbury.

The priory appears to have derived little benefit from its Irish estates, in comparison with its lands in England.[58] Its determination to assert its rights in the face of local opposition and usurpation over a period of four centuries has left a substantial amount of material which enables us to trace its history in broad outline. De Montmorency had been granted this land by Diarmait Mac Murchada (MacMurrough), king of Leinster,[59] and scant regard had been paid to the rights of the incumbents, including those of the church. This led to a bitter dispute with successive bishops of Ferns and Canterbury's difficulties in establishing title to some of its Irish property is illustrated by a dispute over the manor of Fethard. Between 1228 and 1245 Bishop John St John of Ferns initiated proceedings against the prior and convent of Canterbury for the recovery of certain churches belonging to the see which had been granted to them by de Montmorency. The proceedings appear to have taken place in Ireland in the presence of Archbishop Luke of Dublin

---

58. R. A. L. Smith, *Canterbury cathedral priory: a study in monastic administration* (Cambridge, 1943), pp 100-112; Barrie Dobson, 'The monks of Canterbury in the later middle ages, 1220-1540' in Patrick Collinson, Nigel Ramsay and Margaret Sparks (eds), *A history of Canterbury Cathedral* (Oxford, 1995), pp 69-153. Reference at p 142.

59. P. H. Hore, *History of the town and county of Wexford* (6 vols, London, 1901-), i, pp 3-73.

with the monks' interests being represented by their proctor, Brother William Ferbras. A compromise was reached whereby the monks granted the bishop and chapter the manor of Fethard in return for the churches of Bannow, Kilcowan, Kilmore, Kilturk and Tagmagre.[60] However c 1200 the priory had granted the manor of Fethard to Richard of London in return for an annual payment of four marks.[61] Nothing further is heard of this arrangement until over a century later when Bishop Robert Walrand of Ferns informed the prior of Canterbury that a John Lyneyt had come forward claiming, in his wife's name, to be the heir to Richard of London's estate. To support his claim to Fethard he produced an ancient charter sealed with a priory seal, but one different from that currently used by the community. As Lyneyt had already initiated court proceedings to recover the manor, Bishop Robert requested that a diligent search be made of the Canterbury archives for any record of the transaction. He also invited the prior to make alternative proposals as to how the arrangement between the priory and the diocese might be defended.[62] Unfortunately neither the prior's reply nor the decision of the court survives, but as Fethard continued in the possession of the bishop it can be taken that Lyneyt's challenge was unsuccessful.

It is not known how the monks actually exploited their estates for the first fifty years they possessed them. The returns appear to have been sporadic and the Canterbury treasury records only one payment of twenty-seven pounds from their Irish property in 1213.[63] In 1245, the priory's Irish interests were leased to the Cistercians of Tintern for an entry fee of six hundred and twenty five marks and an annual payment of ten marks to the treasury of the Benedictine priory of Bath. The Cistercians also undertook to pray for the deceased Irish benefactors of Canterbury as well as providing the mainten-ance and travel expenses of the Canterbury monk appointed proctor and those of his household.[64] To strengthen the agreement, both Tintern abbey in Ireland and its motherhouse, Tintern in Wales, agreed to submit to the authority of the Archbishop of Dublin and the Bishop of Llandaff who could then use ecclesiastical censures to enforce the agreement.[65] In 1255, at the sug-gestion of Archbishop Boniface of Canterbury, Abbot William of Tintern in

60. Canterbury Cathedral Archives [CCA], DCc/ChAnt I 242; Colfer, *Arrogant trespass*, p 188.
61. CCA DCc ChAnt I 239; *Lit. Cant.*, iii, pp 360-1.
62. CCA DCc ChAnt I, 243; *Lit. Cant.*, iii, pp 363-4; Colfer, *Arrogant trespass*, p 211.
63. *Lit. Cant.* iii, pp xlii-iii.
64. CCA DCc ChAnt I 231; *Lit. Cant.*, iii, p 361.
65. CCA DCc ChAnt I, 232.

Ireland agreed to increase the annual rent to thirteen marks.[66] The arrangement with Tintern also proved unsatisfactory and eventually the prior of Canterbury appealed to the Cistercian general chapter which laid responsibility for ensuring payment, or for making it themselves, on Mellifont Abbey and Tintern in Wales. This arrangement seems to have been more satisfactory and regular payments ensued. In 1407 payment had fallen into arrears for seven years and the Archbishop of Canterbury sequestered the rectory of Lydd, which belonged to the Welsh Tintern, in order to satisfy the debt.

In the fourteenth century, one of the major weaknesses of the Anglo-Irish colony was absenteeism, whereby landowners drew revenues from Irish estates but made no contribution to the colony and its wellbeing. As holder of extensive lands in Ireland, Canterbury fell into this category, and in 1360 its revenues, and those of other absentees, were confiscated. They were restored after an appeal to the king, but this was done as a personal favour to the prior and out of devotion to St Thomas Beckett. The arrangement had to be renewed by successive priors and on the accession of each new monarch.

By the latter half of the fifteenth century the arrangement with Tintern seems to have broken down irretrievably, and in 1470 the priory appointed James Sherlock as its agent in Ireland for an annual fee of nine marks.[67] This arrangement also collapsed as Sherlock faced local opposition in the person of Gilbard Talbot, who asserted that he had rights as the descendant of the founder. Here the Canterbury records fall silent but the priory maintained its stake in Ireland in some attenuated form until the sixteenth century.

Glastonbury

The abbey of Glastonbury in Somerset was the beneficiary of two distinct grants of land in Ireland in the early thirteenth century. The details of these are recorded by a contemporary monk-chronicler, John of Glastonbury, and the estates' subsequent history can be traced through a small number of surviving sources.[68]

At the beginning of the thirteenth century Philip of Worcester, constable of Ireland and holder of extensive lands in south Tipperary, granted the vill of Kilcommon with approximately twelve thousand acres, rights of ecclesiastical patronage and sundry other privileges to Glastonbury, for the establishment of a priory in honour of Sts Philip and James and St Cumin. There is

---

66. CCA DCc ChAnt I 237; *Lit. Cant.,* iii, p 363.
67. *Lit. Cant.,*iii, p 248.
68. Eric St John Brooks, 'Irish daughter houses of Glastonbury' in *Proceedings of the Royal Irish Academy,* 56 (1953-4) pp 287-295.

some uncertainty as to where in Tipperary this land lay, but the most likely location is Kilcommon in the parish of Caher in the barony of Iffa and Offa, which formed part of the Worcester fief. A group of monks from Glastonbury, under the leadership of Prior James, established conventual life there and a number of subsequent grants were made to the foundation.[69] These included additional grants of lands by Philip of Worcester and other benefactors as well as donations of mills, tithes and other incomes from churches. The latest of these benefactions dates from after 1244, though it is not clear if a resident community still existed at this stage. The estate at Kilcommon figured in a dispute between the monastery and Bishop Savaric of Bath and Wells in 1203, when it was awarded to the bishop.[70] The monks must have regained possession of it sometime after that.

During the same period Brother Richard, another monk of Glastonbury, was granted land in Limerick by William de Burgo, the ancestor of the Burke family, for the purpose of establishing a priory in honour of the Blessed Virgin. This was at Ardaneer in West Limerick. The Glastonbury chronicler does not give the extent of the lands donated, but notes that the grant included the rights to the various churches and chapels as well as to the fisheries, mines and mills. Apart from the initial references, nothing further is heard of this foundation and Aubrey Gwynn suggests that it failed as a conventual establishment shortly after William de Burgo's death in 1206.[71]

That Glastonbury maintained its interests in Ireland is evident from letters issued between 1275 and 1281 giving power of attorney to monks of Glastonbury and other representatives in Ireland. In 1275, Brother William de Luckumbe and Henry de Ginelton were granted power of attorney for three years to act on behalf of the abbot of Glastonbury.[72] In June 1278, a letter of protection was issued to the abbot himself who was about to go to Ireland, while William de Luckumbe's and Henry de Ginelton's letters of attorney were renewed for another three years. At the same time further letters of attorney for Irish affairs were issued for William de Ginelton, monk of Glastonbury and Richard Pike.[73] The tone of the entries suggests that these were not members of a well established priory in Ireland but monks of

---

69. Ibid., pp 290-93. This refers to a schedule listing fifteen charters relating to Glastonbury's Irish possessions among the Glastonbury muniments in the library of the Marquis of Bath at Longleat. The charters themselves do not appear to have survived.

70. Aelred Watkins (ed), *The great chartulary of Glastonbury*, (3 vols, Frome, 1947-1956 [Somerset Record Society, vols 59, 63, 64), i (vol 59), p 78, no 126.

71. Gwynn & Hadcock, *MRH*, p 104.

72. Sweetman, *CDI* ii, no 1188.

73. Ibid., nos 1454, 1456, 1457.

Glastonbury delegated as proctors to look after the abbey's interests. The flurry of activity in June 1278, with the presence of the abbot himself, two monastic proctors and two lay officials in Ireland may be indicative of some unspecified crisis. That some disaster later befell the Irish holdings is indicated by a reference in the *Great Chartulary* in 1332, when Pope John XXII wrote to the Bishop of Bath and Wells referring to the visit of King Edward III to Glastonbury in the previous year. During the visit the abbot and community secured royal support for their plea for a grant of properties in England to compensate for the loss of their estates in Ireland.[74] This is the last reference to Glastonbury's Irish estates and the monastery held no Irish property at the time of the Dissolution.

Little Malvern and Castleknock

The priory of St Brigid, Castleknock, Co Dublin, was established c 1185 by Hugh Tyrell, Lord of Castleknock, as a dependency of the Benedictine priory of Little Malvern, Worcestershire. The endowment was an extensive one and included lands and spiritualities in Dublin and Meath. In 1219 the monks were granted the great tithes of the parish by Archbishop Henry de Londres on condition that an additional five monks were added to the foundation. In 1227 they surrendered their claim to the vicarage of the parish, which may indicate that this augmentation had not occurred. This agreement was finalised in 1249.[75] Though Little Malvern had been established as a dependent house by Worcester cathedral priory, it enjoyed almost complete autonomy and the support and protection of the bishops of Worcester.[76] The surviving references in the Worcester episcopal registers indicate that a sojourn in Ireland was not viewed with enthusiasm by the brethren. In 1323, following a visitation of Little Malvern priory, Bishop Thomas de Cobham castigated Br Nicholas de Molendis for refusing to go to Ireland with the result that the priory's interests suffered through the maladministration of his less competent replacement. The bishop also instructed that in future two monks be sent to Ireland as it was not good for one to be alone; failing this, they were to appoint a competent layman to act as proctor.[77] In 1336, Br Nicholas de Upton was dispensed by Bishop Simon de Montacute from having to take up the Irish appointment, living as he did in fear of crossing the sea and living

---

74. Watkins, *Great chartulary*, i, pp v-vi, 194-5.
75. Gwynn & Hadcock, *MRH*, p 105.
76. Heale, *Dependent priories*, p 104.
77. E. H. Pearse, *The register of Thomas de Cobham, bishop of Worcester 1317-1327* (London, 1930), p 155.

in a barbarous land.[78] Br Nicholas had earlier been reprimanded for conspiring against the prior with two other monks, which may provide the context for his appointment to Ireland and his refusal to accept it. This dispensation was renewed in 1339 by de Montacute's successor, Wolstan de Bransford.[79] An unidentified monk of Malvern, presumably the proctor of Castleknock, was among the dignitaries entertained to dinner by the newly elected Augustinian prior of Christ Church, Dublin, in 1346.[80]

The Irish lands seem to have been the cause of longstanding difficulties as in 1368 Little Malvern was granted possession of the church of Whatcote in Worcestershire to compensate for the loss of some of its Irish possessions.[81] In 1483, Sixtus IV ordered an investigation of the seizure of its Castleknock tithes by the prior of the Hospitallers of Kilmainham. Eventually in 1486 the possessions of Little Malvern at Castleknock, as well as its churches and lands in Meath, were purchased for 450 marks by Walter Champfleur, abbot of St Mary's Cistercian abbey, Dublin.[82]

Fore

Fore priory, in Co Westmeath, was endowed by Hugh de Lacy (d 1186) for the Norman abbey of St Taurin at Evreux sometime before 1185, when it is mentioned by Gerald of Wales.[83] Like other contemporary Augustinian and Cistercian foundations it occupied the lands of the earlier Celtic monastery of St Fechin, something reflected in its unusual twin dedication to Sts Taurin and Fechin. The extensive endowments of the priory and its subsequent administration have been the subject of detailed study by Rory Masterson.[84] While the initial endowment only makes reference to the site of the priory

---

78. R. M. Haines, *Calendar of the register of Simon de Montacute, bishop of Worcester, 1334-1337*, (Kendal, 1996), p 62.

79. R. M. Haines, *A calendar of the register of Wolstan de Bransford, bishop of Worcester, 1339-1349* (London, 1966), p 147.

80. M. J. McEnery and Raymond Refaussé, *Christ Church deeds* (Dublin, 2001), p 79 no 235.

81. M. M. C. Caltrop, 'The priory of Little Malvern' in J. W. Wills-Blund and William Page (eds), *The Victoria county history of the County of Worcester* (4 vols London, 1901-24), ii, p 145.

82. Gwynn & Hadcock, *MRH*, p. 105; John T. Gilbert (ed) *Chartularies of St Mary's Abbey, Dublin* (2 vols, Rolls series, London, 1884), ii, pp 16-18.

83. J. H. Round, *Calendar of documents relating to France 918-1216* (London, 1899) p 105; Scott & Martin, *Expugnatio*, p 193. See also Louis Debidour, *Essai sur l'histoire de l'abbaye Benedictine de Saint-Taurin d'Evreux* (Évreux, 1908), pp 59-64.

84. Rory Masterson, 'The alien priory of Fore, Co. Westmeath, in the middle ages' in *Archivium Hibernicum*, 53 (1999), pp 73-79; idem, 'The Church and the Anglo-Norman colonisation of Ireland: a case study of the priory of Fore' in *Ríocht na Midhe*, xi (2000), pp 58-70, idem, 'The early Anglo-Norman colonisation of Fore, Co Westmeath' in *Ríocht na Midhe*, xiii (2002), pp 44-60.

Fig 3: Fore Priory, remains of a monastic mill in the foreground. © Department of the Environment, Heritage and Local Government

and tithes of what were to become eight parishes, the inclusion of the rights to St Fechin's mill at Fore indicate that a substantial grant of land was also included. This was further augmented by de Lacy and his son Walter, who granted the priory eleven parishes in Bréifne sometime before 1224. The community at all times seems to have been a small one, numbering no more that four or five monks but, as Peter Harbison's article demonstrates, the surviving monastic buildings are the most extensive of any Benedictine monastery in Ireland.[85]

The *Annals of St Mary's Abbey* contain an interesting illustration of the symbiosis between monastery and patron. Sometime before 1210 Walter de Lacy and his brother Hugh incurred the wrath of King John of England on account of their involvement in the murder of John de Courson. They fled to Normandy and were given sanctuary in St Taurin where they worked as gardeners and latrine cleaners. Their restoration to royal favour was negotiated by the abbot of St Taurin who claimed, somewhat unconvincingly, not to have recognised his guests.[86]

The loss of Normandy in 1204, and deteriorating relations between

85. See also H. G. Leask, *Fore, Co Westmeath*, (Dublin, 1938); Tadhg O'Keeffe, *Medieval Fore: an archaeological wonder in the Westmeath landscape*, (*Archaeology Ireland*, heritage guide, no 28, Dublin, 2005).
86. Gilbert, *Chartularies*, ii, p 311.

England and France in the thirteenth and fourteenth centuries, put institutions such as Fore in a particularly difficult position. Now seen as alien priories they were particularly vulnerable to confiscation and exploitation in times of war. In 1294, on the outbreak of war with France, the prior of Fore was ordered to account to the Irish exchequer for the customary apport or annual render to the abbot of St Taurin. With the outbreak of the One Hundred Years War in 1337 the properties of all alien priories in England and Ireland were seized and in 1343 and 1344 Prior William Tessone had to account to the Irish exchequer for the priory's income and pay £1 17s 0d. The remainder of the income was allotted for his support and that of four monks and a servant. In 1352 custody of the priory was granted to Br Wiliam de Cesterford and Br Richard de Fontayne for an increased payment of £2 6s 0d. This may indicate that the community was reduced in size, possibly as a result of the Black Death. In 1355 custody of the priory was granted to a lay official, Roger Rodierd, for a farm of £2 16s 0d and in 1357 and again in 1360 it was granted to another royal official, John de Pembroke. The purpose of appointing laymen to this position was to pressurise the community into accepting an increase in the amount they had to pay to the exchequer. In each case the stratagem worked and the prior agreed to accept custody for an increased fee. Between 1360 and 1369 there was peace between England and France and all alien properties were returned to their owners. With the outbreak of war again in 1369, the alien priories were again confiscated and, while there is no immediate reference to Fore, it was in the custody of Bishop Stephen of Meath in 1375. In 1377 custody had passed to Michael de Plessy, described as the proctor of the abbot of St Taurin.

The emergence of John Crose as prior in 1382 is the first time that an Anglo-Irishman is recorded as superior of the foundation. He encountered opposition from other interested parties in the locality and, in 1385, was deposed briefly in favour of Walter Prendergast, vicar of Granard. By c 1385 the foundation was so impoverished that a chantry consisting of the prior and three chaplains was erected.[87] Crose was confirmed as prior in 1388, but died soon afterwards and the priory was granted to Simon, Bishop of Achonry, working as a suffragan in various English dioceses. In 1391 custody was granted to Alexander, Bishop of Meath, who complained of the demands made of him by the exchequer so convincingly that he was granted free custody in 1396. In 1400 the priory came into the possession of the royal favourite, Janico Dardis, but the following year was granted to John de Buckton for a farm of £2 13s 4d.

The division in the western church caused by the Great Schism also had an impact on the priory. On the death of Prior Simon Crose, Ralph de Gometis was nominated prior by the abbot of St Taurin. As France followed the Avignon papacy and Ireland and England the Roman obedience, he was unable to take possession, and Walter Prendergast was recognised as prior until his deposition in favour of William Anglond in 1417.

The Gaelic resurgence and decline of the Anglo-Norman colony had a more severe effect on Fore than on most of the other Benedictine foundations, given its proximity to the territories of ascendant Gaelic lords. In 1402 an assembly was held at Fore to discuss measures for the protection of the area. In 1412 and 1417 the priory and town were attacked, and between 1421 and 1423 the Uí Fhearghail (O'Farrells) and Uí Raghallaigh (O'Reillys) burned two of the priory granges. In 1426, Prior William Anglond was granted custody of the priory rent free as a reward for the number of castles he had built on the priory lands for the protection of the colony. It was at this period that the priory acquired its distinctively military appearance as the buildings were re-ordered with a view to defence (Fig 5). The claustral buildings were also extensively renovated with superfluous structures like the original refectory and portions of the church being abandoned. An attractive fifteenth-century cloister formed the centrepiece of the remodelled complex (Fig 6).

The process of encastellation was continued by Anglond's successor, William Crose, who was appointed by papal provision in 1440 and the monastic buildings were renovated. In 1448 the priory was granted denization or naturalisation, by parliament, thereby breaking the remaining links

87. St John D. Seymour, 'Some priors of Fore, Co Westmeath' in *Journal of the Royal Society of Antiquaries of Ireland*, 64 (1934), pp 64-71. Reference at pp 66-7.

with St Taurin in Normandy. However, this was not recognised by the papacy, which continued to reserve the right to appoint priors. In 1455, Prior Crose was replaced by Edmund Fitzsimon, a member of a Gaelicised Norman family who in turn was replaced c 1478 by Christopher Fitzsimon. The annals record the death of Prior Edmund Dorcha Fitzsimon in 1505 and a Raymond Fitzsimon was a member of the community in 1529. The community at Fore, though small, seems to have been reasonably well ordered and observant. At the time of the Dissolution the priorship of Fore had passed into the hands of another prominent Anglo-Norman family, the Nugents of Delvin, and the monastery was surrendered to the Baron Delvin by his son Prior William Nugent in 1539.[88]

88. Masterson, 'Alien priory', *passim*.

St Nicholas of Exeter

Along with Canterbury Cathedral, the grants of lands to the Benedictine priory of St Nicholas, Exeter, are the best documented of the early grants to English Benedictine houses.[89] In all, seventy documents relating to the Irish properties survive: ten individual charters and a chartulary roll containing thirty charters and twenty-eight deeds. The grants can be dated for the most part to between 1177, when Robert FitzStephen and Miles de Cogan were granted the kingdom of Cork, and 1182, when de Cogan was killed. The properties granted were concentrated in the city and county of Cork, with smaller grants in counties Wexford, Kilkenny and Kildare. Why Exeter should be so favoured is not clear, but in the person of Brother Adam, referred to in a number of the grants, the priory seems to have found a persuasive procurator. The Cork grants are of particular significance for establishing the early topography of the city[90] and indicate that the monastic interest centred on the Hiberno-Norse church of St Sepulchre outside the walled city on the south bank of the river Lee, near the Benedictine priory hospital of St John the Evangelist. Significantly, the church was rededicated to St Nicholas and seems for a time at least to have had a resident monastic community.[91] Recent archaeological excavations indicate that it was rebuilt some time after the Exeter community took possession, with the presence of dressed Dundry stone indicating that some of the building material was imported from England.[92] The priory's churches at Ballyvourney, Co Cork, and Mothell, Co Kilkenny[93] were also dedicated to St Nicholas and at the Dissolution it also possessed the churches of Corkbeg and Aghada.[94] These references occur in the Elizabethan *Fiants* as no Irish possessions are listed for Exeter in the *Valor ecclesiasticus*.

The priory's lands in Wexford consisted of four carucates of land and the church and island of Begerin in Wexford harbour granted by the Roche (de

---

89. Eric St John Brooks, 'Unpublished charters relating to Ireland, 1177-82, from the archives of the City of Exeter', *Proceedings of the Royal Irish Academy*, 43 (1935-7), pp 313-66; Colfer, *Arrogant trespass,* pp 105-6, 208; Evelyn Bolster, *A history of the diocese of Cork: from the earliest times to the Reformation* (Shannon, 1972), pp 121-24.

90. John Bradley and Andrew Halpin, 'The topographical development of Scandinavian and Anglo-Norman Cork' in Patrick O'Flanagan and Cornelius G. Buttimer (eds) *Cork: history and society* (Dublin, 1993), pp 15-44.

91. Brooks, 'Charters', p 324.

92. Rose M. Cleary, 'Medieval graveyard and boundary wall at Cove St, Cork' in *Journal of the Cork Historical and Archaeological Society,* 101 (1996), pp 94-111, at p 95.

93. William Carrigan, *The history and antiquities of the diocese of Ossory* (4 vols Dublin, 1905 [reprint Kilkenny, 1981]), iii, pp 458-9.

94. Brooks, 'Charters', p 315

Rupe) family in the 1180s, and two further unidentified carucates granted by Roger son of Christopher. According to Colfer the origins of the parish of St Nicholas in Fernegenel can be traced to this grant. It appears that this was intended as a conventual foundation as the donor, Adam de Rupe, reserved the right to appoint the prior there. Begerin was an ancient foundation associated with St Ibar. It too was intended to be a conventual priory with Brother Adam, the monk of Exeter who had procured the grant, as its first prior. The grantees, the brothers Adam, David and Henry de Rupe, reserved the right to a voice in the appointment of his successor.[95] Though the monks are credited with building a church on the island, it does not appear to have functioned as a conventual foundation, with the property eventually passing to the Augustinian Canons of Selskar abbey in Wexford town c 1400.[96]

Glascarrig

The congregation of Tiron emerged in the early twelfth century under the direction of St Bernard, abbot of St Cyprien de Poitiers who, in 1109, established a reformed monastery at Tiron in the diocese of Chartres. The order was represented in Ireland by the priory of St Mary, Glascarrig, in the diocese of Ferns, which was founded in 1190 or 1199 as a dependency of St Dogmells priory in Pembrokeshire.[97] Details of the initial endowments as well as later grants to the priory are contained in a charter approved by Bishop Thomas Den sometime after 1363. This lists the principal founders as Griffin de Cauneton, his wife Cecilia Barry and David Roche. The priory was granted lands and the rights to fourteen churches and seven chapels in the dioceses of Ferns, Cloyne, Leighlin and Glendalough.[98] Though there is an early reference to the presence of monks at Glascarrig, the foundation, like so many others of the Irish Benedictine monasteries, does not appear to have been a large one. Conventual life, if it ever existed, had lapsed completely by 1401 when Imarus Oduyud, abbot of the Cistercian house at Kilbeggan, was given papal permission to transfer to Glascarrig as prior. The letter granting this permission states that the monastery was then non-conventual. In 1441-4 the position of prior, vacant by the death of Andrew Occurrin, was granted to Patrick Occurrin who was first to be received into the monastery and then

95. Colfer, *Arrogant trespass*, p. 208; Brooks, 'Charters', nos 1, 2, 39, 42.
96. Grattan-Flood, *Ferns*, pp 154-5; Gwynn & Hadcock, *MRH*, p 104.
97. Gwynn & Hadcock, *MRH*, pp 112-3; Emily M. Pritchard, *The history of St Dogmaels abbey* (London, 1907), pp 159-167; W. H. Grattan Flood, *History of the diocese of Ferns* (Waterford, 1916), p 70.
98. For the extent of these holdings see Billy Colfer, 'Anglo-Norman settlement in County Wexford' in Kevin Whelan (ed) *Wexford: history and society* (Dublin, 1987), p 88.

Fig 7: Down Cathedral c 1830, from J. D. Harding *Picturesque views of the antiquities of Ireland.* Reproduced with permission from Down County Museum.

appointed prior. In 1448 Prior Thady Ua Broin (O'Byrne) was accused by Fergal Occurin, a monk of Millau in the diocese of Rodez. The occurrence of the same surname in these three petitions indicates a strong family connection with the property and it is likely that it had passed to their control.

Downpatrick

The Benedictine Cathedral Priory of St Patrick, Down, and the smaller foundations at Nendrum and Ards were among the religious foundations established by John de Courcy after his conquest of the Dál Fiatach kingdom of Ulaid in 1177. De Courcy is one of the most enigmatic figures of the Anglo-Norman invasion and his conquest is all more remarkable in light of his relatively modest rank.[99] He consolidated his position by attracting settlers from the north of England, with the endowment of religious houses forming a particularly significant element in the process.[100] The publication of a number of early charters and other primary sources by William Reeves and Gearóid Mac Niocaill, and J. Frederick Rankin's recent history of Down Cathedral, give a clear picture of the process of foundation and the subsequent life of the Benedictine community.[101] Peter Harbison's article above discusses the complex building history of the site.

99. For an important reassessment of his origins and career see Seán Duffy, 'The first Ulster plantation; John de Courcy and the men of Cumbria' in Terry Barry, Robin Frame and Katherine Simms (eds) *Colony and frontier in medieval Ireland* (London, 1995), pp 1-28.
100. Marie-Therese Flanagan, 'John de Courcy, the first Ulster plantation and Irish church men' in Brendan Smith (ed.), *Britain and Ireland 900-1300* (Cambridge, 1999), pp 154-78.
101. Gearóid Mac Niocaill (ed) 'Carta Dunenses XII-XIII Céad' in *Seanchas Ard Mhacha*, vol

Fig 8: Shrine of
St Patrick's arm.
© Ulster Museum,
Belfast.

As with a number of the other Anglo-Norman Benedictine foundations, Down was an ancient Christian site and a cathedral dedicated to the Holy Trinity already stood there at the time of de Courcy's arrival in 1177. In 1183 he introduced monks from St Werburgh's abbey in Chester to form the cathedral chapter under the leadership of Prior William de Etteshall.[102] The dedication of the foundation had by now been changed from the Holy Trinity to St Patrick and in 1185 the bodies of Sts Patrick, Brigid and Columba (Colum Cille) were miraculously discovered buried in the cathedral precincts by Bishop Malachy III. The relics were elevated and enshrined and a reference from 1220 indicates that they may occasionally have been brought on circuit, even as far afield as England.[103] The fine medieval shrine of St Patrick's arm in the Ulster Museum in Belfast is believed to have been preserved in Down (Fig 8).[104] To commemorate the discovery and promote the cult, de Courcy commissioned a new life of Patrick by the Cistercian monk Jocelyn of Furness. These events greatly enhanced Down's standing as a place of pilgrimage and throughout the middle ages it functioned as the starting point for the pilgrimage to St Patrick's Purgatory.

As well as the income accruing from pilgrims' offerings, the new Benedictine foundation was generously endowed with various rights, privileges and exemptions by de Courcy and his followers. A charter dating from the late 1180s granted the community the right to every tenth animal from de Courcy's herds or taken by him in booty. It also received the income from a number of lucrative ferry crossings in the vicinity.[105] The extent of the lands actually granted by the founder is not certain. Though the *Annals of Chester* refer to an initial grant of ten carucates[106] it appears that apart from his initial grant of a site, most of the community's land was not granted by de Courcy but, perhaps under duress, by Bishop Malachy III of Down.[107] This

5:2 (1970), pp 418-28; J. Frederick Rankin, *Down cathedral: the church of St Patrick of Down* (Belfast, 1997).

102. J. T. Tait (ed), *The chartulary or registers of the abbey of St Werburgh, Chester* (2 vols, Manchester, 1920-23[Chetham Society, vols 79 & 82]), ii (vol 82) pp 471-2, no 886; A. J. Kettle, 'The abbey of Chester' in B. E. Harris (ed) *A history of the county of Chester* (3 vols, Oxford, 1980-87), iii, pp 132-47. Reference at pp 134-5.

103. On the later medieval relics of St Patrick see Cormac Burke, *Patrick: the archaeology of a saint* (Belfast, 1993), pp 48-56.

104. Note on the 'Shrine of St Patrick's hand' in *Down and Connor Historical Society's Journal*, iv (1931-2), pp 53-54. I am grateful to Dr Raymond Gillespie for this reference. Cormac Bourke, 'The shrine of St Patrick's hand' in *Irish Arts Review*, 4, no 3 (1987), pp 25-7.

105. Mac Niocaill, 'Carta Dunenses', nos 4 & 8.

106. Cited in R. V. H. Burne, *The monks of Chester: the history of St Werburgh's abbey* (London, 1962), p 11.

107. Mac Niocaill, 'Carta Dunenses', no 3. The bishop reserved for his own use all offerings

presumably was because it was already ecclesiastical land and the bishop was the competent authority to grant it. The lands granted were extensive, amounting to forty-six named places and six churches, and Rankin has identified thirty-eight townlands in the present-day vicinity of Down and the Lecale peninsula as being included in it.[108] De Courcy also confirmed the grant of land made to the monastery by Amauricius de Hannekke and granted the community the proceeds of all court cases involving their tenants in his territory on condition that his representative was present to oversee proceedings. This latter concession, as Flanagan notes, was tantamount to conferring ecclesiastical immunity.[109] Sometime between 1227 and 1242 Hugh de Lacy, Earl of Ulster, granted the prior and community the right to operate a fishing boat with a single net on the river Bann.[110] In 1220, the prior and community petitioned asylum in England from Henry III and assistance in rebuilding the monastery which had been destroyed by war. Further damage was caused in 1245 by an earthquake and, like many other religious houses, the priory suffered greatly at the hands of Edward Bruce and his Scottish force during 1315-16.[111]

From the outset the foundation was free of all obligations to its mother house in England. Unlike Chester, Down was established as a cathedral priory, specifically modelled on those at Coventry and Winchester. These institutions were an almost uniquely English phenomenon with only Monreale in Sicily and, for a period in the eleventh century, Dublin, having comparable arrangements.[112] The monks staffed the cathedral, taking responsibility for its upkeep, for the needs of pilgrims and maintaining a high standard of liturgy. They also formed the electoral body within the diocese and their assertion of this right to elect later led to frequent disputes, initially with the Augustinian Canons of Saul but later with the Crown and the archbishops of Armagh. The bishop of the diocese was nominally the abbot of these institutions, a fact Bishop Malachy mentions in the charter,[113] but the actual religious

made in the cathedral on the feasts of Christmas, the Purification of the Lord, St Patrick, Easter and Pentecost.

108. Flanagan, 'de Courcy', p 165; Rankin, *Down cathedral*, p 214.

109. Mac Niocaill, 'Carta Dunenses', pp 420-21, nos 6 & 7; Flanagan, 'de Courcy', p 167.

110. Mac Niocaill, 'Carta Dunenses', p 422, no 9.

111. Gwynn & Hadcock, *MRH*, pp 105-6.

112. Knowles, *Monastic order*, pp 129-34, 619-31; Joan Greatrex, 'The cathedral monasteries in the later middle ages' in Rees, *Monks of England*, pp 118-34.

113. 'Episcopus ero custos et abbas sicut fit in ecclesia Wyntoniensi vel Coventrensi' (I, the bishop, will be custodian and abbot as is the practice in the church of Winchester and Coventry), Mac Niocaill 'Carta Dunenses', no 3.

superior was the prior who served as the cathedral dean. The prior of Down sat as a spiritual peer in the Irish parliament and a number became bishops of the diocese. As a senior ecclesiastical figure, he was frequently called on to witness deeds or act in some official capacity and the Calendar of Papal letters and registers of the archbishops of Armagh contain numerous references to them as plaintiffs and defendants or acting as judges delegate.[114] The first prior, William de Etteshall, was almost immediately succeeded by Prior Andrew who is mentioned in an 1183 de Courcy charter. A Prior D. is mentioned some time after 1183 and a Prior W. in 1224. In 1237 Prior R. was among the witnesses to a charter granted in favour of the Cistercian community at Newry. He is possibly the Prior Robert involved in a visitation of the Augustinian monastery at Bangor in 1237, which recommended the deposition of the abbot there. He may also be the Prior R. mentioned in a papal letter of 1266 in connection with the election of Bishop Thomas Lydel as Bishop of Down. In 1277 Prior Nicholas le Blound was elected bishop. Prior Roger or Robert ruled the community in the first decade of the fourteenth century and was succeeded by Prior Thomas Bright who was elected bishop in 1314. Three years later Prior John of Down is mentioned in the Patent and Close Rolls of the Irish Chancery. He is probably the Prior John Sazarin who was fined £4 for trespass in 1329. In 1336 Prior Roger was a witness to a grant to the Hospital of St John the Evangelist at Down, while in 1353 Prior Roger Calf was elected bishop of the diocese.

The Register of Primate John Sweteman of Armagh contains a lengthy account of a dispute between the archbishop and Prior Nicholas Langtoun and his followers that occurred c 1367. While the cause of the dispute is not clear, the fact that it occurred during an episcopal vacancy in Down may indicate that it concerned rights of election and appointment.[115] The prior, having been cited to appear before the archbishop, went into hiding to avoid being served the summons. On being discovered by the archbishop's chaplain and another messenger, the prior beat and tortured them, forcing the messenger to eat the citation along with its wax seal. Further attempts by the archbishop to assert his authority led to the deaths of two of his servants at the hands of a priest named John Dommgan and a mob raised by the prior.

114. For the succession list of the Priors of Down and the sources from which it is compiled see Reeves, *Antiquities*, pp 176-7 and Rankin, *Down cathedral*, pp 55-60, 224.
115. The Archbishop was already engaged in litigation with Prior Nicholas over the administration of the diocese during the vacancy. Brendan Smith (ed), *The register of Milo Sweteman, archbishop of Armagh* (Dublin, 1996), p 86, no 85; p 94, no 93.

After excommunicating the offenders the archbishop, wisely, referred the case to Rome.[116]

In 1369 another prior called Richard Calf was elected bishop. The degree, if any, of his relationship to the prior of the same name elected bishop in 1353 is not clear but it again demonstrates a close family connection with the monastery. He was succeeded as bishop in 1380 by Prior John Ross. In 1395 John Cely, a monk of Down and bishop-elect of the diocese, complained that Prior Walter Calf had abandoned the Benedictine habit and gone to Scotland as an adherent of the antipope. Cely succeeded Calf as prior, eventually becoming bishop in 1413. It was during his episcopate that the process of amalgamating the dioceses of Down and Connor was initiated. Cely has justifiably been described as 'one of the most notorious and colourful characters ever to have occupied the see of Down'.[117] The first decade of his episcopate passed without incident and in 1425 Henry VI appointed him chancellor and treasurer of the Liberty of Ulster. In 1430 he was ordered by Archbishop Swayne of Armagh to resume wearing the Benedictine habit which he had abandoned.[118] He refused and was threatened with excommunication. Further conflict emerged in 1434 when Cely was ordered to dismiss his concubine, Letys Thomas, with whom he was publicly co-habiting in Kilclief castle near Down. He ignored this threat and those of Swayne's successor, Archbishop John Prene, and was finally deprived of his see by papal authority in 1441. Primate Swayne also encountered similar difficulties with Prior William Stanley who c 1434 was accused of neglecting divine service, sending monks away from the monastery and living in public concubinage.[119] Thomas Brekway was prior in 1470 and may also have held the Abbacy of Saul indicating that pluralism was another problem facing the community. In 1474 Oliver Walsh, a monk of Down, was appointed prior in the face of opposition from Brekway. On Walsh's death in 1478 the priory was papally provided to Thomas, bishop of Annaghdown, as prior *in commendam*. In 1484 Robert Breanus was prior. A decade later he was the recipient of a letter from Archbishop Octavian of Armagh outlining the manner in which the church of Down had suffered as the result of war at the hands of nobles. In 1495 an unsuccessful attempt was made to oust him by Gelasius Magennis, a cleric of Dromore diocese and member of a powerful local family. In 1496 the

116. Smith, *Sweteman*, pp 216-20, no 219; Rankin, *Down cathedral*, pp 56-7.
117. Rankin, *Down cathedral*, p 45.
118. D. A. Chart (ed), *The register of John Swayne, archbishop of Armagh and primate of Ireland 1418-1439* (Belfast, 1935), p 123.
119. Chart, *Swayne*, p 151.

poverty of the community was the reason given for appointing Senequinus Suerdus, monk of Down, to the perpetual vicarage of Ramalyn in Down diocese. In 1501 William Mangan was appointed prior in succession to Prior Robert Breanus. He too faced opposition from Magennis who appears as prior in 1519. He also held the priorship of Saul and was presumably a relative of Bishop Eugene Magennis of Down. He was killed in a family dispute in 1526.

In 1179 de Courcy granted two thirds of the lands of the ancient monastery of Nendrum on Mahee Island in Strangford Lough to the monks of St Bees priory in Cumbria, a dependency of St Mary's Abbey, York.[120] The donation was confirmed by Bishop Malachy III who received the remaining third of the properties and revenue. The foundation seems at all times to have been a small one and seldom figures in the surviving sources. Further grants of land were made by Roger de Dunesford in 1194 and Brian de Eschallers in 1202.[121] The 1222 dispute between the abbot of St Mary's, York, and the bishop of Down presumably related to these properties. In 1288 two monks were resident and the cell seems to have been surrendered some time afterwards, as the 1306 taxation lists the church as a parochial rather than monastic foundation.

The priory of St Andrews in Ards was founded by de Courcy as a cell of St Andrew's priory, Stogursey (Stoke Courcy) in Somerset, a daughter house of Lonlay Abbey in France.[122] The Stogursey priory had been established by William de Falaise between 1100 and 1107 and was patronised by his descendants the de Courcy family.[123] As Prior William of Down is witness to the earliest surviving charter, the date of foundation must have been some time after 1183. The grant was quite extensive, consisting of ten carucates of land with rights to tithes.[124] In 1204 the Irish possessions of Stoke were confirmed by Pope Innocent III.[125] Its connection with Lonlay meant that, like Fore, it was regarded as an alien priory and was taken into the king's hand in 1342. In 1356 Archbishop Fitzralph of Armagh purchased it from Lonlay Abbey for £200, but after his death it was again taken into royal custody. Reference to a prior occurs in 1382, and in 1389 it was governed by Prior Thomas. In 1390

120. Gwynn & Hadcock, *MRH*, p. 107; Reeves, *Antiquities,* pp. 187-97; Rankin, *Down cathedral,* pp 30-31; Flanagan, 'de Courcy', pp 168-70.

121. Reeves, *Antiquities*, pp 190-94.

122. Gwynn & Hadcock, *MRH*, p. 108; Reeves, *Antiquities*, pp 18, 382-3, p 1019; Duffy, 'Ulster plantation', pp 4-6.

123. Duffy, 'Ulster plantation', p 5.

124. William Kerr, 'Black Abbey, the archbishops of Armagh and the church of Derraghy' in *Lisburn Historical Society,* i (1989), pp 45-49.

125. Sheehy, *Hibernia Pontificia,* i, pp 126-7.

Archbishop Colton pursued his claim to the priory and was granted it in 1395 for an annual rent of ten marks. The priory, however, continued to be regarded as an alien foundation and in 1411 it was granted to John Chenele having been seized by the king on account of the war with France. In 1474 the priory, which was described as without prior or monks and a long time in the possession of laymen, was granted to the Premonstratensian community at Woodburn whose superior, Dermit, was appointed prior *in commendam.*

Waterford, Cork and Youghal

The hospital of St John the Evangelist at Waterford and its dependencies at Cork, Youghal and Legan are perhaps the most unusual Benedictine foundations established in medieval Ireland. The Waterford foundation was the subject of a comprehensive article by Canon Patrick Power in 1897, but he was unaware of the extensive material relating to the Irish houses contained in English archives.[126] In particular he overlooked the extensive series of entries relating to the houses contained in a thirteenth- and fourteenth-century chartulary of the Benedictine priory of Bath, which sheds considerable light on the internal affairs of the Irish properties.[127] The Waterford foundation was established sometime before 1190, when it was taken under the protection of Prince John, count of Mortain, who issued three charters guaranteeing its rights.[128] It does not appear to have been a Benedictine foundation before 1204, when the community under their superior, Master Peter, agreed to submit to the authority

Fig 9: Doorway, St John's Priory, Youghal. *Photograph Mary Gibbons, Youghal Tourist Office*

126. Patrick Power, 'The priory, church and hospital of St John the Evangelist, Waterford' in *Journal of the Waterford and South-East of Ireland Archaeological Society,* 11 (1896), pp 81-97.
127. William Hunt (ed), *Two chartularies of the priory of St Peter at Bath* (London, 1893 [Somerset Record Society, vol viii]).
128. *Chartae, privilegia et immunitates being transcripts of charters and privileges to cities, towns, abbeys and other bodies corporate: 18 Henry II to 18 Richard II, 1171-1385* (Dublin, 1889), pp 9, 10, 39.

of the Benedictine priory of St Peter in Bath. In accepting them Prior Robert and the monastic chapter issued regulations governing the running of the Waterford priory and hospital. The prior or warden of Waterford was to be appointed by the prior of Bath, all male members of the community were to travel to Bath, there to make profession and promise obedience to the prior. The sick and infirm in the hospital were to be supported from the resources bequeathed for that purpose and any surplus income was to be devoted to the exercise of hospitality.[129] This agreement was ratified by royal authority for a fee of five marks.[130]

Despite this Benedictine connection, the actual running of the hospital devolved on a group of male and female religious known as the brethren and sisters of St Leonard. Such joint arrangements were not unusual in medieval hospitals and the famous Dublin foundation of St John's at the New Gate was similarly constituted.[131] A document of 1299-1300 suggests that the community was then entirely male in composition, but the sisters are again mentioned in 1468. At the Dissolution the community consisted of the prior, Sir Nicholas, who was a monk of Bath, and four sisters and three brethren of St Leonard.[132]

The foundation was one of the oldest religious houses in Waterford and was well endowed with lands, rents, mills, docks and spiritualities, giving its name to a suburb of the medieval city. A measure of its importance was the appointment of two of the thirteenth-century priors as bishops of Waterford: Prior Walter in 1227 and Prior William in 1255.

The prior of Bath maintained a watchful eye on his Irish possessions and the *Calendar of Documents relating to Ireland* contains a number of grants of licence for him or his representatives to go and inspect them. The Bath chartulary also gives a number of tantalising glimpses into the appointments, disciplinary matters and financial affairs of the hospital priories of Waterford, Cork and Youghal. In 1306 Prior Robert de Clopcote of Bath was in Ireland to investigate allegations of irregularity in the administration of the Irish estates, while in 1332 an incompetent warden was recalled to Bath. Unfortunately the Irish entries in the chartulary stop before the Black Death

129. Sweteman *CDI*, i, no 220.
130. Ibid., no 219.
131. Mark Hennessey, 'The Priory and Hospital of New Gate: the evolution and decline of a medieval monastic estate' in William J. Smyth and Kevin Whelan (eds), *Common ground: essays on the historical geography of Ireland* (Cork, 1988), pp 41-52.
132. John Bradley, Andrew Halpin and Heather King (eds) *Urban archaeology survey of Waterford city* (Waterford, 1988), pp 254-59, at p 255. I am grateful to Eamonn McEneaney for this reference.

so it is impossible to assess what effect this calamity had on the life and administration of the Irish houses. The very silence of the chartulary is perhaps its own witness as one can easily imagine how the affairs of troublesome Irish dependencies would be temporarily overlooked. The connection between Bath and the Irish houses was not broken however, as is evident from references in other sources, particularly the *Calendar of Papal Registers*. In 1334 John de Axbridge was papally provided to the vacant Waterford post, and in 1463 Prior John Lamport was unsuccessfully accused of irregularities by the prior of the Trinitarian house in Adare. In 1466 an agreement guaranteeing the rights of the tenants and parishioners of St John's was entered into by Prior Thomas of Bath and the Mayor and citizens of Waterford. In 1474 the house was recorded as non-conventual but in 1480 the prior of St John's attempted to resume by act of parliament leases of various lands and properties held by priory tenants. This led to a vigorous protest by the mayor and corporation. A substantial lease of priory property was granted by Prior John Devereux to Maurice Wyse in 1495.[133] In 1536 the dissolved priory was granted to William Wyse, a prominent burgess, protégé of Henry VIII and twice mayor of the city, and its rights and properties transformed his fortunes and formed the basis of the Wyse estate, the Manor of St John.[134]

The origins and history of the Cork priory hospital and the houses at Youghal and Legan or Monkstown in the county are even more obscure and confused than that of Waterford.[135] Like the Waterford foundation the Cork house seems to have been in existence by the end of the twelfth century and its properties were also confirmed by Prince John. It is not clear what initial relationship existed between the Cork and Waterford foundations, but Waterford's submission to Bath in 1204 seems to have included Cork as well, perhaps indicating that the two properties were united from the beginning. In 1226 King Henry III issued letters of protection for the prior and monks of the hospital of St John of Waterford and Cork[136] and there are further joint references in 1284, 1290, 1335, 1344, 1386, 1485 and 1536.[137]

---

133. Power, 'St John the Evangelist', pp 86-88.
134. Julian Walton, 'Gifts of sword and cap; Sir William Wyse, Mayor – 1533-34, 1540-41' in Eamonn McEneaney (ed), *A history of Waterford and its mayors from the 12th to the 20th century* (Waterford, 1995), pp 104-22. See particularly pp 107-109.
135. Denis O'Sullivan, 'The monastic establishments of medieval Cork' in *Journal of the Cork Archaeological and Historical Society*, 48 (1943), pp 9-19, particularly pp 11-13; idem, 'Three little known monastic establishments of medieval Cork' in Seamus Pender (ed) *Féilscríbhinn Torna: Essays and studies presented to Professor Tadhg Ua Donnchadha (Torna)* (Cork, 1947), pp 203-208; Bolster, *Diocese of Cork*, pp 135-40.
136. Sweetman, *CDI*, vol ii, no. 1343.
137. Bolster, *Diocese of Cork*, pp 137-8.

The spiritual and charitable obligations of the Cork house were outlined in a document of 1330, which stated that it had been established for the 'sustenance of four chaplains performing divine service daily at Cork for the souls of the king's ancestors, and of all the faithful deceased yearly, and twelve beds for paupers, and sustenance for two brethren and two nursing sisters there, forever.' As in Waterford these religious were known as the brethren and sisters of St Leonard. Neglect of these duties formed the basis of a papal investigation in 1364, and in 1484 a complaint was made that the Benedictine monk in charge of the Cork hospital could not understand Irish and would not appoint a chaplain linguistically competent to administer the sacraments and hear confessions.[138]

The extent of the priory's property was outlined in a survey or *inspeximus* taken in 1358 at the request of Prior John Istod of Bath. Like the Waterford house, it had been granted extensive lands and milling rights, along with the right of presentation to a number of parishes, including Kinsale and Youghal, and their attendant spiritualities. Some confusion surrounds the fact that earlier grants record that some of this property had already been granted to Benedictine monks of St Nicholas priory, Exeter. It is possible that this had been transferred by them to the hospital at some stage.

Fig 10: Engraving of a Benedictine nun from Mervyn Archdall, *Monasticon Hibernicum* (Dublin, 1786).

The earliest reference to the Youghal property occurs in 1306 when the prior of Bath ordered an investigation into its affairs and those of the other properties in Ireland. A late medieval building in Youghal is still indicated as the site of the priory to the present day (Fig 9). The manor of Legan was in the possession of the hospital by 1301 when John de Compton was prior.

Benedictine nuns

The evidence for the existence of Benedictine nuns in medieval Ireland is even more fragmentary than that for their male counterparts. While recent publications have done much to elucidate the general topic of religious women in medieval Ireland, specifically Benedictine references are few[139] and reference has already been made to the sisters of St Leonard, who staffed the priory hospitals at Waterford and Cork. Houses of Augustinian Canonesses constitute the majority of medieval Irish nunneries and there are only three references to Benedictine foundations. Of these, the royal Ó Conchobair

138. Bolster, *Diocese of Cork*, p 138.
139. Dianne Hall, *Women and the Church in medieval Ireland* c. *1140-1540* (Dublin, 2003), pp 42-207; Margaret Mac Curtain, 'Late medieval nunneries of the Irish Pale' in Howard B. Clarke, Jacinta Prunty and Mark Hennessey (eds), *Surveying Ireland's past: multidisciplinary essays in honour of Anngret Simms* (Dublin, 2004), pp 129-143.

(O'Connor) foundation of Kilcreevanty in the archdiocese of Tuam, established c 1200 seems to have been Benedictine for a brief period, before unsuccessfully attempting to become Cistercian. By 1223 the community had adopted the observances of Arrouaise and remained the principal Augustinian foundation in Connacht until its surrender by Abbess Devorgilla O'Connor in 1543.[140] The reference to Benedictine nuns in Cork is even less certain. In 1297 Agnes of Hereford, a recluse in Cork, sought permission to establish a convent for herself and some companions. The house is described as Benedictine but it seems more likely that the nuns were Augustinians and that references to Benedictine nuns in Cork relate to sisters of St Leonard serving the priory hospital of St John the Evangelist.[141]

The best documented foundation is the priory of St Mary at Down and here too the Benedictine affiliation is uncertain.[142] William Reeves describes it as a Cistercian foundation, as does Sir James Ware.[143] The founders are given as the Bagnal family. The earliest and only reference to it as a Benedictine foundation occurs in a papal letter of 1353 granting the prioress, Anne de Mandeville and one of the nuns, Margaret de Mandeville, permission to choose a confessor with authority to confer a plenary indulgence at the hour of their deaths.[144] It is possible that it began as a Cistercian house, only becoming Benedictine later. The records are silent until 1368 when, during a vacancy in the see of Down, Archbishop Sweteman of Armagh mentions Matilda Stokys, a nun of Down, cited in legal proceedings against Sir Roger Ogean, a priest of the diocese.[145] In 1463 Prioress Alice of Down was deprived for sexual incontinence by the commissary of Archbishop Prene of Armagh. She was permitted to remain in the convent at the discretion of her successor, Prioress Christina, who is described as being from the diocese of Sodor.[146] Conventual life seems to have lapsed completely by 1513 when Bishop Tiberius, the Italian bishop of Down and Connor, united the rev-

140. Gwynn & Hadcock, *MRH*, pp 318-9.
141. Gwynn & Hadcock, *MRH*, pp 315-6; Bolster, *Cork*, i, pp 194-9. In England anchorites desiring a cenobitic lifestyle generally adopted the Augustinian rule, cf Jane Herbert, 'The transformation of hermitages into Augustinian priories in twelfth-century England' in W. J. Sheils (ed.) *Monks, hermits and the ascetic tradition* (Blackwell, Oxford, 1985), pp 131-45.
142. Gwynn & Hadcock, *MRH*, p 316; Hall, *Women and the church*, pp 87, 127, 138, 166, 212-3; Rankin, *Down cathedral*
143. Reeves, *Antiquities*, p 232.
144. *Cal. pap. letters*, iii, p 509. A similar privilege was granted on the same date to Richard Calf, Prior of Down, and Walter Loche, priest of the diocese of Down.
145. Smith, *Sweteman*, no 81, p 84.
146. Rankin, *Down cathedral*, p 60; Hall, *Women and the church*, p 213.

enues of a number of small religious houses in Down diocese for the purpose of restoring the cathedral. These included the priory of St Mary which was described as being in ruins.[147]

The Dissolution of the monasteries

In 1536 Robert Cowley, Master of the Rolls, wrote to Thomas Cromwell with reference to the Irish religious houses:

> The abbayes here doo not kepe soo good Divine Service, as the abbayes in England, beeing suppressid, did kepe; the religeous personages here lesse contynent or vertuous, keping no hospitalitie, saving to theyme silves, theire concubynes, childerene and certain bell wedders, to eclypse theire pernycious lyevinges and to beare and pavesse theire detestable deedes.[148]

While allowance must be made for the bias of the author, it is evident from a wide variety of sources that the standard of monastic observance in late medieval Ireland was very low. Though attempts had been made to reform the Cistercians in the late fifteenth and early sixteenth centuries, these were ineffective and the principal expressions of vibrant religious life were found among the Observant branches of the orders of mendicant friars.[149] The evidence for the Benedictine houses outlined above concurs with this assessment and 'the strong impression one gets of the monastic establishment on the eve of the Reformation is that there was not much left to reform'.[150] Whatever their spiritual or moral shortcomings, the monasteries were holders of substantial real estate and other sources of income, the redistribution of which was a major feature of Irish ecclesiastical life in the 1530s and 1540s.

The different social and political situation obtaining in Ireland, particularly in the aftermath of the Kildare rebellion of 1534-35, made the Dissolution of the Irish monasteries a more protracted process than in England where the entire monastic edifice was dismantled between 1536 and 1540.[151] The Dissolution in Ireland must be seen against the centralising pol-

---

147. Aubrey Gwynn, *The medieval province of Armagh*, (Dundalk, 1946), p 137.

148. *State papers, Henry VIII* (11 vols, London, 1830-52) iii, part 1, p 370.

149. Ó Conbhuidhe, *Studies*, pp 1-47; For the Franciscan Observant reform see Colmán N. Ó Clabaigh, *The Franciscans in Ireland 1400-1534: from reform to Reformation* (Dublin, 2002).

150. Colm Lennon, *Sixteenth-Century Ireland: the incomplete conquest* (Dublin, 1994), pp 129-30.

151. Brendan Bradshaw, *The dissolution of the religious orders in Ireland under Henry VIII* (Cambridge, 1974); David Knowles, *The religious orders in England*, III, *The Tudor age* (Cambridge, 1959); Peter Cunich, 'The dissolution' in Daniel Rees (ed) *Monks of England*, pp 148-66.

icy of the Tudors and their incomplete conquest of the country, rather than solely as an offshoot of their religious reform programme.[152]

The parliamentary prelude to the Dissolution of the Irish monasteries was an act confiscating the lands of absentee English landlords, including those of the priors of Christ Church, Canterbury, and Bath.[153] The income from Canterbury's Irish lands was valued at £8 13s. 4d. in the *Valor ecclesiasticus* of 1535 where it was stated that nothing had been received for over thirty years because of rebellion in Ireland.[154] The *Valor* makes no reference to the Irish possessions of Bath priory or St Nicholas, Exeter. A number of smaller houses, none of them Benedictine, was dissolved in the period 1535 to 1538. The majority of houses in the Pale and in the territories of the Earl of Ormond were suppressed in the period 1539 to 1541, and those suppressed in 1540-41 were the subject of detailed surveys of their lands and revenues. These included the Benedictine properties of Ross Carbery, St Nicholas of Exeter, Fore, Bath and Glasscarrig.[155] The priory at Fore was surrendered in 1539 and granted to William King in 1540. The extensive list of its properties and rights indicates that it was well administered and of all the Irish foundations it seems to have been the most vibrant as a religious house.[156] The cathedral priory in Down was dissolved between May 1541 and October 1542.[157] The priory of Sts Peter and Paul at Athlone appears to have escaped the first wave of suppressions and the monks may have remained in possession there until the arrival of Sir William Brabazon as constable of Athlone castle in 1547.

Conclusion

By the end of the first wave of suppressions in 1541 almost sixty percent of Irish religious houses, chiefly in Gaelic territories, had not been dissolved and a number of these survived throughout the sixteenth century. The increased continental contacts of these religious, particularly the mendicant friars, created an important channel for Counter Reformation ideas to percolate back to Ireland. Young Irish men and women entered religious houses on the

---

152. R. Dudley Edwards, 'The Irish Reformation parliament of Henry VIII, 1536-7' in T. W. Moody (ed) *Historical Studies* VI (London, 1968) pp 59-84; Lennon, *Incomplete conquest*, pp 65-164.

153. Philomena Connolly (ed) *Statute rolls of the Irish Parliament* (Dublin, 2002), p 167.

154. John Caley and Joseph Hunter (eds), *Valor ecclesiasticus temp. Henr. VIII auctoritate regia institutus*, (London, 1810), i, p 16.

155. Newport B. White (ed) *Extents of Irish monastic possessions, 1540-1541* (IMC, Dublin, 1943), pp 152, 154, 270-74, 352, 374-6.

156. Ibid., pp 270-74.

157. Rankin, *Down cathedral*, p 82.

continent and from the early seventeenth century a network of continental colleges was established for the training of friars and secular clergy. An attempt was made to revive Cistercian life in Ireland with the return of small numbers of Irish monks professed in Spanish monasteries to the vicinities of some of their pre-Reformation houses. They also laid claim to Benedictine properties at Waterford and Fore, in the former case arousing the ire of the Catholic Bishop of Waterford.[158] During the Confederation of Kilkenny (1641-53), a number of religious orders attempted to reclaim property lost at the Dissolution. In 1646 the abbot general of the Spanish Benedictine congregation wrote to the papal nuncio in Ireland, Giovanni Battista Rinuccini, asking him to restore a number of houses to Irish monks professed in Spanish Benedictine monasteries, whom he wished to appoint abbots. Though his stated aim was to restore Benedictine life in Ireland, it is equally likely that he was concerned about maintaining claims to Irish Benedictine property in the face of Cistercian encroachments. The monks named were an interesting mix of old English and Gaelic stock: Patrick Salinger, Mansuetus of St Columban, Anselm Egan, John O'Donnell, John O'Duffnan and Columbanus Duffy.[159] The project foundered on the opposition of Catholic parties in Ireland who were unwilling to surrender the monastic land they had acquired. Of those listed in 1646 it is possible that one, Mansuetus of St Columban, is identical to the Mansuet Powel, referred to below by Aidan Bellenger: an Irish monk of the English Benedictine house at St Malo, who died c 1664.

Unlike their earlier confrères in the *Schottenklöster* or their contemporaries, the Irish Benedictine nuns, the Irish monks of the seventeenth century were unable to establish an Irish monastery on the continent. In 1665 the Franciscan friar Peter Walsh listed the numbers of regular clergy working in Ireland: 'And in the last place, for what concerns the Benedictin [sic] Monks (who, if I had ranked the Orders according to their antiquity should be, together with those Chanons Regular, treated of before any of the mendicant orders) there are not known to be above two or three in the whole Kingdom'. Unfortunately he does not give their identities or the areas in which they were active.[160] With this reference the medieval and early modern period of

158. Ó Conbhuidhe, *Studies*, pp 224-27.
159. Barnabas O'Ferrall and Daniel O'Connell, *Commentarius Rinuccinianus* ed. John Kavanagh (6 vols, IMC, Dublin, 1932-1949), ii, p 487. The Augustinian Canons Regular also appealed for the restoration of their Irish properties.
160. Peter Walsh, *The history and vindication of the Loyal Formulary or Irish Remonstrance* (London, 1674), p. 575.

Benedictine Ireland, at least in its male expression, came to an end. Though neither as numerous as the Cistercians and Augustinian Canons, nor as influential as the mendicant friars, *Hibernia Benedictina* was nonetheless a reality that found a surprisingly wide and diverse variety of expressions.

Acknowledgements
In addition to those acknowledged in the footnotes, I am grateful for advice and corrections to those who read drafts of this article, in whole or in part: Dr Billy Colfer, Dr Peter Harbison, Dr Pádraig Lenihan, Dr Colm Lennon, an tOllamh Dáibhí Ó Cróinín, Professor Pádraig Ó Riain, Dr Brendan Smith and Dr Bernadette Williams. In the course of research the courtesy of Siobhán Fitzpatrick, librarian, and Karl Vogelsang, Royal Irish Academy, Dublin, an tAth Ciarán Ó Sabhaois OCSO, librarian, Mt St Joseph Abbey, Ros Cré and Dom Daniel Rees OSB, librarian, Downside Abbey, Somerset, was much appreciated.

CHAPTER FIVE

The Irish Benedictine Nuns: From Ypres to Kylemore

Kathleen Villiers-Tuthill

The abbey of the Immaculate Conception of the Blessed Virgin at Kylemore in County Galway, is the oldest of the Irish Benedictine monasteries. The community, established in Ypres in 1665 as an English foundation, was formally designated as an Irish house in 1682. This long history, from Ypres to Kylemore, comprises over three hundred years of unbroken Irish Benedictine tradition. During the course of its history, the community has had eighteen abbesses, three of whom were English, two Belgian and thirteen Irish.

Fig 1:
Affiliation Table from
Dom Patrick Nolan,
Irish Dames of Ypres
(Dublin, 1908)

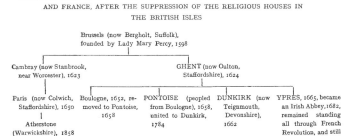

The Abbey at Ypres was a daughter-house of Ghent, one of the English houses set up in the Low Countries in the sixteenth century, which recognised Lady Mary Percy as their founder. Lady Mary, daughter of Thomas Percy, Earl of Northumberland, founded a Benedictine community for English women in Brussels in 1598. As numbers at Brussels increased, it became necessary to establish additional houses at Cambrai and Ghent. From Ghent, foundations were made at Pontoise, Boulogne, Dunkirk and Ypres.

All of these monasteries were independent and subject only to the diocesan bishop. The monastery at Ypres was set up at the request of the Bishop of Ypres, Martin de Praets. The bishop was acquainted with the English Benedictine abbey at Ghent and it was his wish to establish a similar house at Ypres. When making his request to the abbess of Ghent, the bishop asked specifically for Dame Marina Beaumont, because of her fluency in languages, and she went on to become the first abbess of Ypres.

Nuns were sent from Ghent and Dunkirk to assist Abbess Beaumont in setting up her community but, from the beginning, the house was beset with difficulties. The bishop promised to contribute liberally to the foundation of the monastery and had provided a house close to the city wall. However, within a year, Bishop de Praets died, leaving the fledgling community struggling to survive.

In the years that followed, Abbess Beaumont had great difficulty in attracting novices to her community. She requested and received nuns from the abbesses of Ghent, Pontoise and Dunkirk, but none of these would stay. The abbess, it would seem, was a difficult lady to get along with. In 1671, the community was forced to give up its house, which was required by the city for new fortifications, and move to Rue St Jacques. The new abbey at Rue St Jacques would remain the community's home for the next 243 years. However, at the time of the move to Rue St Jacques there was little to indicate that it would survive that long, consisting as it did of just Abbess Beaumont, Dame Flavia Carey, and one lay sister.

Having failed to establish an independent community, Abbess Beaumont again sought assistance from the other English Benedictine houses and eventually received two nuns and several postulants from Paris. The abbess then transferred Ypres Abbey to Paris conditionally, an act which greatly angered the abbess of Ghent (Lady Abbess Knatchbull), who had always intended Ypres for the Irish nation.[1]

On the death of Abbess Beaumont in 1682, a struggle ensued between, on the one hand, the two nuns from Paris, who wished to retain the house for their abbess, and on the other, Dame Flavia Carey, supported by the abbess of Ghent. Eventually, with the intervention of the abbesses of Dunkirk and Pontoise, their bishop and the President of the English Benedictines, agreement was reached. The Paris nuns were forced to depart and nuns from Ghent, Dunkirk and Pontoise were sent to assist the Ypres community in the election of a new abbess. The community elected Dame Flavia Carey on 19 November 1682.[2] The house was then formally designated an Irish monastery, dedicated to the Immaculate Conception of the Blessed Virgin, under the title of Gratia Dei.[3]

1. Dom Patrick Nolan OSB, *The Irish Dames Of Ypres* (Dublin, 1908), pp 52-3.
2. Ibid., p 53.
3. E.W. Beck, FSA Scot, *Irish Ecclesiastical Record*, 3rd Series. 1891, xii, pp 109-16; Nolan, *Dames,* pp 53-4.

Irish nuns from the other monasteries were sent to increase the numbers at Ypres and from then on the community became known as *De Iersche Damen* – the Irish Ladies or the *Irish Dames of Ypres*.

For almost 250 years, this community would remain the only Irish community of the Order of St Benedict. The purpose of the abbey was to provide an education and religious community for Irish women, although other nationalities were also welcome. The abbey attracted the daughters of the Irish nobility, both as students and postulants, and enjoyed the patronage of many influential Irish families living in exile. In their school, the nuns permitted no more than thirty students at any one time so as to provide individual attention for the girls. Many of the students came direct from Ireland at a very young age, sometimes two and three sisters came together. Several of the students went on to become nuns and abbesses. Dom Patrick Nolan in his book, *The Irish Dames of Ypres*, lists the names of some of the Irish students and nuns to be found at Ypres down through the centuries.

Prior to the establishment of Ypres as an Irish monastery, an attempt had been made by two Irish nuns to set up an Irish house in Dunkirk. The nuns were members of the Benedictine community in that city and, on learning that their abbess was contemplating selling her abbey and moving elsewhere, they travelled to Ireland to raise funds to help finance its purchase. The nuns succeeded in winning the support of friends and relatives in Ireland. However, on their return they discovered that Dunkirk abbey was no longer for sale and so the Irish monastery did not materialise. One of the two nuns, Dame Mary Joseph O'Ryan, was among that first Irish community at Ypres.

Dame O'Ryan, accompanied by Dame Ursula Butler, returned to Ireland to secure for Ypres the support promised to set up an Irish house. She returned in 1684 with five or six children for the school and one or two young women for the novitiate. Dame Ursula Butler remained on in England for the coronation of King James II and she died there soon afterwards.

The second abbess of Ypres, Lady Abbess Flavia Carey, died in 1686. At the time there were three choir dames in the community: Dame O'Ryan, who was again absent in Ireland, Dame Joseph Butler and Dame Lawrence Lawson. Again, the assistance of religious, sent from the other Benedictine houses, was necessary for the subsequent election of Dame Mary Joseph Butler as abbess. On learning that her community had elected an abbess in her absence, Dame Mary Joseph O'Ryan delayed her return and remained on in Dublin. Under the patronage of the Archbishop of Dublin, Dr Patrick Russell, Dame O'Ryan opened a school in Channel Row (later North Brunswick St).[4]

4. S. O'Reilly, 'A Famous Dublin Prelate' in *The Catholic Bulletin,* 1916, vi, pp 315-19; Nolan, *Dames,* p 205.

Lady Abbess Mary Joseph Butler (1686-1723) was the first Irish born abbess of Ypres. At the time of her election she was forty-four years of age.[5] She was the niece of Abbess Knatchbull of Ghent, and the cousin of the Duke of Ormond. At the age of eight she had been sent to her aunt to be educated at Ghent and later became a Benedictine nun.

Fig 2: Lady Abbess M. Joseph Butler (1686-1723)

A year after being elected abbess, Abbess Butler received a request from King James II, through the Duke of Tyrconnell, the Lord Lieutenant, to come to Dublin and establish her community there. The king promised her his royal protection and certain privileges as an inducement, and a house was taken for the community at Great Ship Street, close to Dublin Castle. Archbishop Russell still favoured Dame O'Ryan but eventually, perhaps under pressure from James II, extended his support to include Abbess Butler. Dublin, for a time, was to have two Benedictine houses.

Tyrconnell went personally to inspect the community's new house, making sure that all was ready for the abbess and her community. However, at the same time, in a letter to the Grand Vicars of Ypres, he requested that the abbey there be retained for the nuns, in case they should be obliged to return.[6] As the community at Ypres was still small in number, nuns from Pontoise were sent ahead to Dublin to prepare for the arrival of the abbess. On her journey to Dublin Abbess Butler stopped off in London, where she was presented at Whitehall to Queen Mary of Modena, wife of King James II. Her visit there won her the distinction of being the first Benedictine abbess to be seen at Whitehall since the Reformation.[7]

The abbess arrived in Dublin on 31 October 1688 and entered her enclosure in Great Ship Street. Her school was an immediate success and out of the thirty students attending, eighteen expressed a desire to enter. The abbess, however, decided not to accept any postulants due to the political climate of the day. King James attended the consecration of the community's church in

5. Nolan, *Dames*, p 79.
6. Ibid., p 150.
7. Beck, op.cit., p. 405; Nolan, *Dames*, p 150.

1689 and a year later he fulfilled his promise and drew up a royal charter, establishing his 'first and chief Royal Monastery of Gratia Dei' of the Order of St Benedict, with Lady Abbess Butler as its abbess. He also granted the foundation one hundred pounds sterling a year and freedom from rates and taxes.

After James's defeat at the battle of the Boyne in 1690, the Williamite forces rampaged through the city and ransacked the monastery. The abbess had already sent her pupils home and she and her nuns had taken refuge in a neighbour's house. One young nun returned to the abbey disguised in secular clothes and managed to save some of the most sacred and precious objects from the looters.

The Archbishop of Dublin went into hiding in the country and many others followed his example. Abbess Butler made the decision to return to Ypres, although the Duke of Ormond, her cousin, promised her the protection of King William. The abbess, however, could not be persuaded and in the end, the Duke obtained a pass from King William, for herself and her community, offering safe passage to Ypres.

On arrival in Ypres, the nuns from Pontoise returned to their own monastery and left the abbess with four lay sisters and no choir dames. For the next five years the abbess suffered great poverty and hardship. At one time she was encouraged by her bishop to dissolve her monastery and retire to another house, but she refused to do so.[8] Eventually postulants did arrive and financial assistance was received from Pope Innocent XII, the King of France and Queen Mary of Modena. However, small numbers, few postulants and hard times would continue to be the order of the day at Ypres down through the centuries.

Fig 3: Flag of Ramillies

During the term of Lady Abbess Butler the community received a curious gift, the Flags of Ramillies. The flags are believed to have been taken at the Battle of Ramillies in 1706. Originally there were two or possibly three flags. The exact origins of the flags and the exact regiment to which they belonged has been disputed by military historians down through the years. Tradition among the nuns holds that the flags

8. Brick, op.cit., pp 406-9.

were captured by the Irish Brigade from a British regiment at the Battle of Ramillies and deposited at the abbey by Murrough O'Brien, the Lieutenant-Colonel of the regiment of Clare.[9]

For many years they hung in the choir at Ypres and their presence there assumed symbolic significance for the nationalist cause. The poet Thomas Davis refers to the flags and their resting place in his poem *Clare's Dragoons:*

When, on Ramillies' bloody field,
The baffled French were forced to yield,
The victor Saxon backward reeled
Before the charge of Clare's Dragoons.
The Flags we captured in that fray
Look lone in Ypres' choir, they say,
We'll win them company today,
Or bravely die like Clare's Dragoons.

The flags were removed from the choir in the middle of the nineteenth century. There were no Irish nuns in the monastery at the time and the abbess of the day, an English woman, ordered their removal. Some time later, two German lay sisters discovered the flags and, not knowing their history or value, decided to tear them up and use them as decorations to honour the feast of St Martha.[10] Fortunately one of the other nuns found the two before all was lost and succeeded in saving a remnant. The remnant was then moved to a safe place and has remained in the possession of the nuns ever since.

Lady Abbess Butler died on 22 December 1723, aged 82. She had been abbess of her community for thirty-seven years. She was followed by six others of Irish birth; it would be over one hundred years before an abbess of any other nationality would take up the position. For the next forty years, under Lady Abbess M Xaveria Arthur (1723-1743) and Lady Abbess M Magdalen Mandeville (1743-1760), the community again suffered great hardship and poverty. So much so, that at one time they considered leaving Ypres and moving to France, but this idea was later abandoned.[11] Abbess Mandeville was the grand-niece of Abbess Butler and while a novice she returned to Ireland to take action against her brother who was attempting to swindle her out of her inheritance. While in Ireland she recovered the church plate left behind by Abbess Butler. However, on her return journey she was ship-

9. H. V. Gill, SJ, 'The fate of the Irish flag at Ypres, in *Studies* (Dublin, 1919), viii, No 29, pp 119-28.
10. Nolan, *Dames*, p 253.
11. Ibid., p 270.

wrecked off the Isle of Wight, and the plate was lost, though she herself survived.[12]

Conditions improved under Lady Abbess M Bernard Dalton (1760-1783), and numbers increased. Abbess Dalton had great devotion to the Sacred Heart and had all of her community enrolled in the newly established Confraternity of the Sacred Heart at Bruges. The community claimed the distinction of being the first to introduce the devotion into Flanders.[13]

The seventh abbess of Ypres, Dame M Scholastica Lynch (1783-1799), had her enclosure invaded by about forty or fifty armed soldiers during the French Revolution. The soldiers were members of the invading French army and, on 13 January 1793, they threatened 'to point their cannon against the house' if not admitted. Once inside they began placing seals on the door to the church sacristy and anywhere else where they hoped to find anything of value. As the day wore on, they got drunk and were eventually persuaded to confine themselves to the parlour for the night.[14] Next morning, on learning that the General in Chief of the army was an Irishman, thought to have been the Republican general, James O'Moran, the abbess sent word requesting his help. Shortly afterwards the Commander of the town came to make excuses, he took off the seals, paid for all damages and withdrew the soldiers from the monastery. Before leaving, the commander suggested that the nuns might consider taking advantage of the liberty granted by the French nation, break their vows and return to the outside world, but the proposition was rejected by the nuns.[15]

The French were forced to withdraw, but retook the town on 19 June 1794 and, under the new regime, a decree was issued ordering the expulsion of the religious orders. The Irish Dames were given a reprieve, for a time, on the grounds that their members were foreigners, but were subjected to continuous harassment.[16] For many years afterwards the abbey at Ypres was the only monastery left in the Low Countries. The mother house, Ghent, and the other English Benedictine houses had been driven out in the early years of the French Revolution and had re-located to England.

The difficulties in caring for her community during these troubled times proved too much for Lady Abbess Lynch and may well have contributed to her early death, at the age of forty-six, on 22 June 1799. The community

---

12. Beck, op.cit., p 810.
13. Nolan, *Dames,* p 278.
14. Ibid., pp 287-8.
15. Ibid., p 288.
16. Ibid., p 293.

chose her sister, Abbess Bernard Lynch (1799-1830), as her successor. That same year, the order came for the nuns to leave the house on the 13 November, the Feast of All Benedictine Saints. The abbey had been sold over their heads and they were being forced out. However, when the day of departure came, a violent storm prevented the nuns from leaving. The following morning, the Feast of All Benedictine Souls, news that there had been a change of government reached the town. The new government allowed the nuns remain on in their monastery, but they were forced to buy it back from the new owners. The cost of this and necessary refurbishment almost broke the community. Once again they were reduced to 'dire straits of poverty' and for a whole year they were obliged to sleep on the floor, because there were no beds. The nuns, however, met the challenge, never forgetting their primary purpose in life, with prayer and regular discipline continuing as usual.[17]

Things had greatly improved by 1810. The community then consisted of ten choir dames and four lay sisters. They were, they recorded, 'in every respect ... comfortable', they had no debts, 'and enjoyed, in perfect union with one another, every advantage this holy state affords'. All they wished for was 'a greater number of companions to share in their happiness, and perpetuate this establishment for the glory of God'.[18]

Lady Abbess Bernard Lynch died in 1830. She was succeeded by Lady Abbess Mary Benedict Byrne (1830-1840), the last of the Irish abbesses of the Irish Dames of Ypres. Abbess Byrne was in turn succeeded by an English woman, Lady Abbess Elizabeth Jarrett (1840-1888). Over the years the abbey had deteriorated and was falling to ruin. Abbess Jarrett took it upon herself to rebuild the monastery, replacing the old building with an attractive Flemish Gothic styled monastery, of red brick, with square cloisters.[19] She was assisted in her work by her prioress, Dame Mary Scholastica Bergé, who, within a few years, was able to rid the abbey of all debts arising out of the construction of the new building.[20]

At one time during Abbess Jarrett's term, there were no Irish nuns left in the monastery and it was at this time that the Flag of Ramillies came under attack. The abbey's link with Ireland was re-established with the arrival in the house of Mary Josephine Fletcher, in 1854. In later years, Dame Josephine was fond of reminding the nuns that her arrival in Ypres had united the community again to 'old Ireland'.[21]

17. Beck, op.cit., p 812.
18. Nolan, *Dames*, pp 313-4.
19. Beck, op.cit., p 813.
20. Kylemore Abbey Manuscript.
21. Ibid.

Fig 4: New abbey
at Ypres

Lady Abbess Jarrett was forced to resign, due to ill health, in 1885, and the management of the house passed to her prioress, Dame M Scholastica Bergé. On the death of Lady Abbess Jarrett, Dame Scholastica was elected Abbess.

Lady Abbess Bergé (1890-1916), was born in Belgium, and entered the monastery in 1850, at the age of twenty. Although not Irish by birth, Lady Abbess Bergé, according to Dom Nolan, was 'in full sympathy with Irish aspirations', and could be said to be 'more Irish than the Irish themselves'. Which was perhaps just as well, as she was destined to end her days in Ireland when driven from her homeland in 1914. In 1912, Lady Abbess Bergé suffered a severe stroke which left her partially paralysed, unable to speak and confined to a chair for the rest of her life. The prioress, Dame Maura Ostyn, took over the responsibility of running the monastery and it was she who co-ordinated the community's departure from Ypres and eventual settlement in Kylemore.

In 1914, the community consisted of Abbess Scholastica Bergé, Prioress Maura Ostyn, eight choir dames, eight lay sisters and a novice. The abbess and prioress were both Belgian, as was the novice; the remainder was made up of four Germans, three English, one from Luxembourg and seven Irish.

For the community, the first casualties of the Great War were the four German nuns. They were expelled from Belgium, along with all German nationals, in September 1914. At the time the nuns expected to have them back within three weeks. However, by October, as the first battle of Ypres raged around them, it was becoming apparent that this was one war they

might not be able to wait out. The community's final days at Ypres were recorded by the
nuns and later published, entitled *The Irish
Nuns at Ypres*. The material was gathered
from personal diaries kept by individual nuns
and edited by Dame Columban Plomer. The
introduction to the book was written by John
Redmond MP, leader of the Irish Parliamentary Party, whose niece, Dame Teresa
Howard, was a member of the community.
John Redmond had previously visited the
abbey at Ypres and had presented the community with a statue of St Patrick.

Fig 5: Lady Abbess
Scholastica Bergé
(1890-1916)

Between 11 October and 20 November, Ypres was under attack by the
German forces as they attempted to break through the allied defence, in their
effort to reach Calais. During this time, the nuns listened, and from the high-
est windows of the abbey they watched, as bomb after bomb fell on the town
and the streets filled with soldiers and refugees.

Throughout this terrifying ordeal the nuns were sustained by their
prayers. Day and night they prayed for peace and an end to the war.
Otherwise, they busied themselves making badges of the Sacred Heart for the
soldiers and bandages for the wounded. Food in the town was scarce and yet
daily, large numbers of people appeared at the monastery door requesting
food and, in some cases, shelter. The school was taken over by the English
ambulance service. In their final days at Ypres, the nuns had moved to the
cellars for safety and during the night one nun kept watch while the others
slept.

As the fighting continued, the nuns decided to prepare a hiding place for
their many treasures: religious objects, letters, documents and books.
Towards the end of October, it was decided that for her own safety the abbess
should be moved to Poperinge, a town nine miles to the west. For the entire
community the abbess' departure was a traumatic experience and she herself
was reluctant to leave. Stepping from strict enclosure into a war torn landscape was daunting. In the sixty years since her profession, Lady Abbess Bergé
had never once stepped outside the door of the abbey and it was only with
strong persuasion that she agreed to do so on this occasion. The abbess was
accompanied by two elderly nuns and was placed in the care of Dame Placid
Druhan.

Within two days it became clear that it was no longer safe for the community to remain in Ypres, almost all of the civilians had abandoned the

town and had taken to the roads. The prioress decided to move her community to Poperinge. The time of departure was set for 2 pm on Friday 6 November. In the final hours left to them at the abbey, the nuns wandered through the rooms saying their goodbyes. A paper badge of the Sacred Heart was placed on every window and a statue of Our Lady of the Angels on a niche outside one of the windows.

As the time for departure approached and the nuns gathered at the door to leave, it was discovered that no one had brought the key, and departure was delayed as one nun went to fetch it. When the key eventually arrived and was placed in the key-hole, a loud explosion was heard and many of the nuns were knocked to the ground. The monastery had been hit by two shells, one had exploded in the garden and would have certainly fallen on the nuns had they not been delayed. The second had landed on the building itself and, as the nuns moved out into the street, they could see smoke rising from the upper floor.

Fig 6: Irish Dames of Ypres

The nuns walked the nine miles to Poperinge through thick mud, sharing the road with fellow refugees and soldiers. They found the going tough; weighed down by heavy habits and carrying their possessions in bundles, they were soon tired. Prior to this they had walked no more than six or seven times round their small garden and were in no fit state for the journey. On reaching Poperinge, they were given shelter in a convent, which they shared with three other communities, and they remained there for the next fortnight. Eventually they succeeded in obtaining transport to the coast.

During that time, Dame Josephine Fletcher, the link with 'old Ireland', passed away and was laid to rest in a double coffin before being placed in a vault. The community's intention was to have her remains reburied at Ypres when peace would be restored. By a strange coincidence it was also a Dame Fletcher who died in exile on the only other occasion that the community had moved out of Ypres: Dame Susanna Fletcher died in Dublin in 1689.

While at Poperinge, three of the nuns made a quick trip back to Ypres to collect some of the nuns' clothing and to check on the building. They found a deserted city with many of the buildings in ruins. The abbey looked good enough from the outside, but some shells had pierced the roof and inside

Fig 7: Ypres Abbey in ruins

everywhere was covered with bricks and debris. The nuns loaded whatever they could into a hand cart and made their way back to the road. On the journey back they met a British cavalry regiment coming from the trenches. The soldiers called out to the nuns 'Who are you, sisters, where do you come from', to which Dame Columban replied, 'We are English nuns from the Benedictine convent of Rue St Jacques.' This, apparently, was too much for Dame Patrick, who called out: 'We are no such thing. We are Irish Benedictines!' 'Irish', shouted half a dozen of the soldiers, 'and so are we', and they began singing, 'It's a long way to Tipperary'.[22]

Two ambulances transported the nuns to Boulogne and an Irish priest, Father Flynn, was sent to accompany them on their journey. They broke the journey for two nights at St-Omer where they were given accommodation in the Ursuline convent.

The community boarded a ship at Boulogne, on 22 November. The abbess was carried by stretcher on board and placed in her cabin. Many of the nuns found the crossing difficult and were greatly relieved when the ship docked at Folkestone in the early hours of the morning. They spent a night in London before travelling on to Oulton Abbey, Staffordshire, the home of the Benedictine community formerly of Ghent. The community remained at Oulton for six months and then moved to Highfield House, in Golders Green, London, where they remained for a further nine months.

It was still the intention of the nuns to return to Ypres and rebuild their abbey. A national fund was set up, with the support of John Redmond and

22. Dame M. C. Plomer, OSB, *The Irish nuns at Ypres: an episode of the war,* (London 1916), p 159.

Fig 8: Lady
Abbess Laurentia
of Oulton and
Lady Abbess
Scholastica Bergé
of Ypres, with
Mother Prioress
Maura Ostyn.

others, to help the nuns during their stay in England and to finance any future restoration work at Ypres. However, as the war continued in Europe this possibility began to fade. The future for the community was looking bleak. Friends and supporters proposed that they consider coming again to Ireland and Dom Columba Marmion and John Redmond were instrumental in bringing that about in February 1916. The nuns moved to Co Wexford, close to Dom Marmion's community at Edermine, and opened a school at Merton House. The monastery was housed closeby at Macmine Castle. The time in Co Wexford was extremely energetic and rewarding for the nuns. Their school was popular and well attended and, although this was a time of unrest in the country, the community appreciated the warmth and support of their neighbours in the locality. This support enabled the nuns to farm over 100 acres of land and maintained a two acre walled garden, giving them a degree of independence and self-sufficiency. However, their greatest achievement at Macmine was to receive eleven nuns into the community.

Lady Abbess Bergé died at Merton House in November 1916 and Dame Maura Ostyn was elected as her successor. Lady Abbess Maura Ostyn (1916-1940) had been acting superior for four years and had already shown that she was well capable of doing the job. Two more nuns died in the flu epidemic of 1918, and they were buried alongside Abbess Bergé in the new cemetery in the monastery grounds.

Fig 9: Macmine
Castle. Line drawing
© David Rowe

With the signing of the Armistice in November 1918, the nuns were forced to come to a decision: should they return to Ypres or remain on in Ireland. Dom Marmion's Edermine community was under pressure from the bishop of Ferns to return to their monastery, Maredsous, in Belgium, and eventually did so. The prior of Edermine, Dom Aubert Merten, stayed behind as chaplain to the nuns. After some deliberation, the community decided to make Ireland their permanent home. However, for the majority of the nuns, Macmine was con-

Fig 10: Merton House.
Line drawing
© David Rowe

sidered unsuitable for their needs and the abbess began searching the country for a more satisfactory building. She eventually settled on Kylemore Castle in Connemara, situated in the diocese of Tuam. The castle was on sale for £45,000, but the nuns had nowhere near that amount of money at their disposal. To raise funds, Lady Abbess Maura, accompanied by Dame Teresa, travelled to London in 1920, in an effort to secure compensation from the British government for the ruined abbey at Ypres, but failed. The purchase price was eventually raised through bank loans, with friends of the community acting as guarantors.

From London, the abbess and Dame Teresa travelled on to Ypres. They wished to see for themselves the extent of the damage done to the abbey and to collect some possessions saved from the ruin by neighbours and friends. The nuns took photographs of the ruined building, to show the community back in Ireland what remained of the abbey that had been their home for almost two hundred and fifty years.

The community moved to Kylemore Castle in December 1920. They now numbered nineteen, the German nuns being still absent. Their arrival in Connemara was recognised as a great boon to the area and every effort was made, by clergy and people, to help the refugees settle into their new home.

Taking ownership of Kylemore Castle was an onerous task for the nuns. With the castle came thirteen thousand acres of land, over a hundred tenants, a farm with extensive buildings, several

Fig 11:
Abbess Maura Ostyn
(1916-1940)

other estate houses, a six-acre walled garden, a miniature cathedral in the grounds, along with a mausoleum containing the remains of the original owners of the estate and extensive fishing and shooting rights. It was certainly a big jump from the old monastery garden in Ypres. The transition would be difficult but, with Lady Abbess Maura in charge, not impossible.

On 1 March 1921, the Sacred Congregation for Religious granted permission for the rights and privileges of Ypres Abbey to be transferred to Kylemore, making Kylemore Abbey the first Benedictine abbey to be established in Ireland since the Reformation. In thanksgiving for their arrival at Kylemore, Abbess Maura promised to erect a statue of the Sacred Heart as soon as funds became available. This promise was fulfilled in 1932, when a large statue of the Sacred Heart was placed half-way up Duchruach mountain at the rear of the abbey.

One of the first difficulties presented to Lady Abbess by her new abbey was the question of enclosure. In Ypres, the community practised strict papal enclosure. This required a high wall to enclose the monastery, but at Kylemore this would be impossible. On the advice of Dr Gilmartin, Archbishop of Tuam, at Kylemore the nuns would practise monastic enclosure; instead of a wall, they took the mountains surrounding the abbey as their enclosure.

The nuns were anxious to reopen their school, and did so almost immediately, but it was not formally opened until 11 September 1923. There was a
junior school and a secondary school, with thirty pupils ranging in age from
eight to eighteen. A small number of lay teachers was employed from the
start, but the majority of teachers were members of the community, who had
themselves been educated at Ypres. From the beginning, Kylemore was recognised as offering education of a high academic standard, with all the advantages
of a continental education without the necessity for lengthy travel.

On 20 December 1924, the school hosted its first concert and prize-giving
ceremony, with photographs of visiting clerics and of the students published
in the local press. The newspapers carried the names of many of the students
and the majority appear to have been drawn from the neighbouring counties,
though there were some from other parts of the country. However, within a
few years, Kylemore was attracting foreign students and winning a reputation
as an international school. For the young girls of the district the nuns opened
a domestic economy school. This was later replaced by a day school, which,
in the 1930s, was amalgamated with the boarding school.

The upper floor of the farmhouse, Addergoole House, was converted into
living quarters for Dom Aubert Merten. For a time, the possibility of opening a Benedictine monastery for men at the farm was under consideration
and a number of young monks joined Dom Merten at Addergoole, but this
was abandoned with the opening of Glenstal in 1927.

The remains of Abbess Bergé, and the two nuns who had died at
Macmine, were brought to Kylemore in 1921 and laid to rest in the crypt of
the Gothic church. Three of the four German nuns expelled from Ypres
rejoined the community in 1924, the fourth having died in Holland.

In 1929, the Land Commission purchased that section of the estate leased
out by tenants and the nuns continued to farm the remainder. They also
retained the fishing rights which proved a tremendous asset when they decided
to open a guesthouse at the abbey during the summer months. Utilising the
classrooms and the many other houses scattered around the estate, the nuns
could accommodate up to sixty guests. The guesthouse was popular with
fishermen and clergy, and with honeymooners.

Lady Abbess Maura died in November 1940 and she was succeeded by
Lady Abbess Placid Druhan (1941-1953). Numerically, the community was at
its peak in the 1940s and early 1950s, when there were forty-two nuns in the
monastery. On the death of Lady Abbess Placid in 1953, Dame Agnes
Finnegan was elected to replace her. Lady Abbess Agnes (1953-1981) was the
last abbess to be elected for life. A native of Westport, Co Mayo, she was a

former student of the abbey and the first of the Kylemore nuns to be elected
abbess. During Abbess Agnes' term, a section of the abbey was severely damaged by fire on 25 January 1959. The fire destroyed a large section of the rear
and western end of the building and almost all of the remainder suffered
water damage. Major renovation works were necessary and a new wing added
before the building was habitable again.[23] The nuns then decided to close the
guesthouse and concentrated instead on enlarging the school.

It was Abbess Agnes too who presided over the changes brought to community life following the Second Vatican Council. This was a testing time for
monastic life and the community relied heavily on the abbess for direction.
The changes affected many aspects of community life but some were more
obvious than others, such as the modifications to the habit and the concession that allowed trips home to visit family and friends. Under the changes,
the division of choir dame and lay sister, or converse sister, was dispensed
with and from then on the title 'sister' was given to all. The daily prayer was
shortened and changed from Latin to the vernacular. However, Latin Vespers
continue to be sung each Sunday evening at Kylemore and plainchant
remains the dominant music in the nuns' worship. The title 'Lady Abbess'
was simplified to 'Mother Abbess'. Elections for the position of abbess were
to be held every six years, and not on the death of the abbess, as was the practice up until then. Although elected for life, Abbess Agnes took advantage of

---

23. Kathleen Villiers-Tuthill, *History of Kylemore Castle & Abbey,* (Galway, 2002), pp 199-206.

this climate of change and resigned voluntarily in 1981. In the twenty years that followed, the community had three abbesses; Mother Mechtilde Moloney, Mother Mary O'Toole and Mother Clare Morley.

On 8 December 2001, a new abbess, Mother Magdalena FitzGibbon, was blessed by the Archbishop of Tuam, Dr Michael Neary. During the ceremony, Mother Abbess Magdalena received the symbols of office: a ring and a pectoral cross. She was also presented with the Ypres crozier, a silver Abbatial crozier dating from 1721. To mark the occasion, the community chaplain, Dom Paul McDonnell, wore the seventeenth-century Ypres vestments. The crozier and vestments are just some of the treasures saved from Ypres Abbey and lovingly protected by the nuns at Kylemore Abbey.

Today, the Kylemore community stands at nineteen and is still of mixed nationality. In recent years, the community, in common with other religious orders, is experiencing a serious decline in vocations. However, they are still a vibrant and active community, receiving strong support from a wider community of friends. The abbey school is one of the few remaining girls' boarding schools in the country and continues to provide an education for the young girls of the area. The abbey itself is recognised as one of the country's most beautiful buildings and contributes greatly to tourism in the region. It attracts visitors from all nations and of all religious beliefs. The nuns welcome their visitors in the spirit of St Benedict and invite them to participate in the community liturgy and prayer.

CHAPTER SIX

The Post-Reformation English Benedictines and Ireland: Conflict and Dialogue

Aidan Bellenger OSB

Fig 1: Engraving of a Benedictine monk from Mervyn Archdall, *Monasticon Hibernicum* (Dublin, 1786). He is depicted wearing the habit of one of the seventeenth-century reform congregations, similar to that still worn by monks of the English Benedictine Congregation.

The English Benedictine Congregation as revived in the seventeenth century was a missionary as well as a monastic body. Most of its ordained manpower, bound by the missionary oath taken by contemporary secular priests, worked on the English mission. Its monastic houses were, in effect, continental houses of formation, its monks, solitaries. Until the French Revolution and its aftermath closed the monasteries, and the expanding British Empire gave new missionary opportunities, the English monks rarely ventured beyond England and Wales until the early nineteenth century. Irish connections with the English brethren were few and tenuous.[1] More substantial links were forged between the female monasteries of both nations and, as Kathleen Villiers-Tuthill's article demonstrates, the foundation of the Irish Benedictine house at Ypres owed much to the involvement of the English Benedictine nuns of Ghent.

Mansuet Powel, of the St Malo English monastery, who died in 1664, was said to be an Irishman but biographical details are sparse.[2] Hugh Serenus Cressy (1605-74), of St Gregory's, Douai, one of the most distinguished of Stuart converts, served, while still a Protestant, as chaplain to Strafford in Ireland and received prebends in 1636 at both Dublin cathedrals and became Dean of Leighlin in 1637.[3] Edward Hawett, of St Edmund's Paris, a Lancastrian by birth (like so many of the English Benedictines) went in 1688 to Ireland as chaplain to Colonel Parker's regiment and died in Dublin where he was buried in his habit with great pomp.[4] George Anselm Touchet, of St Gregory's, was the second son of the notorious Mervyn, ninth Lord of Audley and second Earl of Castlehaven (County Cork) in the Irish Peerage who was

---

1. For an historical overview of the English Benedictine Congregation see Bernard Green, *The English Benedictine Congregation* (London, 1980) and Daniel Rees (ed) *Monks of England* (London, 1997). For more detailed background see David Lunn, *The English Benedictines 1540-1688* (London, 1980) and Geoffrey Scott, *Gothic rage undone: English monks in the Age of Enlightenment* (Bath, 1992).
2. Athanasius Allanson, *Biography of the English Benedictines*, ed Anselm Cramer, (Ampleforth, 1999), p 75. But see Colmán Ó Clabaigh's article above, p 120.
3. Ibid., p 87.
4. Ibid., p 101.

executed for 'unnatural vice' in 1631. The monk son, eventually heir to the titles, was barred from succession on account of his Catholicism and, despite serving for a time as chaplain to Catherine of Braganza in London, seems to have lived a largely cloistered life. He was dead by 1689.[5] These few personal connections suggest by their rarity the inherent Anglo-centricity of the English Benedictines well summed up by their peppery first chronicler, Benet Weldon (1647-1713):

> In Northumberland died Father Roland Dunn (20 August 1675) a Scotch monk of Würtzburg in Germany, aggregated to the Congregation as have been several others from diverse places as Lorrainers, Flemings, Irish, Scotch, French and Portuguese; yet sparingly, for that such subjects are not the affair of this congregation which might still have retained St Malo's if French had never been taken in.[6]

The bond between Maurus Corker (1636-1715), of the former monastery of Lambspring near Hildesheim (the only English Benedictine house with abbatial status) and Oliver Plunkett, Archbishop of Armagh, is certainly the most significant link between the English Benedictines and Ireland before the French Revolution. Corker was in Newgate prison with Plunkett, and both were under threat of execution following the Popish Plot: Plunkett was executed on 11 July 1681, Corker was released and went on to become President of the English Benedictines, Abbot of Lambspring and a notable maker of converts, the poet Dryden among them. Plunkett, whose last letters to Corker are preserved at Downside, requested the Benedictine to oversee his funeral arrangements: 'My body and clothes etc is at Mr Corker's will and pleasure to be disposed of.' Following his execution, Plunkett's remains were interred at St Giles in the Fields in London. Exhumed in 1683, the body was taken by Corker to Lambspring on his release from prison in 1685. The head was then taken to Rome and give into the care of the English Dominican Cardinal Howard. After some years in the custody of the Dominicans in Rome, it was presented in 1718 to Hugh McMahon, a successor of St Oliver in the see of Armagh, who entrusted it to the care of the Dominican nuns at Drogheda, where in 1881 an ornate Gothic church was built to serve as a shrine for the head of Ireland's only canonised martyr and England's last.[7] The rest of the body was enshrined at Lambspring in the

---

5. Ibid., p 103. See my revised biography of Touchet in the *New Dictionary of National Biography* (Oxford, 2004).

6. Benet Weldon, *Chronological notes* (Worcester, 1881), p 210.

7. M. Murphy, *Saint Oliver Plunkett and Downside* (Downside, 1975), p 11. Plunkett's last letters have been published in John Hanley, *Letters of Saint Oliver Plunkett* (Dublin, 1979), pp

crypt below the choir of the abbey church, a traditional place for saint's tombs, echoing the pilgrim churches of Rome. With the dissolution of the monastery in 1803 the connection between the monks and the archbishop lapsed, but in 1883 the future cardinal, Aidan Gasquet, then prior of Downside, brought the remains to his own monastery, where a purpose built shrine, to the designs of Dom Ephrem Seddon, was dedicated in 1921. Many pilgrimages from Ireland have been arranged, and in 1975, the year of his canonisation, some of the relics of the body were given to Armagh.

Plunkett's long wait for canonisation reflected the complexities of Irish society, as Professor Marianne Elliott has reminded us in her recent book:

> The Ulster clergy (and particularly the Franciscans) resented the appointment of an Old English outsider like Plunkett to the archbishopric of Armagh and they made innumerable complaints to Rome in ensuing years. His absence from surviving Gaelic poetry (when nearly every other archbishop of Armagh was celebrated) is noteworthy. His preference for Protestant gentry and government supporters over his native Irish co-religionists was a particular charge made against him, and he would undoubtedly have attracted the name of 'Castle Catholic' – one who had gone over to the enemy or joined the system – had such a term of abuse then existed.[8]

Plunkett's reforming, Tridentine agenda, moreover, squared uncomfortably with the Irish church of his time and reflected the later work and problems of the English Benedictine bishops who attempted to stamp their authority on the infant Australian church. The eighteenth century Benedictines did not inherit the heroic witness of their seventeenth century forbears, who included three canonised martyrs and six *beati* among their dead. Life in quiet country retreats, gentle scholarship, a Jacobite antiquarianism, characterised a period which witnessed a gradual decline in English Benedictine numbers and influence. The French Revolution changed all that.

> The nineteenth-century Benedictine experience was a subtle blend of the home and colonial with a strong dose of Euro-scepticism. Continental Europe was seen as a potential source of political trouble ... The wider world of the industrial cities and the far-flung Empire was the true milieu of the nineteenth century English Benedictine.[9]

568-583 and include his correspondence with Corker. Plunkett's 'last speech' is also preserved in Downside in a manuscript in Plunkett's hand.

8. Marianne Elliott, *The Catholics of Ulster* (London, 2000), p 144.

9. D. A. Bellenger, 'Revolution and emancipation' in D. Rees, *Monks of England*, p 206.

It was in these contexts that the English Benedictines and the Irish people encountered each other.

The great overseas missionary work of the English Benedictines in the nineteenth century was in Australia, where the two first archbishops of Sydney, John Bede Polding (1794-1877) and Roger Bede Vaughan (1834-1883), both monks of Downside (the St Gregory's, Douai, community had settled in Somerset in 1814), built up a strong institutional church, but failed to establish what Polding had always dreamed of – a Benedictine diocese or province with a monastery as its quiet but vital centre. The English Benedictines were favoured by both Rome and London as being more supportive of the Establishment than their Irish co-religionists and in the short term, co-operation between the monks and the colonial government benefited the Australian Catholic community. The Church Act of 1836, introduced by Richard Bourke, an Irish Protestant who served, full of reforming ideas, as Governor of New South Wales, boosted Catholic status. He was an opponent of an Established Church but a believer in the civilising mission of Christianity which would be recognised in the giving of state aid to all recognised denominations: 'The people of these different persuasions will be united together in one bond of peace, and taught to look up to the government as their common protector and friend, and that thus they will be secured to the state good subjects and to Society good men'.[10]

Looking up to government sounded like Ascendancy language and a 'bond of peace' was sorely lacking in the Catholic community itself. English Benedictine management sat uncomfortably on a predominantly Irish priesthood and faithful. In 1839, for example, there were thirty-two Catholic priests in the colony, of whom six were English and twenty-six Irish. The Irish constituency in Australia's population was highly significant, 'little short of 25% of the immigrants from 1788 down to the early twentieth century'.[11] Australian Catholicism, fed by a constant flow of priests, sisters and brothers from Ireland, had an intensifying and enduring 'Hibernicity' which found its first great icon in the Irish-born Australian cardinal, Patrick Francis Moran (1830-1911), third Archbishop of Sydney, nephew of Cardinal Cullen of Dublin; and its triumphant symbol in St Mary's Cathedral, Sydney, in appearance a great monastic cathedral transplanted from rural England, in reality a shrine to Irish Australia:[12] 'Unfortunately, the Irish and English

10. Quoted by J. Gascoigne, *The Enlightenment and the origins of European Australia* (Cambridge, 2002), p 29.
11. O. MacDonagh, 'The Irish in Australia: a general view,' in O. MacDonagh and W. F. Mantle (eds), *Ireland and Irish Australia* (London and Sydney, 1986), p 159.
12 See Patrick O'Farrell, *St Mary's Cathedral Sydney 1821-1971* (Sydney, 1971).

characters are very different in their nature and when any difference takes place between an English Bishop and an Irish Priest, their national antipathies and cultural distaste spring up and prevent proper understanding.'[13] Indeed, 'at the core of Irishmen lay the conviction that God was on the side of the Irish'.[14]

Australian Catholic history is gradually moving towards a 'revisionist' stage, which might make it easier to see the stand-off between English monks and Irish priests in a less nationalistic perspective. Patrick O'Farrell's concise and pithy history of the Australian Catholic Church comments quite bluntly: 'To the Irish, the Benedictines were pretentious snobs who did not understand the real work of the mission.'[15] Whether this is fair comment given the heroic missionary energy of Polding, one of the great monastic and imperial figures of the nineteenth century, I leave to others to say. Dom Norbert Birt, in his two-volume *Benedictine Pioneers in Australia* (1911) had tried to redress a balance and answer Cardinal Moran's *History of the Church in Australia* (1896) which distorts and devalues Polding's contribution: 'This seemed to be the more necessary as His Eminence's enormous volume has no index of any kind, this making it a matter of extreme difficulty to gather together widely separated references which, in reality, will be found to be closely connected or co-related.'[16]

Polding remained convinced of the Benedictine destiny of Australia. Some of his fellow monks came early to the conclusion that Australia should be left to the Irish. William Bernard Ullathorne, Vicar General in Australia as a young man, saw the balance between the races in Australia as quite clear: 'Ireland, as of old, supplied her saints, and England gave her money.'[17] Thomas Joseph Brown, Vicar Apostolic and later Bishop of Newport in Wales, writing to the Prior of Downside in June 1842, put the problem succinctly:

> The clergy and people in Australia are almost all Irish, having a strong national feeling. Dr Ullathorne, and I think Dr Polding, told me that the Australian Irish clergy, and their countrymen, including the Bishops in Ireland, were sore at being under an English Bishop and a regular ... what will it be when new bishops, foreigners as they may be termed, shall be

---

13. Ibid., *The Catholic Church in Australia* (London, 1969), p 71, quoting a letter of 1851 from the Irish Australian priest, John McEnroe, to Pope Pius IX.
14. Ibid., p 48.
15. Ibid., p 22.
16. H. N. Birt, *Benedictine pioneers in Australia* (2 vols, London, 1911), i, p ix.
17. O'Farrell, *Catholic Church*, p 44.

appointed, and the resident clergy and even their nation of which the Irish are most jealous shall be overlooked, let Dr Polding recommend Irishmen for Bishops, and more good will be done.'[18]

The Australian Catholic Church was only one place in which the English Benedictines encountered the Irish diaspora. Another, and increasingly important one, was on the English mission. In 1838 there were some thirty Benedictine missions in England and Wales, served by some fifty-five priests. By 1900 the number of missions with resident missioners had increased to sixty-two and the number of priests to one hundred and eight. Moreover, alongside the rural chaplaincies and the genteel towns like Bath and Cheltenham, traditional Benedictine places, there were many urban missions, especially in the areas of the new industrial economy with their immigrant populations.

The second half of the nineteenth century witnessed a great growth in the number of Irish immigrants in Lancashire, the most Catholic and most Benedictine of English counties. The number of Catholics counted at Mass in Lancashire on Sunday 31 March 1851 was 102,812, 42.5% of the total number of 241,482 Catholics in England. This reflected the doubling in size of the Irish immigrant population of Lancashire to over 191,000 in the decade 1841-51, one tenth of the county's population. In 1851, Irish immigrants made up 17% of the population of Manchester and in 1881, 13% of the population of Liverpool.[19]

The first post-Reformation Catholic mission in Liverpool was established by the Jesuits and taken over by the Benedictines in 1783. Unlike Preston and Wigan, Lancashire's other two great centres of Catholic population, Liverpool's Catholic history was largely a development of the eighteenth and nineteenth century. The Benedictine missions increased in number in Liverpool parallel to secular chapels and those of other religious orders. St Mary's, the Benedictine mother church, was splendidly rebuilt to Pugin's design and in 1844, a call was made for 'the persecuted Saxons of Lancashire and the persecuted Celts' to get on with each other and build a united church community.[20]

Shared suffering may have contributed to that ideal and in 1847, three of the ten martyrs of charity, priests who died ministering to the typhoid vic-

18. Ibid., p 57.
19. J. A. Hilton, *Catholic Lancashire* (Chichester, 1994), pp 92-3.
20. T. Burke, *Catholic history of Liverpool* (Liverpool, 1910), p 75.

tims, were Benedictines; some 15,000 died in that year alone.[21] A church dedicated to St Augustine, in Great Howard Street in the midst of Liverpool's dockland, was opened in 1849, a memorial to the 'martyrs'. Several more of its clergy were to die in the pursuit of their ministry, the last, Maurus Potter, in 1882. The account of his last days makes impressive reading:

> A friend accidentally met him at half-past seven the next morning, has-tening along Great Howard Street on his way to the fever dens of Carlton Street. Here and in the adjoining streets he laboured incessantly day after day administering spiritual, and no less temporal, consolation to the sick and dying. Then the necessity came, of carrying in his own arms the fever-stricken victims and some children out of Dublin Court ... no ade-quate help was near or available, and having braved the dangers of so many fever-stricken homes, and feeling secure in the strength of a good constitution, he fearlessly carried in his arms each of those who were otherwise without a friend to help them to the fever van ... On the Monday following he was again in full activity in the courts and alleys of his district, and for a whole week worked amongst the sick, of whom there were some days twenty cases, but on the Saturday after, in the after-noon, fagged and weary, he called at the house of one of his communi-cants and begged a drink of water for what he called 'an unusual thirst'. The friend saw at a glance he was changed and ill, and knew by the appearances what she dare not tell him, but in gentle words advised him to return home and get medical aid. 'I think it is only fatigue and hope it will pass off', he replied, 'for I must not be ill now when the poor need so much help.' On the following day he still struggled hard to overcome his sense of sickness, and preached twice. The evening discourse, which was his last, being a touching one from the text, 'Thou shalt love thy neighbour as thyself.' On the Monday he strove hard to be at his work again, but the fever had secured its hold on him, and all that kindness and medical aid could do were unavailing.[22]

Such work among the largely Irish immigrant community of Liverpool was heroically atypical, but the solid contribution of the English monks to the Irish diaspora can be found in many parts of the country. The career of Dom Bernard Harrington, most closely associated with the Irish 'area' of Swansea, appropriately called Greenhill, might serve as an example both of an Irish-born monk and of a priest of the diaspora. Timothy Harrington was born in

---

21. A. Hood, 'Fever in Liverpool' in *English Benedictine History Symposium II* (1992), pp 2-21.
22. ibid., pp 17-18.

1862 at Castletownbere, County Cork, and educated at St Michael's College, Listowel and St Edmund's, Douai. He entered Downside in 1884 and was ordained priest in 1893 in Rome where he had taken a doctorate in divinity the same year. He spent the years 1894-1902 at Belmont in Herefordshire, the Benedictine congregational house of studies, as a professor. In 1903 he was sent to St Joseph's, Greenhill, Swansea, as an assistant priest and he was to remain there, with the exception of two years at Beccles, Suffolk, (1911-13) until his death in 1932.[23]

His energetic pastoral zeal was reflected in his fund-raising tour of the USA during his curacy and his ability to build and to develop his parish. Returning to Swansea in 1914 as rector, he opened a boys' school in 1915, to be followed in 1928 by a new girls and infants' school. When complete, St Joseph's had 'the distinction of being the largest recognised school in Great Britain'. He set up a domestic science centre, enlarged the presbytery (the church, now the cathedral of the Menevia diocese had been opened in 1888), built a new mission church in the parish and also started new centres in the outlying districts of Pontardulais and Gorseinon. He was on the Swansea Board of Guardians, of which he served as Chairman. In conversations with Dom Roger Huddleston, who was to be his obituarist, he reflected, not long before his death: 'I thank God for all that material work, the schools and the rest; but most of all I thank him that he made it possible for some of our boys from St Joseph's to become priests.'[24]

Harrington was one of an increasing number of Irishmen who joined the English Benedictine Congregation in the second half of the nineteenth century. An earlier generation had produced a few Irishmen, including the formidable Placid Sinnott (1803-96), who had spent fifty-five years on the mission and who although 'so long in England' had remained a keen advocate of Home Rule.[25] Sinnott, a Wexford man, had met a fellow Wexford man, William Clery, a student from the school of Downside, who encouraged him to become a monk. He travelled by sea to Bristol from Wexford and walked the twenty miles or so from Bristol to Downside to join the monastery.[26]

The monastic schools conducted by Ampleforth, Douai and Downside in the nineteenth century were small, homely establishments lacking the professionalism of their modern counterparts. They provided, however, not only a source of vocations to the monastery, but a good, classical education for the

23. Obituary of Dom Bernard Harrington, *The Downside Review,* 50 (1932), pp 28*-33*.
24. Ibid., p 33*.
25. *The Downside Review,* 15 (1896), p 109.
26. Ibid., p 108.

rising Catholic middle classes. The school at Ampleforth, the largest of the three for most of its history, seems to have been the least Irish. Looking, for example, at the school lists for 1855-1860, with well over a hundred names, only eleven boys came from Ireland;[27] most were Lancastrians. At Douai, in France until 1903, the Irish were a far more significant constituency, and St Patrick's Day was marked not only by 'the usual patriotic style of bunches of shamrock and much greenery', but also by an English versus Irish football match; inter-racial or inter-tribal rivalry was never far away.[28]

At Downside, convenient to the port of Bristol, there seems to have been a consistently large Irish contingent, a group which becomes more difficult to assess when Irish surnames become such a common feature of all English Catholic communities. They represented a professional Irish class, with strong links with the armed forces (the association of the English Benedictine schools with the Irish Guards is a continuing sign of this connection) and to the local magistracy, many of them adherents to English rule. Among the distinguished alumni noted in the centenary number of *The Downside Review* (1914) were three Irish Privy Counsellors, Richard More O'Ferrall, Rowland Blennerhasset and Charles Owen O'Conor Don, who all played an active part in Irish public life. The last mentioned, it was noted, had carried the standard of Ireland at the coronation of King Edward VII in 1902.[29] *The Downside Review*, with a judicious balance, also notes Richard O'Gorman, who came to the school in 1836 and joined Smith O'Brien in his rebellion of 1848, 'held up' the Wicklow and Wexford mail coach, opened the mail bag and destroyed the warrants issued for the arrest of a number of his fellow-conspirators. A warrant was therefore issued for his own arrest on the charge of treason, but he escaped and made his way to America where he pursued a successful career in the Law.[30] A sample of Downside pupils in 1875, an elite group of thirteen who formed the first 'committee' of the school's Abingdon Debating Society, indicates how Irish the English Benedictine schools had become. Eight of the thirteen were Irish, two from South Africa, one born in India, and only two English-born. Of the Irish, three became monks: William Ildephonsus Campbell, of Dublin; John Joseph Colgan, of Cappagh; and Edward Cuthbert Butler, of Dublin, later second abbot of

---

27. *The Ampleforth Journal* 2 (1897) 'Ampleforth lists, 1855-60,' pp 129-33. 'Of the 1,634 boys known to have attended Ampleforth between 1802 and 1895, 81 (nearly 5%) came from Ireland and a further 123 from overseas.' (David Goodall, 'Ampleforth Alumni,' in Anthony Marett-Crosby, *A school of the Lord's service* (Ampleforth, 2002), p 127.
28. *The Douai Magazine*, 2 (1894), p 108.
29. *The Downside Review*, 33 (1914), pp 212-220.
30. Ibid., p 214.

Downside and one of the most distinguished of modern Benedictine scholars and writers.[31]

With such a strong Irish contingent it was not surprising that, in 1905, the Downside Benedictines began to consider an Irish foundation. Their caution in this enterprise probably reflected the failure of the Ramsgate Abbey settlement at Leopardstown on the outskirts of Dublin, discussed by William Fennelly below.[32] The Downside house, in theory, owed its inspiration to Dom Edmund

Fig 2: Dom John Francis Sweetman

Ford, the first Abbot of Downside, who hoped to open an Irish school which 'might gradually develop and enable us to establish a priory'. The school would be 'intended for the class of boys who are now sent to England'.[33] The Bishop of Ferns, in whose diocese the chosen property was to be found (Mount Nebo, near Gorey), had no objection 'if you will not interfere with our diocesan school or with parochial work and rights.'[34] The prelatical correspondence led in 1907 to the opening of Mount St Benedict, as the new foundation was christened.

It may have been Abbot Ford's blessing which made it possible, but it was Francis Sweetman who inspired the Mount's character and made it the singular place it was. John Sweetman (Francis in religion) was born at Clohammon, County Wexford, on 22 May 1872, the third son of Walter and Mary (née Butler) Sweetman, prosperous landowners with strong local roots. A kinsman, Nicholas Sweetman (1700-1806), was Bishop of Ferns from 1745 to 86.[35] John Sweetman was a pupil at Downside for two years (following his

---

31. D. A. Bellenger, 'Two Abingdon Photographs 1875 and 2001' in *The Raven,* 282 (2001), pp 54-6.
32. D. Parry, *Monastic Century: St Augustine's Abbey Ramsgate* (1861-1891), (Tenbury Wells, 1965), p 76.
33. Downside Abbey Archives, Abbot's Archives, Gorey Files. Printed Evidence, 1925. Copy of letter from Abbot Ford to Bishop Browne, 7 April 1905
34. Ibid., copy of letter to Bishop J. Browne from Abbot Ford, 10 April, 1905.
35. Biographical details from D. A. Bellenger, 'An Irish Benedictine Adventure: Dom Francis Sweetman (1872-1953) and Mount St Benedict, Gorey' in *Studies in Church History* 25 (1989), pp 401-415 and from *The Benedictine Almanac and Guide* (1954), pp 13-14.

Fig 3: Mount St
Benedict, Gorey

three brothers) and entered the novitiate on leaving school in 1891. In the
school he had played for the first XI at cricket, a game for which he never lost
his enthusiasm, and acted in several plays – his performance as Sir Lucius
O'Trigger in Sheridan's *The Rivals* was said to be particularly memorable. He
studied at S. Anselmo in Rome from 1897-9 and was ordained priest in 1899,
the year Downside became an abbey. In 1900 he went to South Africa as a
chaplain to the forces and was wounded in the foot. He taught at Downside
for a period, but his dream was always to make an Irish foundation:

> Mount St Benedict, Gorey, is a Benedictine school, founded by Downside
> Abbey, Somerset, England, some twenty years ago. The project originated
> amongst certain Irish monks in the Downside community who were
> anxious to work in Ireland, and was warmly welcomed by leading Irish
> Catholic laymen, many of whom had been educated in Benedictine
> schools abroad, and wished for the same opportunity for their sons in
> Ireland. Such schools play a conspicuous part in Catholic education at the
> present time in Italy, Austria, France, England, Belgium, America and
> other countries, and if any other proof were needed it could be found in
> the history of the Order during the past 1400 years. Numerous Popes and
> not less than 200 Cardinals have been chosen from its ranks, 37,000
> monasteries have been established, and the memorials of its activities are
> scattered over the face of Europe. The work of reconstruction and evang-
> elising Europe after the collapse of the Roman Empire was, in conjunc-
> tion with our own Irish monks, largely the work of the Benedictines. To

this day, Boniface, Willibrord, and to some extent Augustine, are revered as the apostles of Germany, Sweden and England, respectively.

The monasteries which the monks established became centres of progress and work, especially in the education of the young, and agriculture. The monk, following St Benedict's precept to live by his own labour, became an example of industry. No work is foreign to Benedictine life, but from the very character and spirit of this Rule, which aims at common family life with the permanent attachment of the monk to his monastery, the first call on his labour was the development of the neighbourhood in which his monastery was built. The Benedictines carry the idea of home life into their schools, and it is a special feature of Benedictine education that boys are given a wide measure of freedom in order that, by being trained in habits of personal responsibility, they may be fitted to exercise the greater freedom of the university and after life.

It was with such objects in mind that the monks of Downside Abbey, recognising the debt of Catholic England towards Ireland in the past, obtained permission from Dr Browne, the then Bishop of Ferns, to establish a school and ultimately a monastery, in his diocese, and sent three of their number with Dom Sweetman, a native of Wexford, as Superior, and Dom Cuthbert Butler, a native of Dublin, as his assistant, to carry out the foundation. The money necessary for the purchase of suitable premises was lent by Mr John Sweetman of Dublin and at no subsequent date has financial assistance been sought from Downside.[36]

Mount St Benedict was never a properly monastic community. It only had two or three resident monks at any time and its school had fifty as its typical roll. Its educational methods were somewhat haphazard, somewhere between eccentricity and inspiration, and reflected Sweetman himself:

A big man in every sense of the word; 'the Reverend man', as he was known to the boys, or 'His Reverence' as he was known to the local people, who loved him dearly, had nothing mean or petty about him. There were no school bounds at the Mount, and the boys were trusted and taught to respond, not to a strict school discipline, but to the ideal which was expected of them by Dom Francis.[37]

It had a number of famous alumni, Seán MacBride and many of the Dillon family among them.[38] Others entered the novitiate at Downside, including

36. Downside Abbey Archives, Printed Evidence, 1925.
37. *The Benedictine Almanac and Guide* (1954), p 13.
38. Including Fr Matthew Dillon, later headmaster of Glenstal.

Dom Wulstan Philipson, who chose the Abbey over the Abbey Theatre, remaining a noisy republican in his seventies and frequently disrupting the singing of the *Salvum Fac* at the end of the school Mass; and Dom Brendan Lavery, a lovable and eccentric man, who, in 1977, was sent to Mount St Benedict to oversee the sale of the property. Dom Patrick Nolan, a controversial Irish monk of Maredsous, was also resident at the Mount in the late 1920s. His presence there, as Mark Tierney demonstrates below, was the cause of considerable unease for Msgr James Ryan, the principal benefactor of the new Maredsous foundation at Glenstal.

It was Francis Sweetman's political entanglements that gave the Mount its notoriety and led to its many years of half-life. The years of revolution and civil war which formed the background to the Mount's history were hardly propitious ones for an English transmarine foundation. Involvement with Irish politics, much encouraged by Miss Aileen Keogh, Sweetman's formidable matron, led to Sweetman's later reputation as a republican hero. In 1925, when the school was closed, it was as much about diocesan politics (the new Bishop, Dr William Codd, did not want a dangerous 'exempt' religious on his patch) and monastic obedience (Sweetman was too prone to 'do his own thing') as it was about national politics. The very English John Augustine James, the founder of St Gerard's Bray, and later, as a widower, a monk at Downside,[39] describes his seven years (1911-18) at the Mount, providing an interesting perspective on the place:

> As a school it never grew into anything more than that – the place failed. With individual boys it certainly succeeded. Many of them made their names in subsequent years: and many more cherished, and still cherish, their memories of Mount Saint Benedict. But its numbers barely reached the score of fifty. Promising boys were removed, sometimes after residence of a term or two: the second Downside, which was to outshine all other Irish educational establishments, never came into being. There were two main reasons for this. One, I am bound to say, was inefficiency: not inefficiency in work, but in the ordinary domestic details of life. Parents expect a reasonable standard of cleanliness and comfort for their children. They forget that their boys are happy and well taught when they perceive them to be cold and dirty. One mother, in whose house I was often welcomed, confided to me that when the boy came home for the holidays, she invariably had to burn every scrap of his outfit and completely refit him. The boy was, in fact, removed for a time to the Oratory, but became

---

39. This was a return to the cloister. He had previously been a novice and junior at Downside from 1908-11.

so wretched at the loss of his beloved and earlier school that his parents relented and allowed him to come back to us.

The second reason which retarded the development of the Mount was the intrusion of politics into school life. This is not the place to discuss Irish politics. When I was sent to Ireland I was warned – as far as I can remember by my pupils – that no Englishman can possibly understand the Irish. That may be true, but it is equally true that many of them think they do, and consequently do not require enlightenment from me. But during the war years, and throughout the 'troubled times' which followed them, Irish boys are not good politicians; and the tendency for both boys and staff to get embroiled in political matters was far from healthy. It is the duty of school authorities to keep boys out of politics: at the Mount the tendency was in the opposite direction. Fathers and mothers do not, as a whole, favour influences which tend to arouse political rivalries among their children. Nor were those whose convictions leant towards union with England much delighted by the Sinn Féin or separatist attitude adopted by the ruling forces at the Mount. What parents needed was a school, reasonably well run and free from those disturbances which were affecting the more turbulent members of the nation. As time went on – I experienced seven and a half years of the Mount – it became obvious that our school was going to fulfill neither of these requirements. I conducted my classes during the winter in a heavy great coat, new shoes and mittens. The story that the bath water was heated but once during the term and that the entire school was required to wash all over in one bath full was probably an exaggeration: but it was a story whose telling should not have been justified by any suspicion of inefficiency. The political situation, too, became more and more tense; sermons were preached and demonstrations were staged.'[40]

Sweetman had supported the Home Rule Party early in World War I, but after Easter 1916, his politics changed. He attended the funeral Mass of Thomas Ashe in 1917 and the Mount soon became the chosen school of the children of many involved in the 1916 Rising including the sons of executed rebels John McBride and Tom Clarke, and the son of Countess Markievicz.[41]

40. J. A. James, *The light and warmth within: an informal biography*, c 1951. Typescript in Downside Abbey Library, Ch 20, 'Mount St Benedict,' not paginated.

41. Brian P. Murphy, *St Gerard's School Bray* (Bray, 1999), pp 19-20. For the place of clergy in radical politics in Ireland see G. Moran (ed), *Radical Irish Priests 1660-1970* (Dublin, 1998). Sweetman is given a passing mention by B. S. Murphy in his chapter, 'The Stone of destiny: Father John Fahey (1894-1969), Lia Fáil and Smallholder Radicalism in modern Irish society', at p 217. Murphy discusses the context of rural radicalism.

Despite determined efforts the school closed, but the Mount continued. Father Sweetman remained in residence until his death in 1953. From 1925-39, he was technically a fugitive monk, under the ecclesiastical ban of diocese and abbey, but in 1939 Abbot Sigebert Trafford, Abbot of Downside and Abbot President of the English Benedictine Congregation, reconciled him. The Mount was his true home and monastery. He was the father figure, a resident landowner, providing work to many in the vicinity and encouraging local co-operative ventures, including a tobacco plantation. Family money had endowed the Mount and Sweetman continued to feel responsibility for its continuance. It was less a monastery that a hermitage and an austere one at that; an empty school does not provide the height of domesticity and certainly no luxury. Sweetman's declining years were aided by the presence of another monk. Sigebert Trafford (1886-1976) who, having failed to be re-elected as abbot of Downside, went in 1950 to reside at the Mount and looked after Sweetman in his declining years. Trafford, English squire by nature and appearance, and a forceful, even overwhelming, personality spent twenty years at the Mount 'entertaining all comers with his wonderful hospitality, running the farm (profitably too), carrying on a vast correspondence and doing a great deal of hard physical work as his health permitted.'[42] Trafford worked on the farm, his gaunt profile indistinguishable from any other farmer, except for the golden pectoral cross – which was as much a part of his working dress as his boots – and, when necessary, his gun. The titular abbot of St Albans, as he became, may have seemed like some monastic colonist, but his instincts and inclinations were those of a countryman at ease with his adopted soil. The two hermit monks at Mount St Benedict, Gorey, were the nearest that the English Benedictine Congregation got to establishing an Irish house. Its failure was a complex affair and, to some extent, was compensated for by the success of St Gerard's, Bray. Here, a Benedictine spirit pervaded and for a while, another Downside monk, Dom Alphege Shebbeare, acted as chaplain.

As Colmán Ó Clabaigh has shown, Ireland in the Middle Ages may have seemed an appropriate place to send difficult monks from England and, in a modern sense, both Sweetman and Trafford fell into this category. Yet their exile could have borne fruit. Gorey might have prospered in different times and circumstances. The social makeup of Ireland in the first half of the twentieth century seems to have favoured the agricultural bias of the reformed Cistercians and it is perhaps significant that if Gorey flourished at all it was

42. *The Raven* (1977), Obituary of Abbot Trafford, p 4.

as a farming enterprise. Even so, Cardinal Newman appears to have thought Ireland ripe for a Benedictine future – it was in Dublin that he wrote his much quoted treatise on the Benedictines.[43]

Celtic spirituality and the English Benedictine tradition both encouraged solitude. Dom Augustine Baker, the celebrated mystic and author of *Hagia Sophia*, in his lifelong search for isolation, considered settling in Ireland[44] but was dissuaded: seventeenth-century Ireland was hardly a safe haven. A later English Benedictine spiritual master, John Chapman, Abbot of Downside, was not only a correspondent of Columba Marmion, but a confrère of his at Maredsous. A number of English monks of that monastery and of Erdington, its English satellite in Birmingham, transferred to the English Congregation during World War One. Marmion himself preached retreats to many Benedictine communities in England during the First World War. His monks also received hospitality at Downside *en route* to their refuge at Edermine in Ireland.

The revival of the Benedictine life in Ireland has been principally a twentieth and twenty-first century phenomenon and in that movement, the English Benedictines played a not inconsiderable part. Large numbers of Irish pupils continued to attend English Benedictine schools until the twentieth century's last quarter and Glenstal's alumni include many whose fathers attended Downside and Ampleforth. Sweetman's Gorey adventure showed the possibility of a Benedictine school in Ireland. Overall, however, perhaps the chief importance of the English Benedictines for Ireland was to keep alive for a few Irish monks and nuns, and a much wider circle of Irish laypeople in the diaspora, a faint Benedictine presence, the awareness of an ideal which would not quite go away.

43. J. H. Newman, 'The mission of St Benedict' in idem, *Historical sketches* (3 vols, London, 1873), iii, pp 365-430.
44. J. McCann and H. Connolly, *English Benedictines* in *Catholic Record Society* (London, 1933), p 115. 'And one of his friends offered him commendations to go over into Ireland, and be entertained there, at Waterford, in the home of an English Catholic gentlewoman … [he was] dissuaded … and invited … to pass into the Low Countrys'.

CHAPTER SEVEN

Abbot Columba Marmion

Placid Murray OSB

Ireland has contributed a great deal to modern Benedictine history – and indeed to the church at large – in the person and spiritual teaching of Blessed Columba Marmion (1858-1923), who was beatified by Pope John Paul II on 3 September 2000. During the beatification ceremony the Pope singled out Marmion's writings as 'an authentic treasure of spiritual teaching for the church of our time' and he prayed for 'a rediscovery' of Marmion's spiritual teaching.[1] Any such attempt at rediscovery cannot hope to recapture the 'age of innocence' that first welcomed his books so enthusiastically.[2] Marmion currently is not so much out of date as out of fashion.[3] The prevailing spiritual fashion nowadays is the urge on all sides to achieve self-realisation, to build up self-esteem. All is centred on the self, on the 'me'. Marmion, by contrast, invites the contemporary Christian to a liberation from the self by rediscovering the 'unsearchable riches of Christ'.[4] Marmion's was a *prayed* spirituality, chanted with his monastic brethren in the daily liturgical round of the Divine Office and Mass. It was there that he discovered the message that he preached in so many retreats and which found a permanent expression in his books. It was a 'seeking for Christ in his mysteries' rather than a 'quest for the historical Jesus', a *faith* trying to understand, rather than an *intellect* looking for faith. If in fact this has turned out to be Marmion's 'mission' in the church, how then did he understand his original and personal 'vocation' to become an Irish Benedictine?

His origins and background: Dublin and Rome
Marmion was born on 1 April 1858, the seventh child of William Marmion and his French wife, Herminie. Baptised Joseph on 6 April in St Paul's Church, Arran Quay, his early life was passed entirely inside a few square miles of his native Dublin. The Marmion household was devoutly Catholic

---

1. *L'Osservatore Romano,* weekly edn., 6 Sept, 2000, p 8.
2. Placid Murray, 'A blessed Dubliner' in *Studies,* lxxxix (2000), pp 380-8.
3. Marmion is not included in the survey by William P. Loewe 'From the humanity of Christ to the historical Jesus' in *Theological Studies,* 61 (2000), pp 314-31.
4. *Ephesians* 3:8.

and three of Marmion's sisters later entered the Congregation of the Sisters of Mercy. In 1868 he attended the primary school run by the Augustinian Friars in St John's Lane, Dublin, before proceeding, in January 1869, to the Jesuit-run Belvedere College, where he received an excellent grounding in Greek and Latin. In 1874, at the age of fifteen years and nine months, he entered Holy Cross College, Clonliffe, the Dublin diocesan seminary, and commenced his studies for the diocesan priesthood. In 1877, having completed his studies in philosophy, he was conferred with the

Fig 1: Blessed Columba Marmion (1858-1923)

Bachelor of Arts degree by the Catholic University, Dublin. In 1879 he proceeded to Rome to complete his theological training living in the Pontifical Irish College and studying at the College of Propaganda Fide for eighteen months. Here he was recognised as a brilliant student, being awarded the gold medal for academic excellence in 1881. Although invited by the college authorities to present himself for the doctorate programme, he turned the offer down for health reasons, on account of the extra year in Rome that this would have entailed. He received minor orders in February 1881, was ordained subdeacon on 12 March, deacon on 15 April and, at the early age of twenty three years and two months, was ordained priest on 16 June. He returned to Ireland in July 1881, with his theological course completed and with a reputation for brilliance, but without any experience of studying at a secular university, and with little direct knowledge of adult lay life outside his own family. In September 1881 he was appointed curate in Dundrum parish in Dublin, where he remained for a year until his appointment as Professor of Metaphysics and French in Holy Cross College, Clonliffe in September 1882. He was also appointed chaplain to the enclosed nuns of the Redemptoristine convent at Drumcondra, a position he retained until 1886.

He served for a short period in 1886 as chaplain to the women's prison in Mountjoy in Dublin.

The Monte Cassino experience: anima naturaliter benedictina

It was while he was a student at Rome that Marmion felt for the first time the call from God to the Benedictine life. Appropriately enough, it happened at Monte Cassino, although the occasion itself was simply a return journey from Naples to Rome from a summer outing with some fellow students from the Irish College in 1880, when Marmion was aged twenty-two.[5] This experience shows that Marmion's vocation, even in his seminary days, was never that of a clear cut call to the diocesan priesthood, so much so that he could later write about Msgr Kirby, who ordained him: '... I fear he looks on me as a kind of apostate for having left the secular mission. However I heard the words *Magister adest et vocat te* and I obeyed.'[6] It was in front of a painting in the Monte Cassino abbey refectory, depicting St Benedict at prayer in the Sacro Speco (of Subiaco), that the divine call appeared to him to be beyond doubt. However, the realisation of the call came in a roundabout way, and only six years later, through his friendship with François Moreau, a Belgian student in Propaganda, who was fired with enthusiasm for the combination of Benedictine and missionary ideals promoted by Dom Salvado, founder of the monastery of New Norcia in Western Australia. Shortly before his ordination to the priesthood, Marmion wrote a long letter from Rome to Dom Salvado, in which he traced the history of his vocation. He began by saying that he wished to make known to Dom Salvado 'what I believe is my vocation to your mission of Western Australia'. Although in the event he did not join the Australian venture, nevertheless one passage in the letter is worth quoting in full, since it shows clearly that he was already considering becoming a Benedictine before his ordination, albeit with some misgiving:

> Even though I had always felt a great desire for the religious state, I used to feel however at the same time a certain unease or scruple as regards becoming a Benedictine, seeing that God had given me an immense desire to work for the salvation of souls; and I used always feel deeply moved when I used to hear or read something about those thousands of human beings for whom Jesus had shed his blood, and who die without knowing him. And so, when I read the details concerning your mission,

---

5. Dom Raymond Thibaut, *Un Maître de la vie spirituelle: Dom Columba Marmion, Abbé de Maredsous (1858-1923),* (Maredsous, 1953) p 27.
6. Idem, *Abbot Columba Marmion: a master of the spiritual life* (London, 1932), p 40. The Latin sentence is from John 11:28 'The Master is here and is calling you.'

I realised that it was exactly that to which I was called, because I should satisfy my desire to be a religious, and at the same time work for *the most forsaken* souls, and in obedience.[7]

The first Maredsous period

On 25 October 1886 Marmion received permission to join the Benedictine Order from Dr William Walsh, the newly appointed Archbishop of Dublin. On 21 November 1886 he entered the newly founded Belgian abbey of Maredsous, with which, by virtue of his Benedictine vow of stability, he was to be associated for the rest of his life. The first thirteen years of his monastic life (1886-99) were spent at Maredsous itself, beginning with a particularly exacting novitiate under Dom Benoît D'Hondt. After a rather unsuccessful start in the abbey school as surveillant (a kind of housemaster to the junior boys), he found his feet within the community through more congenial work, notably the teaching of Thomistic philosophy to the junior monks. He also gradually built up a reputation in the surrounding district as a spiritual guide, through the exercise of ministry on a small scale. Throughout his protracted exile in Belgium he remained unmistakably, although not defensively, Irish in person and character, even after French had become the language of his daily life. Furthermore, though he became a member of the German Beuronese Congregation (by virtue of his vow of stability for Maredsous), nevertheless the local people around the abbey quickly christened him 'the Irish Father'. Such was Marmion's lot – to be a solitary Irish Benedictine on the continent before his time.

The Louvain period

At some stage between 1896 and 1899 Marmion had already worked out his distinctive understanding of the doctrine of divine adoption, which was later on to be the kernel of his published works. Dom Idesbald Ryelandt[8] once described to the present writer how it had been a soul-searing experience for him to have lived for years alongside Marmion, a man whose whole life was dominated by the intuition of that one line from St John, *The Word was made Flesh*. Marmion did not preach from a written script; Dom Idesbald described his style as a freely ranging *concatenatio*, pouring out from an interior abundance. Marmion disclaimed all originality in what he had to say. The

7. Full (French) text in Thibaut, *Maître*, pp 29-30. This is Marmion's earliest extant letter.
8. Dom Idesbald Ryelandt (1878-1971), monk and prior of Maredsous, prior of Glenstal (1938-45) and noted spiritual writer.

Dominican writer, Père M. M. Philipon, has preserved a remark made by Marmion during a retreat he preached in 1916, 'The doctrine is not mine, *non est mea doctrina*. I have drawn it from the Gospels, the Epistles, from tradition and the Holy Rule.'[9] In a letter of May 1917 he wrote, 'It was in the liturgy that I learned to know Saint Paul and the Gospels.'[10] In 1899 he was sent as one of the founding monks from Maredsous to the monastery of Mont-César in Louvain. He remained in Louvain for ten years, during which time he fulfilled the duties of prior, prefect of clerics and professor of dogmatic theology. This decade in Louvain provided a wide outlet for his matured spiritual doctrine, through his lectures on dogmatic theology in Mont-César, his retreats to priests and religious, and his wide private correspondence.

Marmion the Writer

Marmion published little throughout his life, unlike most writers who gradually build up a reputation by continuous publications. He was in his late fifties when *Christ, the Life of the Soul* first appeared in 1916. At that time, as abbot, he was weighed down by the cares of office, with little leisure for literary pursuits, and censorship under German occupation during World War I made it necessary to alter the date of publication. The immediate and phenomenal success of the book has been described by Dom Bernard Capelle as a silent plebiscite.[11] This was followed by *Christ in his Mysteries* (1919), *Christ the Ideal of the Monk* (1922), and *Sponsa Verbi* (1923). The books were able to appear in rapid succession because they were compiled from notes taken down during his weekly conferences to his monastic community. The final editing was done by Dom Raymond Thibaut, and was in each case authenticated by Marmion, who even remarked about the text of *Christ, the Ideal of the Monk,* 'c'est bien moi'.

The abbacy 1909-23

The third and final phase of his monastic life began when the Chapter of Maredsous elected him as its third abbot in 1909. As abbot, over and above the spiritual guidance of his community and of many individual correspondents, Marmion was involved in four major public events. The first was the invitation by the Belgian government in 1909-10 to undertake a Benedictine foundation in Katanga, which was part of the Belgian colony of the Congo.

9. M. M. Philipon OP, *The spiritual doctrine of Dom Marmion,* (London, 1956), p 79.
10. Thibaut, *Maître,* p 404.
11. Dom Bernard Capelle in *La Vie Spirituelle,* no 325, Jan 1948, p 127.

Fig 2: Abbot Marmion with the Maredsous monks in exile, Edermine, Co Wexford

In spite of pressure from government quarters, the chapter of Maredsous refused the offer, and Marmion, who would have favoured such a foundation, accepted this negative decision. The next important external event occurred in 1913 when nearly the whole community of Anglican Benedictines of Caldey Island, off Tenby in Wales, transferred their allegiance from Canterbury to Rome. Marmion became deeply involved in the spiritual and canonical process of the reception of the community into the Catholic Church. The outbreak of the Great War in 1914 ushered in four years of grave anxiety for Marmion. Unlike the military situation in World War II, Belgium was able to retain its sovereignty over a small coastal strip of its own territory. This enabled those young monks of Maredsous for whom Marmion had found a temporary home at Edermine in County Wexford, to travel to and from the front, where they acted as *brancardiers* (stretcher bearers). Marmion made every effort to maintain the bond of community between those monks who had remained behind in Maredsous under German occupation, and those based in Edermine, even travelling in disguise through the German lines to reach Ireland. One final piece of important monastic, ecclesiastical and even political business absorbed much of Marmion's later energies, although strictly speaking it was not of his remit. His strenuous efforts to install Belgian monks in Dormition Abbey in Jerusalem,[12] following the internment of the original German community by the victorious British forces, were of no avail, the question being finally settled by the re-install-

12. Nikolaus Egender,'Belgische Benediktiner in der Dormitio in Jerusalem 1918-1920' in *Erbe und Auftrag,* lxxvii (2001), pp 155-64.

ation of the German (Beuronese) monks in 1921. The anti-German sentiment in Belgium after World War I made it impossible for Maredsous and the other Belgian houses to remain in the German Beuronese Congregation. Marmion played a central role in the process of withdrawal, to this end visiting the other Belgian houses after the Armistice in November 1918. On 23 December 1918 the monastic chapter in Maredsous voted in favour of separation from Beuron and in February 1920 the Belgian Benedictine Congregation of the Annunciation was formally erected. Throughout this period, and in spite of failing health, Marmion maintained his hectic schedule of retreats and sermons and his extensive correspondence. He died at Maredsous on Tuesday 30 January 1923 after a brief illness which originated in a chill and developed into bronchial pneumonia. He would have been sixty-five on the following 1 April.

CHAPTER EIGHT

The Origins and Early Days of Glenstal Abbey

Mark Tierney OSB

Glenstal Castle, in the parish of Murroe, Co Limerick, was built by the Barrington family in the 1830s. The architect, William Bardwell, designed it in the Norman-Revival style, with a gate-tower, keep, and impressive front façade.[1] The Barringtons had acquired the Carbery estate in 1831, which stretched from the Mulcair River at Barrington's Bridge, to the Clare River on the Limerick-Tipperary Border. In 1870, the estate consisted of 9,485 acres.[2] This holding was considerably reduced, following a series of Land Acts, passed between 1881 and 1909. Thus, by the year 1925, when Sir Charles and Lady Barrington decided to leave Glenstal, they owned less than 1,000 acres, in and around the castle demesne. They were finding it more and more difficult to maintain the castle and estate, especially in the new Ireland, which emerged from the War of Independence (1919-21) and the Civil War (1922-23).

One of the main reasons why the Barringtons left Glenstal was the sad death of their only daughter, Winifred ('Winnie'), who was killed in an unfortunate incident in May 1921. She was travelling in the company of a Black and Tan officer, Captain Biggs, when the car was ambushed by the local IRA unit near Newport, Co Tipperary. Winnie, who was in the front seat of the open car, was shot by mistake, and died that evening in Glenstal. The family was devastated. Lady Barrington, who was a Scot and a Unionist at heart, urged her husband to leave Ireland as soon as possible, and take up residence in England.

When eventually, in 1925, the time came to leave, Sir Charles made a magnificent gesture. He wrote to the Irish Free State government, offering Glenstal as a gift to the Irish nation, specifically suggesting that it might be a suitable residence for the Governor-General. Mr W. T. Cosgrave, the President of the Executive Council of the Irish Free State, and Mr Tim Healy, the Governor-General, visited Glenstal in July 1925, and 'were astonished at

---

1. Mark Tierney and John Cornforth, 'Glenstal Castle, Co Limerick' in *Country Life,* October 2, 1974, pp 934-37.
2. *Return of owners of land in Ireland,* (Dublin 1876), p 146.

Fig 1: Glenstal castle

its magnificence, which far exceeded our expectations'.[3] However, financial restraints forced them to turn down the offer. Mr Cosgrave wrote to Sir Charles, stating that 'our present economic position would not warrant the Ministry in applying to the Dáil to vote the necessary funds for the upkeep of Glenstal'.[4]

Soon after this, the Barringtons held an auction of the furniture and books in the castle, and let it be known that they were about to leave Ireland for good. The news soon spread to the village of Murroe, and caused much comment and dismay, as the Barringtons had been a major employer in the area for nearly a hundred years. It would be a local disaster, if the Glenstal demesne and castle were to be abandoned and become a ruin, like so many other Big Houses in Ireland. There thus began a local campaign to save Glenstal. It should be said that the Barringtons never intended abandoning the place, and kept a skeleton staff in the castle, in the hope that someone might come along to buy it.

By a strange coincidence, two eminent Catholic clergymen, both natives of Murroe, then stepped in, and showed an immediate interest in saving Glenstal. The first was Fr Richard Devane, Professor of Church History at St Patrick's College, Thurles, and the second was Dr Harty, the Archbishop of Cashel and Emly. Fr Devane had studied at the Irish College, Paris, spoke

3. W. T. Cosgrave to Sir Charles Barringtoon, 29 July 1925. *Glenstal Abbey archives.* Boxfile no 1: 'Origins of Glenstal Abbey'.
4. Ibid.

fluent French, and had recently visited the Abbey of Maredsous, in Belgium, where an Irishman, Dom Columba Marmion, had been abbot from 1909-23. He was interested in the history of Irish monasticism, and regretted that there were no Benedictine monks in Ireland in modern times. Archbishop Harty, a man of wide vision, had noticed how many Irish Catholic boys still went to boarding schools in England. He hoped one day to have, in

Fig 2: Castle door depicting Queen Eleanor of Aquitaine (left) and King Henry II of England (right).

his diocese, a school that would attract the kind of boy who might otherwise have gone to England. It was Fr Devane who took the initiative. He approached Dr Harty, suggesting that the latter might acquire Glenstal, and offer it to some Benedictine community, with a view to their establishing a boarding school, similar to the ones run by the Benedictines of Ampleforth and Downside, in England.

In August 1925, a third priest came into the picture, Msgr James Ryan, a wealthy Cashel priest, reputed to have a personal fortune of about £50,000.[5] He had retired as President of St Patrick's College, Thurles, and was living at his home, The Hermitage, Cappagh, Thurles. He was well-known for his generosity, and had recently bought a property for the Pallotine Order in Thurles. He was also involved in the restoration of the Irish Franciscan House, St Anthony's, in Louvain, Belgium, which had been seriously damaged during World War I. Archbishop Harty approached Msgr Ryan, and asked him if he would be prepared to buy Glenstal Castle, with a view to its becoming one day a Benedictine monastery. Dr Harty, at the prompting of Fr Devane, proposed that the monks of the Abbey of Maredsous, in Belgium, be approached, with a view to making a foundation in Glenstal. Msgr Ryan fell in with the idea. He is reputed to have replied to Dr Harty: 'Maredsous! I know the place well. My friend, Cardinal Mercier[6] took me there years ago,

---

5. James Ryan was a member of the Scarteen Ryan clan. He had no brothers or sisters, and had inherited a fortune from his grandmother.
6. Cardinal Mercier was archbishop of Malines, Belgium.

Fig 3: Msgr James Ryan

to meet my old friend Abbot Columba Marmion.[7] I'll purchase Glenstal for the Benedictines.' Msgr Ryan immediately got in touch with Sir Charles Barrington, and. early in September 1925, Glenstal Castle was sold to him for the nominal sum of £2,000.

On 29 September 1925, Msgr Ryan wrote to Dom Celestine Golenvaux, the Abbot of Maredsous, putting forward the proposal of Dr Harty, for a Benedictine foundation in Ireland, and offering Glenstal Castle and demesne to the monks of Maredsous for this purpose.[8] The Abbot of Maredsous replied to Msgr Ryan on 9 November 1925, saying that it was impossible to take up the offer, because one of his monks, Dom Aubert Merten,[9] was at that very moment (1925) in Ireland, trying to make a foundation near Kylemore, Connemara.[10] In fact, this Connemara venture never got off the ground, as Dom Aubert failed to get the necessary permission from the Archbishop of Tuam, in whose diocese Kylemore was situated. Fr Aubert also failed to get any of the monks of Maredsous to join him.

This delay in the negotiations had an unfortunate twist to it, for a whole year went by before there was any further contact between Msgr Ryan and the Abbot of Maredsous. During this time, Msgr Ryan became attached to his new acquisition. He took up temporary residence in the castle, and began to look upon himself as a kind of lord of the manor. He apparently decided that, even if he eventually handed over the property to the Benedictines, he

---

7. Dom Columba Marmion, Abbot of Maredsous 1909-23.
8. Msgr Ryan to Abbot Celestine Golenvaux, 29 Sept 1925. *Archives of Maredsous,* Glenstal papers.
9. Dom Aubert Merten had come to Ireland in 1915, and was superior of the house (Edermine) in Co Wexford, where Abbot Marmion had established his younger monks during the war years. After the war, all the Belgian monks had returned to Maredsous, except Dom Aubert Merten. He accompanied the Irish Dames of Ypres to Kylemore, and remained in Ireland as their chaplain.
10. Dom Celestine Golenvaux to Msgr Ryan, 9 Nov 1925. *Arch. Mar.* Glenstal papers, no 2.

would retain for his own use all the hunting, fishing and shooting rights, as well as two of the larger rooms in the castle.

Early in October 1926, Msgr Ryan was in Louvain, in connection with the restoration of St Anthony's Franciscan Friary. While there, he took the opportunity to visit the Abbey of Mont César (Kaisersberg), where the abbots of the Belgian Benedictine Congregation were assembled for their second General Chapter. He was invited to address the abbots and took the occasion to repeat his proposal of the previous year, offering

Fig 4: Dom Celestine Golenvaux, Abbot of Maredsous, 1923-1950

Glenstal Castle to the Benedictines as a free gift. At the same time, he made all kinds of promises of financial help for the Irish foundation, with special reference to a sum of £5,000 from an anonymous American donor. Dom[11] Celestine Golenvaux, the abbot of Maredsous, who the previous year had turned down the offer was now so moved by the words of Msgr Ryan that he decided to go to Glenstal, as soon as possible, to see the place for himself. He was encouraged to do so by Dom Theodore Neve, the abbot of Saint André, who offered to accompany him to Ireland.

Abbot Celestine Golenvaux wrote a long letter to the prior of Maredsous, dated 19 November 1926, in which he spoke of his favourable impressions of Glenstal.[12] He had been received graciously by Dr Harty, who gave him every encouragement to proceed with a foundation. Furthermore, he visited Kylemore and met Dom Aubert Merten. The latter made it clear that he was not going to make his own independent foundation in Connemara, so that obstacle had now been cleared away. This letter may be considered as a turning point in the foundation process of Glenstal, in that it implies the first positive 'Yes' to Msgr Ryan's proposal.

The abbot of Maredous confirmed this in a letter to Msgr Ryan, dated 3

---

11. The use of the style 'Dom', was common among English and continental Benedictines, indicating that the monk was also a priest.
12. Celestine Golenvaux to the prior of Maredsous, 19 Nov 1926. *Archiv. Mar.,* Glenstal papers, no 4.

December 1926, in which he said clearly that he now thought it would be possible to make a foundation in Glenstal. The proposal had been discussed by the chapters of Maredsous, Mont César and Saint André, with a positive response from all three. The next step would be for Msgr Ryan to draw up an official document, laying out the conditions of his proposal. This legal document should be sent to Abbot Robert de Kerchove, of Mont César, President of the Belgian Congregation. The Abbot of Maredsous ends his letter with the words:

> Which of the Belgian monasteries will in fact undertake the foundation? It seems most likely that the monastery in question will be Maredsous. And to prove our continued interest, it is proposed to send two monks to Glenstal, next January (1927), to make a more detailed study of the situation. We consider this actual visit by the two monks as a *first taking of possession.*[13]

Throughout all these early negotiations, credit must be given to Dom Theodore Neve, the abbot of Saint André (Zevenkerken), who acted as an adviser and intermediary in several instances. He accompanied the abbot of Maredsous on the fact-finding mission to Glenstal in November, and on his return to Belgium, wrote to Archbishop Harty: 'It seems to us all that this foundation is willed by God. *Digitus Dei hic est.*'[14] He furthermore indicated that it would take about three months for all the deliberations to be completed, and concluded by saying that towards September 1927 'the first classes of the secondary school and of the arts school[15] could begin'.[16]

On 8 December 1926, Archbishop Harty gave what amounted to his charter for the future foundation, in a letter addressed to Abbot Theodore Neve:

> 'With special pleasure, I give the community of Maredsous permission to establish a Benedictine House at Glenstal in the diocese of Cashel. This permission extends to an arts and crafts school, which would be a great boon to ecclesiastical art in Ireland, and also a higher school of general studies, in which Irish subjects would hold a prominent place, and in which the pension of boys would be sufficiently high to make the school very select.' He concluded with these words: 'Although the archdiocese cannot assume any financial responsibility for the house, your fathers can

---

13. Celestine Golenvaux to Msgr Ryan, 3 Dec 1926, *Archiv. Mar.* Glenstal papers, no 5.
14. 'The finger of God is here.'
15. Both Msgr Ryan and Celestine Golenvaux were interested in establishing a school of arts and crafts in Glenstal.
16. Dom Theodore Neve to Dr Harty, 2 Dec 1926. *Archiv.Mar.* Glenstal papers, a copy.

be assured of a warm welcome from priests and people and of practical sympathy in their educational work. To me personally, it will be a most pleasing duty to welcome the Benedictines to the archdiocese of Cashel and to my native parish of Murroe.'[17]

In mid-December 1926, Abbot Celestine Golenvaux wrote at length to Fr Richard Devane, in which he says that 'the Glenstal enterprise is an invitation from God, and not to accept it would be an act of infidelity'.[18] The abbot of Maredsous goes on to make some realistic reflections, cautioning against an expectation of wonderful works undertaken at once by the Benedictine monks in Ireland. 'It would be a grave mistake to found a monastery solely for its works (liturgical, educational, artistic etc). Glenstal must first of all be a centre of interior life and prayer, and only then can one speak of expansion into exterior works.'[19]

The minor setback came at the end of December 1926, when the abbot of Maredsous wrote to Msgr Ryan, repeating what he had said in his letter of 3 December, and wondering if the latter had ever received this letter. He asks that Msgr Ryan send him *an official document*, offering Glenstal to the Benedictines: 'I simply await a word on your part, in order to put into effect the project we all have at heart.'[20] Msgr Ryan had, however, received the letter of 3 December, but had delayed his reply, which he finally wrote on 31 December. In this letter, Msgr Ryan gave two reasons for not writing earlier: firstly, he had not been well, and secondly, he had done some shopping round, looking for financial backing for the Glenstal venture, but had failed so far to get anything worth while. His wealthy American friend, whom he now named as the Marquis Maloney, had withdrawn his offer of help, while other well-wishers seem to have evaporated into thin air. There was only one positive note in Msgr Ryan's letter, namely that Vincent Scully, of Mantlehill, Golden, Co Tipperary, had donated his valuable library to the Glenstal foundation.[21] At the same time, Msgr Ryan also made it clear that the Belgian monks could not expect him to pay for their travelling expenses in connection with the foundation. He also warned about the large sums of money that would be required in establishing the monastery, with its two schools.[22]

17. Dr Harty to Dom T Neve, 8 Dec 1926. *Archiv. Mar.* Glenstal papers, a copy, no 7.
18. Celestine Golenvaux to Richard Devane, 15 Dec 1926. *Archiv. Mar.* Glenstal papers, no 9.
19. Ibid.
20. C Golenvaux to Msgr Ryan, 29 Dec 1926, *Archiv. Mar.* Glenstal papers, no 10.
21. Msgr Ryan to Celestine Golenvaux, 31 Dec 1926. *Archiv. Mar.* Glenstal papers, no 11. The Scully library eventually came into the possession of the Glenstal monks, and formed the nucleus of the monastery library.
22. Ibid.

In the meantime, the Abbot of Maredsous, who was becoming somewhat disillusioned, if not impatient, wrote to Archbishop Harty on 1 January 1927, saying that 'no progress could be made, until such time as Msgr Ryan expresses *in writing* his precise intention of handing over his estate of Glenstal for a monastic foundation'.[23] The abbot followed this with a somewhat forceful letter to Msgr Ryan, dated 12 January 1927, reiterating his need for a precise, written proposal and agreement: 'It is only when this first and absolutely indispensable formality is accomplished that *a preliminary decision may be arrived at by the Chapter of Maredsous.*'[24] He enclosed in this letter a draft agreement, as a basis for Msgr Ryan's official offer of Glenstal to Maredsous.

At this delicate stage of the negotiations, there was need for more than patience on the side of those trying to help out. Fortunately, there was at hand someone who was able to smooth the waters, Fr Richard Devane. He wrote a most encouraging letter to Abbot Theodore Neve on 18 January 1927, saying that 'there is no need to be anxious about the future – everything will be alright … You need not be surprised at the Monsignor's delay in replying to letters, because he is not a very efficient businessman. He does not answer letters promptly. I visited Glenstal recently. Msgr Ryan is making preparations there for the advent of your priests and lay-brothers. He has placed in the library at Glenstal a considerable collection of books'.[25] Devane concluded the letter by giving the following advice:

> As soon as the Monsignor invites your priests to Glenstal, they should come at once, because their presence there will induce Msgr Ryan to conclude matters quickly. When your priests arrive at Thurles, I shall meet them and give them advice as to the manner of acting with Msgr Ryan.[26]

From this letter of Fr Devane to Abbot Neve, one must draw the conclusion that these two men were acting in the background, providing an element of sanity and practicality in a complicated situation. Fr Devane found it easier to deal with Abbot Neve than with Abbot Golenvaux, as one can see from the concluding words of Devane to Neve: 'I am writing to the Abbot of Maredsous, but I think there is no need to tell him all the details mentioned in this letter.'[27]

In the meantime, Msgr Ryan was not idle. He wrote a most helpful letter

23. C Golenvaux to Dr Harty, 1 Jan 1927. *Archiv. Mar.* Glenstal papers, no 12.
24. C Golenvaux to Msgr Ryan, 12 Jan 1927. *Archiv. Mar.* Glenstal papers, no 13.
25. Richard Devane to Th. Neve, 18 Jan 1927, *Archiv Mar.* Glenstal papers, no 14.
26. Ibid.
27. Ibid.

to the Abbot of Maredsous on 20 January 1927, apologising for the delay in writing, and concluded with these words: 'You will, I hope, hear from me with your requirements (i.e. the official documents) in a few days. Having forwarded the necessary papers, I shall, as soon as feasible, go to Glenstal to make preparations for the reception of the two monks (*ie* the prospectors) of whom you wrote.'[28] Indeed, Msgr Ryan sent the draft memorandum to the Abbot of Maredsous on 25 January 1927, concluding with these words: 'I shall sign the memorandum when you let me have it. Please send me an extra copy or two, as I shall have to give one to Archbishop Harty.'[29] This memorandum gives a detailed history of the negotiations up to that moment, as well as stating the propositions and conditions of Msgr Ryan in relation to the transferring of Glenstal to the Abbey of Maredsous.[30]

At this moment of the story there enters a new personality, Dom Patrick Nolan, a monk of Maredsous, who had led a rather peripatetic life, having served much of his time in Erdington Abbey, Birmingham, England, and later in Mount Saint Benedict's, Gorey, Co Wexford,. A difficult character, he had been a thorn in the side of Abbot Marmion. He had, in fact, also got into serious trouble with the Bishop of Ferns some years earlier, over the disposal of Edermine House.[31] He read an account of the proposed Glenstal foundation in the Irish newspapers, and wrote to Abbot Golenvaux from Mount Saint Benedict's on 29 January 1927: 'Allow me, an Irishman, who has always prayed and worked for the establishment of the Benedictines in Ireland, to go and help in this new foundation (i.e. Glenstal) and fix my stability for it.'[32] However, Abbot Golenvaux turned down this offer from Fr Patrick Nolan, saying that he could not accept the latter as a member of the Glenstal community, because Msgr Ryan, who apparently knew all about Fr Nolan, had stipulated specifically that Nolan was *persona non grata* with him.[33] On hearing of Patrick Nolan's present intentions, Msgr Ryan added a codicil to the original *Memorandum,* in which he stated: 'Be it understood and accepted as a condition of this donation (of Glenstal), that no member

---

28. Msgr Ryan to Cel. Golenvaux, 20 Jan 1927. *Archiv. Mar.* Glenstal papers, no 15.
29. Msgr Ryan to Cel. Golenvux, 25 Jan 1927. *Archiv. Mar.* Glenstal papers, no 16.
30. 'Memorandum of the negotiations between Msgr Ryan and the abbots of the Belgian Congregation' 25 Jan 1927. Original in French. *Archiv. Mar.* Glenstal papers, 17a and 17b.
31. Abbot Marmion had brought his junior monks to Ireland during the First World War. They settled in Edermine House, near Enniscorthy. Dom Patrick Nolan hoped to make an Irish foundation in Co Wexford, with money he had received from his parents. The local bishop refused permission.
32. Dom Patrick Nolan to C Golenvaux, 29 Jan 1927. *Archiv. Mar.* Glenstal papers, no 18
33. C Golenvaux to Patrick Nolan, 1 Feb 1927. *Archiv. Mar.* Glenstal papers, no 19.

of the community or inmate of Mount Saint Benedict's, Gorey, Monastery be admitted to the proposed community and monastery at Glenstal.'[34]

Everything was now in place for the arrival of the two prospectors: Dom Gregoire Fournier and Dom Odilon Golenvaux.[35] They arrived in Glenstal early in March 1927, and were met by Fr Thomas O'Connor,[36] another Murroe priest, who drove them everywhere and helped them in their work of assessing the Glenstal situation. They sent several reports to the Abbot of Maredsous, but it was the letter of 13 March 1927, signed by both prospectors, that turned the scales and sealed the whole issue of the foundation. They spoke of the 'beauty of the place', and offered very positive arguments for accepting Msgr Ryan's offer. They also confirmed that it was Fr Richard Devane who first thought of having a Benedictine foundation in Glenstal.[37] A similar thought was expressed by the Abbot of Maredsous, in his letter of 31 March 1927, to Fr Devane: 'Now that the foundation of Glenstal is about to be officially accepted by the Chapter of Maredsous, I feel obliged *morally* to turn to you. You deserve to be the first to know about our decision, because *it is to you* that we owe the whole initiative of the great project.'[38] The Abbot of Maredsous also assured Fr Devane that he would send 'monks who were good religious, not angels, but men imbued with the true spirit of their vocation, animated by good will.' He also promised to appoint 'as Prior of the new foundation, a man who was a gifted administrator and experienced and prudent in financial matters'.[39]

On 14 April 1927, the chapter of Maredsous accepted the gift of Glenstal from Msgr Ryan.[40] On 18 April Dom Gerard François was appointed superior of the new community, while other members chosen were Dom Odilon

34. *Memorandum or Agreement between Msgr Ryan and the abbots of the Belgian Congregation.* The codicil is added at the end of this document. *Archiv. Mar.* Glenstal papers, no 22..

35. Dom Gregoire Fournier, was a man of considerable experience, in that he had spent several years in Jerusalem, as superior of the Dormition Abbey venture (1919-21), under Abbot Marmion. Dom Odilon Golenvaux was a brother of the Abbot of Maredsous.

36. Fr Thomas O'Connor and Fr Richard Devane were the two priests, natives of Murroe, who befriended the monks from Belgium, and helped in many ways. At this time, Fr O'Connor was inspector of schools in the archdiocese of Cashel.

37. The actual words used, regarding Fr Devane's role, were: 'celui qui a eu la pensée initiale de la fondation'. G Fournier and O Golenvaux to Cel. Golvenvaux, 13 March 1927. *Archiv. Mar.* Glenstal papers, no 42.

38. C Golenvaux to Fr Devane, 31 March 1927. *Archiv. Mar.* Glenstal papers. It was Devane who had coined the phrase that they should try 'to make Glenstal the Maredsous of Ireland'.

39. Ibid. The prior in question was Dom Gerard François.

40. For a summary of the chapter meeting, relating to 'The foundation in Ireland' see *Archiv. Mar.* Glenstal papers, no 59.

Golenvaux (who had to withdraw as he had been requested for the Greek College, Rome), Dom Omer Van Tours, Dom Mayeul Lang and Dom Winoc Mertens. A short time later, Dom David Maffei[41] and Dom Hubert Janssens were added to make up the six founding monks. On 8 May 1927, the blessing of the Foundation Cross, and its presentation to Dom Gerard François, took place in Maredsous. On 11 May 1927 Abbot Celestine Golenvaux, Dom Gerard François, Dom Winoc Mertens and Dom Odilon Golenvaux arrived by boat in Dún Laoghaire, Dublin, where they were met by the Belgian Consul-General, M. Goor. On 13 May, accompanied by Msgr Ryan, who had come to Dublin to greet them, the party made their first stop at Thurles. There they were met by Fr Devane, and conducted to Archbishop Harty's house. Dr Harty entertained them to lunch and presented them with a motor van.[42] After lunch, among other matters for discussion, the *patron saint* of Glenstal was raised by Dr Harty, who suggested Saint Benedict. However, Fr Gerard François pointed out that this was the name by which the Abbey of Maresous was known, and it would not be right for the foundation to have the same name as the mother-house. Finally, it was agreed that Glenstal should be given two names, Joseph and Columba,

---

41. A monk of Mont César Abbey, who was to be the novice master.
42. This motor van was to prove of inestimable value to the Glenstal community during the early years.

in memory of the Irish-born late Abbot of Maredsous, Dom Columba Marmion.[43]

The first group of monks arrived by train on 13 May 1927. They were conveyed to Glenstal by Michael Kennedy[44] and the post-master of Murroe. It took several months to settle in, as the castle was quite underfurnished. Glenstal was canonically erected on 18 December 1927. Abbot Celestine Golenvaux then confirmed Dom Gerard François as the prior, with Dom David Maffei as subprior and novice master. The regular monastic life at Glenstal can be said to have begun that same day, Sunday 18 December 1927.

It might seem from much of the correspondence at the time that the monks of Maredsous were taking up residence in an empty castle. It was, in fact, quite different. While all the valuable furniture and books had been auctioned in September 1925, a great amount of furniture and fittings remained. According to an inventory, drawn up by W. B. Fitt & Co., on 14 July 1926, under the title 'Valuation for transfer', Msgr Ryan bought from Sir Charles Barrington, a range of household goods, at the cost of £150. Most items were less than £1 and consisted of chairs, tables, wardrobes, wash-stands, rugs, carpets, etc for the interior of the house, and oil tank, grind stone, ladders, wheel-barrows, carpenter's bench, tackling for horses, horse-drawn lawn mower, scythes, saws, shovels, spades, forks, rakes, etc for the yard and gardens.[45] The monks had to buy beds, tableware, and other such items, but the castle was not left desolate. Besides, the Vincent Scully library had been installed in the magnificent library of the castle. The building had its own central heating, run on solid fuel. There was a magnificent kitchen, fully equipped with ovens and ranges.

Sir Charles Barrington wrote to Msgr Ryan on 29 July 1927: 'I am greatly pleased with what you have written as regards the hopes and intentions of the Brothers with reference to my old home. I trust that they will get on well there and be successful and as happy as we were in that beautiful spot. I shall always regret the sale of the trophies of the chase which were sold from the hall, and the guns (i.e. six cannon) on the terrace.'[46] Sir Charles wrote sometime later to the prior of Glenstal: 'If I had only known that your Order was coming, I would have presented all those hunting and shooting trophies to you. I left you the Irish Elk anyhow.'[47]

---

43. Abbot Marmion's baptismal name was Joseph, his name in religion was Columba.
44. Fr Michael Kennedy was the curate of Murroe at the time.
45. *Glenstal Archives,* Boxfile I, 'Goods at Glenstal Castle, 14 July 1926'.
46. *Glenstal Archives,* Boxfile I, Sir Charles Barrington to Msgr Ryan, 29 July 1927, a copy.
47. *Glenstal Archives,* Boxfile I, Sir Charles Barrington to D. Gerard Francois, 17 Oct. 1928. The two Irish Elk horns are still in the entrance hall in Glenstal.

During these early days, Msgr Ryan kept in frequent touch with the monks. He visited Glenstal occasionally, occupying the two rooms which he had reserved for his own use in the castle. He also had the monks call to see him in Thurles. A typical invitation to the prior arrived in late August 1927, delivered by Msgr Ryan's personal courier, Joe: 'Are you free to dine here at 3 o'clock today? If so, please come – arrive – here at that hour. Owing to the day being fine, my horse will be engaged saving the hay and I cannot therefore go for you. Will you walk as you did yesterday? We must make hay while the sun shines.'[48] In fact, one gets the impression that Msgr Ryan was overdoing his privileged position of donor, expecting the monks to jump to attention at his every whim. One such typical case related to the library, which Msgr Ryan considered as much *his* as the monks. Writing to Fr Prior on 14 May 1928, Msgr Ryan stated: 'I hope to visit Glenstal tomorrow (Tuesday) afternoon, with a friend, Dr Callanan.[49] Please tell Fr Hubert, the Librarian, to place the Scully letters and documents[50] on the large table in the provisional sacristy. We shall return tomorrow evening.'[51] Someone has added a note on the margin of this letter, to the effect that 'Dr Callanan has taken several documents on that day, and never sent them back.'[52]

Two other instances of evident interfering can be cited. On 29 February 1927, Msgr Ryan wrote to the Prior of Glenstal, ordering him to 'prohibit Dom Winoc burning any more of the park lands …When driving to Boher Station (with Fr Winoc) I called his attention to the fire burning the parts close to the thorn trees, which must be injured by the fire, as there was no one there to control it.'[53] Some months later, Msgr Ryan orders the prior to 'tell Fitzgibbon to deposit his gun at the Murroe Guard Barracks till I meet him. While in *your* employment, he has no use for a fowling piece, as I have reserved to myself the shooting and fishing of Glenstal property. I trust therefore you not allow *anyone* to shoot on the place till I visit it next week.'[54]

All this time, there was no move made by Msgr Ryan to hand over the

---

48. *Glenstal Archives,* Boxfile I, Msgr Ryan to Dom Gerard François, 24 Aug 1927. Msgr Ryan asked the prior of Glenstal to walk from the Thurles railway station to the Hermitage, i.e. Ryan's house, a distance of over a mile.

49. Dr Callanan was a medical doctor in Thurles. He was very interested in local history.

50. The Scully Library consisted of a large collection of books, as well valuable manuscript letters and documents.

51. *Glenstal Archives,* Boxfile I, Msgr Ryan to Dom Gerard François, 14 May 1928.

52. Ibid.

53. *Glenstal Archives* Boxfile I, Msgr Ryan to Dom Gerard François, 29 Feb 1928. Fr Winoc, the farmer, was trying to get rid of the ferns which covered the deer park, to have some grazing land for the cattle.

54. *Glenstal Archives,* Boxfile I, Msgr Ryan to Dom Gerard François, 19 Aug 1927.

Glenstal property to the monks. He spoke several times of his intention of making a legal transfer of Glenstal to the Benedictines, but as late as 19 August 1927 no steps had been taken to this effect. Finally, at the urging of Archbishop Harty, the deeds were handed over on 19 January 1928, and the Benedictine monks became the legal owners of Glenstal.

These early days of Glenstal Abbey were particularly difficult for the six monks from Maredsous, who found themselves in a very challenging situation, in a strange land. They had to master the language, adjust to Irish and local customs, and cope with considerable financial restraints. Thanks to the prior, Dom Gerard, who succeeded in obtaining help from some of his wealthy friends in Belgium and Switzerland, they managed to keep debt at bay. They also received help and advice from well-wishers throughout Ireland, among whom must be mentioned Mr Stephen O'Mara, who financed the first Glenstal piggery. Fr Gerard planned to build a church or chapel as soon as possible, believing that the temporary chapel, inside the castle, was quite inadequate. However, owing to the Wall Street Crash of 1929, he was forced to wait until 1932 before he could realise this dream.

There was also the delicate question of dealing with Msgr James Ryan, who continued to retain, for his own use, some of the larger rooms in the castle, as well as reserving to himself the hunting, shooting and fishing rights in the grounds. Time and diplomacy were to overcome these latter difficulties. It would be ungracious for the monks of Glenstal to find fault with Msgr Ryan. He was clearly very eccentric, but he was also a gentleman, and very proud of having established the Benedictine monks permanently in Ireland. At the end of the day, both parties had to accept the fact that without Msgr Ryan there might have been no Glenstal as we know it today.

CHAPTER NINE

Monastic Exiles in Ireland

William Fennelly OSB

Four distinct groups of Benedictine monastic exiles arrived in Ireland in the late nineteenth century and early twentieth century. The first group came in the 1880s from the French monastery of La Pierre qui Vire and settled at Leopardstown near Dublin. A second wave, made up of three different groups, arrived during the First World War. The first were the Dames of Ypres who initially set up at Macmine in Co Wexford and later went on to found Kylemore Abbey. The second was a group led by Abbot Columba Marmion from Maredsous in Belgium. They established themselves at Edermine, also in Co Wexford, though they returned to Maredsous after the war. The third group to arrive during the Great War was a group of Parisian nuns seeking a possible place of refuge from the French anticlerical laws. This group settled at Loftus Hall and stayed from 1914 until 1937.

This brief survey will concentrate on the French exiles that came to Ireland from 1880 to 1882 and on the group of Parisian nuns that came during the Great War. These two groups give valuable insights into some of the issues and movements that shaped European monasticism in the nineteenth and early twentieth centuries. The great ideals of the nineteenth century founders often provoked hostility, not least among European legislators. However these ideals failed to take root in Ireland, due to a combination of economic mismanagement and an unhappy confluence of strong personalities. This is remarkable, given the powerful and dynamic resurgence of Irish Catholicism at the time. It would be reasonable to have expected the prevailing Catholic culture to have carried these groups through their difficulties. Perhaps the principal quality to emerge from this recital of difficulty is the perseverance of those who engaged in these brave projects and their fidelity to a style of life whose time did not seem to have come in the Ireland of their day.

Monastic revival in nineteenth century Europe

In order to understand the Leopardstown foundation, it is necessary to sketch in outline the context from which these monks came. As a result of the hostility of the French Revolution and the activities of the secularising governments of Austria, Spain and Switzerland in the early years of the nineteenth century, only about thirty of the 1,500 European monasteries in existence in 1780s survived until 1832 and most of the monasteries that did survive were in poor shape. In the eyes of these civic reformers, who were not necessarily hostile to Catholicism, monasticism served no discernable purpose and was, in their eyes, a parasite on society, which would best be served by the redeployment of the considerable wealth accumulated by the monasteries since the Middle Ages. Not since the Reformation had the monastic movement been so threatened by the hostility of the civil power. This period of suppression and secularisation gave way in the nineteenth century to a dynamic movement of restoration and reform, from the 1830s onwards. This movement began most notably in France, at the abbey of Solesmes and then, in Germany, spreading from the Rhineland abbey of Beuron.[1] The daughter houses of these monasteries were to have a significant impact on the intellectual, spiritual and particularly the liturgical life of the church for the next century.

The first generation of nineteenth-century founders were anxious to recover the fervour of medieval monasticism and they sought to revive much of the aesthetic and observances of their medieval forebears. The core elements of the monastic restorations were a reaffirmation of the importance of stability within the enclosure of the monastery; the re-dedication of the monk's life to the round of monastic duties in a community governed by a resident abbot; and especially the singing of the monastic office. The Solesmes congregation was involved in the revival of Roman Catholic liturgical culture, and Beuron, though also involved in this field, made a noteworthy contribution to church art in the nineteenth and early twentieth centuries.

However, the Benedictine movement has a genius for housing several competing visions of how the monastic life should be most appropriately lived. Therefore, in addition to the French and German currents, a quite different stream developed in Italy. Like Solesmes and Beuron, this stream was also given its initial impetus by a charismatic personality rather than through the emergence of a common programme agreed upon by a group of monks. In this case the founder was Pietro Casaretto (1810-1878), whose reform, starting in 1842, eventually found institutional expression in the 'Cassinese

---

1. For the monastic thought of the founder of Solesmes, see G. Oury, *L'héritage de Saint Benoît: initiation aux auteurs spirituels de l'ordre*, (Solesmes, 1988) pp 262-271. For Beuron, see Benedict Reetz, 'Les principes fondamentaux de la vie monastique et bénédictine d'après Rme. D. Maur Wolter, 1825-1890' in *Théologie de la vie monastique, d'après quelques grands moines des époques moderne et contemporaine* (Vienne, 1961), pp 123-133.

Congregation of the Primitive Observance' later called the Subiaco Congregation.[2]

Casaretto's reform was fostered in some of the Italian houses that survived the upheavals that swept away most of the monasteries of Europe and therefore, because he started from existing communities, he had to work with the existing structures. Solesmes and Beuron had sought to anchor the life of their communities in a reawakened sensitivity to the riches of liturgical spirituality, combined with a renewal of asceticism, fostering the essentially contemplative nature of the monk's life. Casaretto grounded his monastic reform programme on two central intuitions – a rigorous renewal of the ascetic life and a missionary thrust at the service of apostolic works and evangelisation.

Casaretto, though an engaging and devout man, set out a reform programme that lacked the intellectual coherence of his reforming contemporaries. He also lacked the imagination to conceive of structures that would effectively articulate and house the basic intuitions of his reforms. He relied on the heavily centralised structures that prevailed in the monastic reform movements of the seventeenth and eighteenth centuries, which he knew from his own monastic formation. Monks under this system made profession for provinces and not for particular monasteries. Though these structures had addressed particular needs in their own time, they made local adaptation difficult in the rapidly evolving context of the nineteenth century. For this reason, when his reform movement gathered momentum and grew in size, it became necessary to replace him with leaders whose talents could face the challenges of the rapidly growing congregation.

In 1850, after an intense religious experience, Jean-Baptiste Muard (1804-1854) founded the monastery of La Pierre qui Vire. A key element of his vision was the founding of a penitential religious institute, whose members would lead a poor and mortified style of life, while also engaging in preaching in the most de-Christianised parts of France. Muard only slowly came to decide that his institute should live by the Rule of St Benedict, in the congregation headed by Casaretto. Muard died in 1854, exhausted by the rigours of his penitential lifestyle.

An English province of Casaretto's congregation was established in 1856. In 1861, the monastery of Ramsgate was founded on the Isle of Thanet, Kent. The superior of this province was Dom Wifred Alcock (1831-1882) – the first

---

2. Interesting information on the life of Casaretto is provided by E. de Laurentii, 'L'abbé Pier Francesco Casaretto et son oeuvre, 1810-1878', unpublished typescript, La Pierre qui Vire archives.

mitred Benedictine abbot in the British Isles since the Reformation. The precise events concerning the arrival of Casaretto's reform in England need not
concern us here.[3] The English monks of the Subiaco congregation at this
time tended to form several small communities rather than concentrate all of
their resources in one large monastery. These were principally Mass centres,
eventually developing into parishes, and the style of life in these communities was more apostolic and pastoral in character than strictly monastic. Such
work was needed in England at the time, as Catholic Emancipation was a still
recent memory, and the process of establishing parishes and dioceses was still
ongoing.

Benedictine life reaches Ireland

One of Casaretto's first novices in Italy had been a Kilkenny man called
Adalbert O'Sullivan (1838-1930). O'Sullivan was a charismatic figure. This
charisma is attested to by the fact that he succeeded in convincing two of his
sisters, his mother[4] and one of his brothers to enter the monastic life.
O'Sullivan encouraged his sisters to leave the Italian monastery of Rosano
where they had entered, to return to England, to make a foundation under
his guidance. This community quickly ran into financial difficulties and this
should have given his superiors a warning of Fr Adalbert's tendency to let his
energies for making foundations outstrip his financial abilities. Abbot
Casaretto wrote to Fr Adalbert early in 1864 saying that he had been visited
by Msgr Kirby, Rector of the Irish College in Rome, who urged the Subiaco
congregation to found a monastery in Ireland. Fr Adalbert went to Ireland in
1866 for an extended break. He soon sought permission to purchase a farm
called *Tigh Lorcán* at Leopardstown. His superiors counselled caution, owing
to the already precarious finances of the English province. Fr Adalbert
nonetheless went ahead with the purchase in 1867 and he paid for it with the
trust monies of the monastery at Ramsgate. The new foundation was called
St Benedict's Priory. Recruits were entering the English province in a steady
stream and this may have served to foster the ambitious optimism of all concerned that the financial difficulties currently being experienced would be no
more than temporary.

The fluidity of the overall situation is highlighted by the inability of the

---

3. For the history of Ramsgate Abbey see D. Parry, *Monastic century, St Augustine's, Ramsgate
1865-1965* (Tenbury Wells, 1965).
4. With Dame Benedict Luck they founded a convent at Pegwell, and after this venture failed
they established themselves at St Mildred's Priory at Minster in Kent, where the Benedictine
nuns of Eichstätt, Bavaria, later made a foundation.

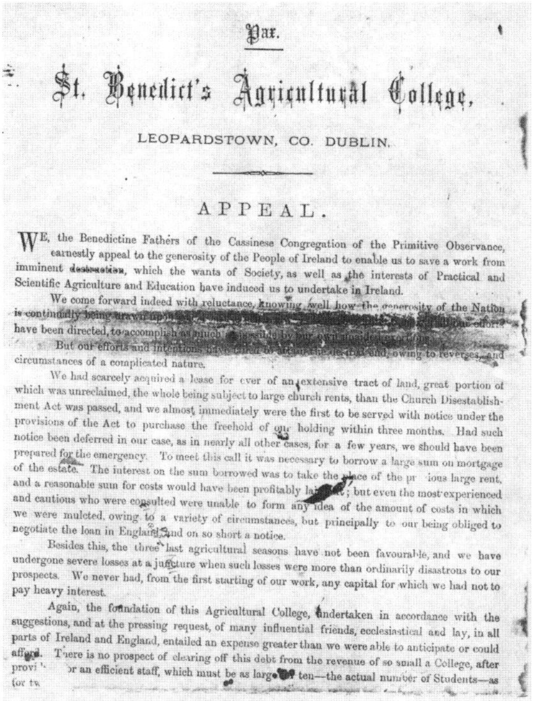

Pax.

St. Benedict's Agricultural College,

LEOPARDSTOWN, CO. DUBLIN.

APPEAL.

WE, the Benedictine Fathers of the Cassinese Congregation of the Primitive Observance, earnestly appeal to the generosity of the People of Ireland to enable us to save a work from imminent destruction, which the wants of Society, as well as the interests of Practical and Scientific Agriculture and Education have induced us to undertake in Ireland.

We come forward indeed with reluctance, knowing well how the generosity of the Nation is continually being drawn upon [illegible] efforts have been directed, to accomplish as much [illegible] by our own unaided exertions.

But our efforts and intentions [illegible] end, owing to reverses, and circumstances of a complicated nature.

We had scarcely acquired a lease for ever of an extensive tract of land, great portion of which was unreclaimed, the whole being subject to large church rents, than the Church Disestablishment Act was passed, and we almost immediately were the first to be served with notice under the provisions of the Act to purchase the freehold of our holding within three months. Had such notice been deferred in our case, as in nearly all other cases, for a few years, we should have been prepared for the emergency. To meet this call it was necessary to borrow a large sum on mortgage of the estate. The interest on the sum borrowed was to take the place of the pr ious large rent, and a reasonable sum for costs would have been profitably laid out; but even the most experienced and cautious who were consulted were unable to form any idea of the amount of costs in which we were mulcted, owing to a variety of circumstances, but principally to our being obliged to negotiate the loan in England, and on so short a notice.

Besides this, the three last agricultural seasons have not been favourable, and we have undergone severe losses at a juncture when such losses were more than ordinarily disastrous to our prospects. We never had, from the first starting of our work, any capital for which we had not to pay heavy interest.

Again, the foundation of this Agricultural College, undertaken in accordance with the suggestions, and at the pressing request, of many influential friends, ecclesiastical and lay, in all parts of Ireland and England, entailed an expense greater than we were able to anticipate or could afford. There is no prospect of clearing off this debt from the revenue of so small a College, after provi or an efficient staff, which must be as large [illegible] ten—the actual number of Students—as for tw

Fig 1: St Benedict's Agricultural College fundraising circular

English monks to agree how much of the monastic office they would sing and at what hours. There was a strong desire to adopt a thoroughly reformed style of monastic life, including the singing of the night office, however it was difficult to establish it with any degree of continuity, owing to limited numbers and changing personnel.

The appetite of the English province for taking on new projects continued undimmed, with the opening of a mission in Hong Kong and the extension of the monastic school at Ramsgate. To compound the problems of the province, fifteen of the sixteen novices in the provincial novitiate left, many to join other Benedictine communities in England. A canonical visitation of the various communities of the English province found the community members somewhat confused and leaderless. The reliance of the Roman authorities on the Fr Adalbert's judgement to guide them was, perhaps, ill-judged, considering the increasing agitation of his Irish creditors. Fr Adalbert's optimism remained undimmed, although Casaretto's successor, Abbot Testa was less than impressed by his sunny and somewhat groundless optimism. Testa sought to impress on him that the grave predicament of the Irish foundation placed the whole English province at risk of financial ruin. O'Sullivan, in addition to his initial purchase in 1867, had added another adjoining farm in 1873. On foot of these two purchases, Fr Adalbert already had difficulty meeting the repayments on his loans. Undaunted, however, he purchased a third estate in 1874.

The purpose of this foundation was approved by Cardinal Cullen, who had authorised Fr Adalbert to found an agricultural college for the sons of gentlemen studying at the Catholic University of Dublin. The idea was that these young gentlemen would attend lectures in Dublin in the morning and spend their afternoons in the country studying farming under Fr Adalbert.

In 1875, Fr John Stutter and Fr Dunstan Sweeney were sent to Leopardstown to assist Fr Adalbert with the establishment of the agricultural college. Neither the students nor the expertise that Fr Adalbert intended to impart to them ever appeared and, despite desperate efforts to raise funds (Fig 1), it became clear that the 1,300 acres that he had amassed in Leopardstown and Foxrock would have to be sold. It is telling that this foundation was characterised by its work rather than by the desire for a monastic style of life.

Fr Adalbert, to his credit, travelled to England and Rome with a confidence that belied the fraught situation of his foundation. Indeed his diary for the time lists his social engagements at length, without referring in any detail to his financial situation. Fr Adalbert left Dublin for the New Zealand mission run by Ramsgate in 1879 and returned to England in 1892, to work in the parish of Cheam in London. He retired to the monastery at Ramsgate in 1925, were he died in 1930 at the age of ninety-eight, bearing the title of oldest Benedictine in the world. Fr Oswald Monti was left the unenviable task of looking after the property and of arranging to pay off its debts.

French primitive observance in Dublin

The next chapter of the Benedictine presence in Leopardstown began when Marshall McMahon retired as president of the French republic in 1879. He was replaced by Jules Grévy. Grévy appointed Jules Ferry as his prime minister and Ferry, in March 1879, ordered the dissolution of the Jesuits and the prohibition of any form of participation by religious in education. He insisted that all religious congregations petition for recognition by the civil authorities. Leo XIII requested that this not be done and so on 29 March 1880, Ferry ordered the expulsion of all unauthorised religious congregations, among them the Jesuits, Dominicans, Franciscans and Benedictines.[5] The eviction of the monks from La Pierre qui Vire in the Morvan was particularly dramatic: on 5 November 1880, the monks barricaded themselves in their cells and the police battered down the doors of the monastery and of the monks' cells with sledgehammers, before taking them into custody. In the Abbey of Solesmes in the Sarthe the police arrived during the singing of vespers and dragged the monks individually from choir as they were singing the Magnificat. The prior of La Pierre qui Vire, Dom Etienne Denis, had written to the Abbot General in early August declaring his intention to move the novitiate to England in the case of dissolution. He visited Ramsgate to seek

5. Denis Huerre, 'Quand la République expulsait les moines... (1901-1920)' in *Collecteana Cisterciensia*, 63 (2001), p 82.

advice concerning a suitable property for the community in exile and the Leopardstown foundation was placed at his disposition. However, since the property was so heavily mortgaged, a question mark already hung over it as a viable option in the long term. The first group of monks arrived at Leopardstown on 28 October 1880, led by Fr Thomas Dupéroux, who was the novice master, Br Athanase Avignon, his assistant, and three novices. Also attached to this group was Fr Adam Hamilton, a monk of Ramsgate who was to help them get established. Fr Adam eventually joined the French community definitively, due to his appreciation of their particularly austere style of life.[6] A second group of six novices and a priest arrived on December 1880, and a third group of five arrived on 29 December.

This group of nineteen re-established conventual life and quickly recommenced the celebration of the full monastic office, including the midnight office. The midnight office and the interrupted sleep it entailed was a badge of honour for the French monks, though their English counterparts had difficulty accepting it with the same enthusiasm. The community lived a frugal existence, as they had neither a regular source of income, nor any work as such. The annalist of the community records little of its internal life, other than the reception of novices and monastic professions, accompanied by lengthy wistful remarks on the poverty of their sacristy and the disagreeable sound of the bells which the monks gave up using, as their peal was so intolerably flat.[7]

The first professions for this community took place in January, which is a remarkable testament to the courage of these exiles, who can have had little idea of what shape their monastic lives would take. In May, Cardinal MacCabe, Archbishop of Dublin, presided at the simple professions of five of the brethren. In all, seventeen monks made their simple profession at Leopardstown, with a further nine receiving the habit. The life of this youthful community was marked by a constant stream of arrivals and departures, as many of the monks were sent on to the Sacred Heart monastery in Oklahoma,[8] where La Pierre qui Vire had made a foundation in 1875. The superior of Leopardstown, Fr Dupéroux, was elected abbot of this American

6. For a manifesto of his position see Adam Hamilton, *A history of St Mary's Abbey of Buckfast 760-1906*, (Devon, 1906).
7. P. Gabriel, 'Annals of Leopardstown and of Buckfast 1880-1884'. Another valuable source of information is the unpublished typescript of Denis Huerre, *Enquêtes sur la Pierre qui Vire*, 1974.
8. For the history of St Gregory's Abbey see Joseph Murphy, *Tenacious monks: the Oklahoma Benedictines, 1875-1975*, (Shawnee, 1974).

community in the late 1880s. Throughout 1881 it became clear that, even if the French monks had wished to stay in Dublin, the administrative tribunal charged with the discharge of the debts of the property was determined to sell it. As the community had failed to find any donors willing to relieve their burden of debt they began to search for suitable alternative accommodation.

In October 1882 they bought the ancient monastic site of Buckfast Abbey, near Plymouth. The community of thirty monks left Leopardstown in stages between October 1882 and January 1883. They were warmly welcomed in the area by Bishop William Vaughan, who involved himself in establishing the new monastery on a firm financial footing.[9] The community that arrived in England was more classically contemplative in character, as many of the more missionary minded monks had been sent on to the Indian mission at Sacred Heart, Oklahoma.[10] This process of natural selection was to have important consequences when the time came to revive the monastery at La Pierre qui Vire, as they never renewed the more active pastoral engagements that had been part of their founder's initial desire for the community. Similarly, the character of the monastic observance at Buckfast was informed by the observant monasticism of their French founders. The foundation in Leopardstown seems never to have been considered as either a permanent home for the French monks or as a possible daughter house. It was in essence little more than a nursery for the exiled community of La Pierre qui Vire. To begin with the house at Buckfast was similarly conceived, however due to the international nature of the recruitment there (German, French, English and Irish) and the sheer numbers of junior monks, it soon became independent. Most importantly, the community found in Lord Clifford, a benefactor willing to endow the monastery with sufficient funds to enable them to begin the extensive reconstruction of the medieval Cistercian abbey on the site, starting in 1884. In 1899 it became a canonically separate community and in 1902 they elected their first abbot, Boniface Natter, who, though a native of Germany, had entered La Pierre qui Vire and had finished his novitiate in Dublin. He was succeeded by the celebrated liturgist and writer, Abbot Anscar Vonier.

After the departure of the troublesome monks with their vexing problems of observance and suitable work, the property at Leopardstown settled down

---

9. John Stephan, *Buckfast Abbey: A new history of the abbey from AD 1018-1968*, (Bristol, 1968).

10. For a fuller treatment of the conflict between missionary monasticism and the more strictly contemplative ideal in the United States see Joel Rippinger, *The Benedictine Order in the United States, an interpretative history* (Collegeville, 1990).

to a more prosperous existence as a racecourse. None of the buildings occupied by the monks survive and the racegoers hardly have much in common with their monastic predecessors. One hopes that they bear their financial losses with the cheerful insouciance of Fr Adalbert O'Sullivan. The abbeys of La Pierre qui Vire and Buckfast continue to exist, as does St Gregory's Shawnee, Oklahoma, the successor monastery to Sacred Heart. The questions of observance which so excited the English and French monks at Leopardstown are less urgent today, but the questions of financial autonomy and meaningful work remain as pressing as ever. If nothing else, this brief Irish monastic experiment provides an example of resilient courage in launching into the deep and uncharted waters of an uncertain monastic future. The annalist may have been guilty of boring posterity with his exacting remarks on the sacristy, but his emphasis on the monastic receptions and professions tells the essential truth of this community's collective dedication to the monastic way as the form chosen to structure their search for God.[11]

Loftus Hall
The convent of Benedictine nuns at Loftus Hall represents a slightly different case.[12] This convent was founded from the famous Parisian convent of St Louis du Temple, at the Rue Monsieur. This convent had been founded after the French Revolution by Princess Louise de Condé. She had been in Russia with the celebrated Dom de Lestrange and his Cistercian colleagues, who were fleeing the Revolution. She entered and made profession in Warsaw, in the convent of the Benedictines of the Blessed Sacrament. Forced to flee by the Napoleonic invasion of Poland, she returned to France in 1814. With the approval of the newly restored Louis XVIII, she established her convent in the former Templar convent, where the French royal family had been imprisoned during the Revolution. The nuns had been forced to leave with the fall of the monarchy of Louis Philippe in 1848 and they moved to the Rue Monsieur. The community was closely linked to various monarchist groups. However, this was to change as the chance of a monarchist restoration became increasingly remote.

This convent enjoyed great prestige in France and is referred to in the writings of Paul Claudel, Jacques Maritain, Julien Green and many other

11. I am grateful to my confrère Fr Mark Tierney who generously placed his extensive dossier of material relating to the Leopardstown community at my disposal.
12. On Loftus Hall see Thomas P. Walsh, 'The history of Loftus Hall' in *Journal of the Old Wexford Society*, 4 (1972-3) pp 3-12; 5 (1974-5) pp 32-38; Billy Colfer, *The Hook peninsula* (Cork, 2004) pp 176-79.

leading figures in Catholic literary and philosophical circles in early twentieth-century Paris. Much of this fame rested on the beauty of the chant and on the personal friendships forged by several of the nuns with leading French intellectuals of the day. Notwithstanding this, the community was in a delicate position since the introduction of a fresh raft of anti-clerical laws in 1904 by Emile Combes. Combes was a former clerical student who, as prime-minister, was determined to break the power of the church. His attack came about in the context of the failure of the *ralliement* to the Republic encouraged by Leo XIII (1878-1903). Leo XIII was succeeded by Pius X, who resolutely turned his back on the accommodation with the new political and intellectual climate in Europe. Pius X provoked the modernist crisis which hit French Catholic intellectuals, particularly with the condemnation of Alfred Loisy, a professor at the Institut Catholique in Paris. The nuns were not formally expelled from France. However their legal position was tenuous. Their position was doubly complicated, caught as they were between the fraught intellectual climate within the church and the overt hostility of the government.

Before the First World War, Abbot Columba Marmion had preached a retreat to the community, and the nuns of the Rue Monsieur were aware of his efforts to establish a community in exile from the Belgian Abbey of Maredsous. In view of the prevailing political climate, one of the nuns, Mother Marie Joseph, who had been the Marquise de Bizien du Lézard

Fig 3: Mother
Marie Joseph:
Marquise de
Bizien du Lézard

before she became a nun, proposed that the convent should establish an independent base outside of France. De Bizien had inherited a large fortune, as she was the only child of a wealthy family. She received permission from Cardinal Billot to dispose of her inheritance for the purposes of the establishment of Benedictine monasteries for men and women in Ireland. De Bizien purchased the property of Edermine in Co Wexford for Marmion and she proposed that the Belgian monks should help in the foundation of the convent of Parisian nuns, as a possible refuge in the event of their expulsion from France.[13] Marmion, in fact, had to go to Brittany in 1915 to collect several hundred thousand francs in cash and he carried it through customs, as it was not possible to get this money to Ireland due to the disruption caused by the war. Wexford seems to have been a magnet for homeless Benedictines, as can be seen in Kathleen Villiers-Tuthill's account of the Irish Dames of Ypres and Aidan Bellenger's account of Mount St Benedict's in Gorey. Despite their diverse origins, each of these Wexford Benedictine houses was full of strong characters, who were armed with the tenacity to weather the difficult climate in the diocese of Ferns and in Ireland at the time.

De Bizien came to Ireland accompanied by an Irish member of the monastery at the Rue Monsieur, Mother Augustine Savage. Mother Savage had been born in Belfast and had entered the Parisian con-vent, but had always cherished the hope of returning to Ireland. To this end, she had left Paris and was living with the Benedictine nuns at St Mary's Abbey, Colwich in Staffordshire, England.[14] These nuns, when they came to Ireland in 1914, lived in the gate lodge attached to the

Fig 4: Mother Augustine Savage

monastery at Edermine for some months. They eventually managed to pur-chase the impressive property of Loftus Hall near Hook Head, also in Co Wexford, in 1916. They called the new monastery St Mary's Priory. The situ-ation in Ireland grew progressively more uncertain, due to the difficulties of communicating with continental Europe and this was further aggravated by the 1916 Rising. Marmion was unable to offer this community much assis-tance, as his own foundation at Edermine quickly ran into significant diffi-culties of its own. The fact that de Bizien had purchased Edermine was to play a significant part in the crisis that eventually led to the closure of Edermine, as it was done without the permission of the abbot's council at Maredsous and contravened canon law. Marmion was forced to allow a canonical visitation by Abbot Cabrol of Farnborough in England in an attempt to resolve this complex situation. Cabrol recommended the closure of the new foundation in 1918 and this was duly done in 1919. De Bizien her-self had acted without the approval of the chapter of her own community in Paris and this taint of canonical invalidity hung like a pall over the new foun-dation. The monastery had been founded in similar circumstances to the Leopardstown foundation in as much as it was in anticipation of difficulty

13. For the foundation at Edermine see Mark Tierney, *Dom Columba Marmion* (Dublin, 1994) pp 159-87.
14. I am grateful to Sr Benedict Rowell OSB, archivist of St Mary's Abbey, Colwich for assist-ance in researching this brief interlude in her community's history.

with the French government. However the ambitious foresight of Mother de Bizien did not correspond to the needs of her Parisian monastery. This divergence became even more explicit with the reconciliation of the French government and the Catholic Church in the 1920s when they exchanged diplomatic accreditation. Mother de Bizien was left to construct her new monastery without the support of the Parisian mother house.

The nuns of Loftus Hall also had difficulty establishing themselves in the public mind, as the Irish Dames of Ypres had a much higher profile in Ireland. The Dames' plight excited wide public sympathy. John Redmond, the leader of the Irish Parliamentary Party, whose niece was a member of the community, involved himself in a public appeal for funds for them. Notwithstanding their eclipse, relations between the two communities of nuns would appear to have been good. The nuns of Loftus Hall made no objection to the application of some of the revenues from the liquidation of Edermine to fund the purchase of Kylemore by the Dames of Ypres. However, despite their lower public profile, they succeeded in attracting several recruits, and by 1919 they had fourteen young postulants.

Mother de Bizien and Mother Savage, however well intentioned, did not possess the requisite skills and grounding in the Benedictine tradition to foster the element of stability necessary for the survival of this young community. They wisely sought the help of the English Benedictine nuns of Colwich, who sent three nuns to help the struggling foundation. When Mother de Bizien made clear that she would be sole superior of these nuns and decide all matters of observance in their regard, irreconcilable differences arose and the Colwich nuns withdrew, albeit on amicable terms.

Aid was similarly sought from the Benedictine nuns of Dumfries in Scotland (formerly of Arras in France). These nuns were from a tradition that placed great value on Perpetual Adoration of the Blessed Sacrament. This tradition had been strong among contemplative women since the seventeenth century, and Mothers de Bizien and Savage sought to place Eucharistic Adoration at the centre of the work of the new foundation. Again disputes arose over observance and the exercise of authority. These forced the Dumfries nuns to reconsider their position in taking part in the Wexford foundation. The Scottish nuns thought they had come upon a potentially fruitful supply of postulants for their ailing foundation. Mother de Bizien on the other hand thought that she had found a handy supply of a few nuns to tide her over during a temporary difficulty. Throughout this period Mothers de Bizien and Savage seemed to have had little difficulty in identifying what they did not want for their community. However the formulation of more positive statements of the community's purpose and style of life eluded them.

In addition, dissensions within the community also caused considerable difficulties: the lengthy process of exclaustration of one sister proving particularly divisive. Sr Mary Conway had been received as a lay sister in 1919, but when her sister was received as a choir nun she sought to change her canonical status. The refusal of this request led to considerable acrimony. In 1944 Sr Mary was still writing to Bishop Codd of Ferns attempting to regularise her situation from Dublin, where, though she was living in a hotel, she still wore the monastic habit and considered herself a nun. She eventually became a Presentation sister.

In 1937, the community reluctantly decided to disperse and the remaining nuns were scattered among various convents in England and France. Loftus Hall was occupied by Rosminian Sisters who came from Loughborough in England.[15] De Bizien herself, with some of her closer disciples, joined the congregation of St Bathilde, recently founded in the Paris suburb of Vanves. This congregation had been founded by Mother Bénédicte Waddington Delmas.[16] This institute was one of a number of Benedictine missionary congregations for women founded in the 1920s across Europe, such as the St Lioba congregation in Germany and the Bethany Benedictines and the nuns of Ermeton sur Biert in Belgium. The connection with Loftus Hall lived on in France, in the person of Sister Philomena White, who had entered in Ireland, and continued her monastic life in St Thierry, near Rhiems, until her death in 2004.

Conclusions

The recital of the events surrounding the two foundations examined in this essay reveal more than just the eccentricities of the people involved. The Benedictine monasteries of Europe in the nineteenth century had forged an identity in the context of a profound change in civic culture. The founders of these monasteries were only moderately successful in achieving the goals that they set themselves. They were subject to the influence of the situations in which they lived and the people who felt drawn to live in their monasteries. Likewise, colourful figures like Adalbert O'Sullivan, Thomas Dupéroux and Marie Joseph de Bizien sought to implant in Ireland those forms of European monasticism that they found so life-giving. Despite their great optimism and

---

15. I am grateful to Fr Séamus de Vál of Bunclody, Co Wexford, diocesan archivist of the diocese of Ferns, for his invaluable assistance in providing informed and convivial access to the extensive files relating to the Loftus Hall foundation in the diocesan archives.
16. Yvonne de Pourtalès, *Histoire d'une vocation: Marguérite Waddington-Delmas* (Paris, 2000).

BENEDICTINE
FOUNDATIONS
& Places of Refuge
in Modern Ireland

+ Monks
⁘ Nuns
Place of Refuge

Rostrevor

+Kylemore Abbey

Leopardstown+

Mount St Benedict+

+Glenstal Abbey
Macmine Castle⁘

+Edermine House

Merton

Loftus Hall

Cobh Priory

competence, in objective terms, they failed. It is nonetheless interesting to see so many of the prinicipal currents of European Benedictine monasticism attempting to find an Irish expression.

No institution has a right to survive or succeed. The great monasteries of St Columban in Luxeuil and Bobbio had been swept away by the French Revolution. Similarly in Switzerland, St Gall, one of the greatest of Irish monastic foundations, on completion of a massive building programme, was closed down by the local government in 1798, having been a centre of monastic life and learning for 1,200 years. From the Leopardstown foundation, monks who made profession there brought monastic life to Oklahoma and Buckfast in England and back to La Pierre qui Vire. From Loftus Hall, nuns contributed to the life of the new congregation of St Bathilde and of Colwich Abbey in England. If these individual monasteries foundered then they contributed to the endurance of the style of life they were set up to promote. Monasticism is less about the promotion of Benedictinism than it is about the living of the Christian life. It is the life of the monastic and not of the monastery that matters. In this sense, when one considers the monks and nuns who lived their early monastic lives in Ireland, it is the fidelity to their vocation that impresses. In a very real sense, they formed a modern expression of the ancient Irish tradition of *peregrinatio pro Christo* – the holy wandering of those earlier monks and nuns who left their homeland to sing the song of the Lord on alien soil.

CHAPTER TEN

Glenstal Abbey 1930-2004

Mark Tierney OSB

Fig 1: Glenstal Abbey

On 1 October 1928, the monks opened a small school for arts and crafts at Glenstal. Boys from the surrounding district came each day on bicycle or on foot, but it was hoped eventually to provide boarding facilities for them. Fathers Winoc and Mayeul, along with a young Belgian, Henri Mouton, taught in the school.

The next important event in the history of Glenstal was the building of the first chapel. The decision to build came during the visitation of the monastery in May 1930. Thanks to the generosity of one of Fr Gerard François's Belgian friends, it was possible to purchase several of the huts in which the workmen were lodged during the construction of the hydroelectric generating station at Ardnacrusha, County Clare. These were used in the new building and the first stone of the chapel was blessed by Fr Gerard on the Feast of the Sacred Heart, 27 June 1930.

Fig 2: Fr Winoc
Mertens and
Fr Finbar O'Mahoney
(back row) with
students of the
Glenstal Arts School

In order to raise money to complete the work on the chapel, it was decided
to hold a bazaar in the grounds of Glenstal on 28 and 29 June 1931. Most of
the work connected with the bazaar was done by Fr David Maffei, the subprior, who organised local committees. The amount of money collected during the two days of the bazaar exceeded all expectations, coming to over
£2,000. This was sufficient to defray the cost of completing the new chapel,
and also to help in extending the accommodation for the school of arts and
crafts. The school had been growing all the time, mainly thanks to the interest shown in it by the Limerick County Council, who offered ten scholarships for the academic year beginning September 1931. Several of those boys
who won scholarships were unable to take them up, because of travel difficulties or lack of boarding facilities in Glenstal.

The year 1932 saw three important events in the history of the monastery.
First of all there was the ceremony of the blessing of the new chapel on
Wednesday 13 April. Archbishop Harty performed the ceremony, which was
followed by Mass, sung by Fr Gerard François. The preacher was Fr M. J.
Lee. He said that the opening of the chapel marked the end of the pioneering days for the Glenstal monks. They had now sunk roots and the chapel
was an abiding testimony that the Order of Saint Benedict had come to stay.

The second event was the opening of the secondary school in September
1932. Earlier in the year Fr Columba Skerret, who had come to Glenstal from
Maredsous in 1931, was appointed rector, or headmaster, of the new school.
Fr Columba was an Irishman, although he had lived most of his life in
England and on the Continent. The school started with seven boys. The first

lay master was Mr Vincent Quirke, a native of Wexford, who remained on the staff in Glenstal until his retirement some thirty years later.

The third event was the reception into the novitiate of the first Irish choir-novice, Brother Bernard O'Dea. The ceremony took place on Michaelmas day in the new chapel. Brother Bernard did his novitiate in Glenstal, but had to go to Belgium for his studies. The question of recruitment for the Irish Benedictine monastery had always been a difficult one, since the monks did not have any great contact with people outside their immediate neighbourhood. In 1933, Fr David Maffei undertook to lecture in secondary schools all over Ireland and to seek out any possible vocations. A small booklet was produced, explaining the Benedictine way of life, and slowly but surely more young men came to offer themselves to God and St Benedict in the Glenstal community.

At the beginning of March 1934, Miss Mary Martin came to Glenstal as matron to the boys of the boarding-school. She brought with her a number of other young women, who formed the nucleus of the future Medical Missionaries of Mary. She was to remain in Glenstal for two-and-a-half years. She received great help and spiritual advice from the second prior of Glenstal, Dom Bede Lebbe, who succeeded Dom Gerard as prior in July 1934. Fr Bede was also appointed headmaster of the secondary school, as Fr Columba Skerret's health was not very good. In fact, Fr Columba had developed cancer and died in Belgium on 3 November 1936.

Fr Bede remained as prior and headmaster, but soon found that it was impossible to combine the two jobs, especially as the monastery was growing and there were many administrative duties and problems. In May 1937, Fr Matthew Dillon was appointed headmaster. He had joined the Glenstal community two years previously, and was already ordained priest, having worked for some time in the Southwark diocese in England. Fr Matthew may be considered the real father of the school. When he took over there were less than twenty boys, but he built it up to over a hundred within the next ten years. He undertook various building programmes and proved himself a most dynamic and successful teacher and headmaster.

In the meantime the monks were moving into new quarters in what were formerly the stables and out-houses of the castle. The work of reconstruction was undertaken by Fr Daniel Duesberg, a monk of Maredsous, who arrived in Glenstal on 6 August 1937. He was a man of great energy and excellent artistic taste, and successfully built the new monastic quarters, a new guesthouse and a sawmill. At the same time he was director of the school of arts and crafts, and under his guidance the pupils reached a high degree of excellence.

Fr David Maffei, who had been one of the six founding fathers of Glenstal, was recalled on 14 August 1937, to take up a post in his monastery at Mont César in Belgium. On October 1937 Dom Idesbald Ryelandt, a former prior of Maredsous, came to Glenstal and was immediately appointed subprior in place of Fr David. Although it was intended that Fr Idesbald should remain a short time in Ireland, he stayed on for more than eight years, and was appointed prior of Glenstal in October 1938, in succession to Fr Bede Lebbe. Fr Idesbald, who spoke no English, asked that Fr Bernard O'Dea, who had only just been ordained, should be made his subprior.

During these early years, Fr Winoc Mertens was perhaps the best-known of the Glenstal monks. Possessing a beautiful voice, ideal for church singing, he used his talents to great effect. He was in constant demand to train choirs in the proper performance of plainchant, while he acted as one of the judges at many local and national competitions and *feiseanna*.

On 19 May 1939 Mgr James J. Ryan died at his residence, The Hermitage, near Thurles. It is no secret that his relationships with the monks of Glenstal cooled as the years went by. Perhaps be became disillusioned when the community did not attract as many young Irishmen as he expected.

The war years (1939-45) brought considerable hardship and loneliness for the Belgian monks in Glenstal. For the most part they were cut off from their relatives and friends. As was customary in Belgium, priests were called upon to act as chaplains in time of war, and Fr Daniel Duesberg, who had spent hardly two years in Glenstal, left Glenstal in December 1939 to serve as chaplain in the Belgian army. He later served in the Maquis, the Belgian Underground movement, but was captured and died in a German concentration camp in November 1944. Another member of the Glenstal community, Fr Athanasius, was called to serve as chaplain to the Belgian forces in exile in London during the latter part of the war.

Quite a number of building programmes were undertaken during the war. A complete new storey was added to the main square keep of the castle. This gave much needed accommodation for the boarding-school. In the monastery area, a large new wing was erected and helped to complete the monastic quadrangle, thus providing the much desired 'enclosure' and privacy for the monks.

Perhaps one of the happiest days in the annals of Glenstal and one which must have put great hope into the hearts of the pioneering monks, was the ordination to the priesthood in the monastery chapel of four Irish monks on the one day. On Sunday 18 July 1943, Dr Kinnane, the co-adjutor archbishop of Cashel ordained Fathers Finbar O'Mahoney, Malachy Maguire, Peter Gilfedder and Oliver Quirke.

When the war in Europe ended in May 1945, the abbot of Maredsous decided to recall Fr Idesbald Ryelandt to Belgium. The monks of Glenstal in the meantime awaited the decision of the abbot of Maredsous regarding their new prior. Abbot Celestine Golenvaux spent a month in Glenstal in October 1945, and decided that the time had come to appoint an Irish monk to lead the Glenstal community. The official appointment of Fr Bernard O'Dea as the new prior of Glenstal was made on 8 December 1945. Two years later, on 6 February 1948, Glenstal was made an independent or conventual priory, and Fr Bernard thus became the first independent superior of the Irish Benedictine community. Up to this, Glenstal had been a simple priory, and the abbot of Maredsous was its real superior. It was a great step forward, and one which would allow the monks in Glenstal to make their own decisions and plan their own future.

One of the first decisions made by the independent Glenstal chapter was in connection with the opening of a university hostel in Dublin. At the request of many parents of past pupils of the school, as well as the university authorities and the archbishop of Dublin, Glenstal opened a hostel in Palmerston Park, Dublin on 9 October 1948. Father Matthew Dillon, who had been Headmaster of the school since 1936, was in charge of the hostel. Almost at once, Balnagowan, as the Dublin house was called, flourished and, by 1962, had forty-six students.

Another major decision made under the priorship of Fr Bernard was to build a monastic church. The chapel, which had been in use since 1932, was found quite inadequate for the increasing number of monks – now almost thirty – not to speak of the growing number of people who came to Mass on Sundays and feastdays. The architect was Dom Sebastian Braun, a monk of Maredsous. Before embarking on such a large undertaking, the question of money had to be faced. Fr Gregory Barry was put in charge of the fundraising campaign. He and Fr Bernard made a successful six-month tour of the USA during February-September 1951. Fr Bernard, from Inagh, Co Clare, got very considerable help from the Clare exiles in America.

During the absence of Frs Bernard and Gregory, the first sod of the foundation of the church was turned in Glenstal on 28 May 1951, the ceremony being performed by Fr Athanasius, the subprior. Fr Bernard was back in Glenstal in time for the solemn ceremony of laying the foundation-stone of the new church. This was on Sunday 14 October 1951, in the presence of a large gathering of people. President Seán T Ó Ceallaigh attended and the ceremony was performed by Dr Kinnane, the archbishop of Cashel.

On 1 August 1952, Fr Bernard O'Dea, who had been in office for seven years, resigned as prior for health reasons. He had been a very popular prior, both at home and abroad, and had done much to bring Glenstal within the radius of an ever-widening circle of friends and well-wishers. Glenstal may be said to have come out of its shell during his term of office as prior.

The community held their first election for a new superior on 6 August. Their choice fell on Fr Placid Murray, who held the office of prior until 1957, when Glenstal was raised to the status of an abbey. It was during Fr Placid's priorship that the first Glenstal Liturgical Congress was held on 6-7 April 1954. Over seventy priests from all over Ireland attended, and it was considered such a success that similar Liturgical Congresses were held annually in Glenstal for the next twenty years.

One of the last public acts performed during the priorship of Fr Placid was the opening and blessing of the new church in Glenstal. The ceremony was performed on Sunday 24 June 1956 with Dr Kinnane, the archbishop of Cashel, as the officiating prelate.

It was evident to most people that with the completion of the monastic church, and the increase in numbers, Glenstal might soon be raised to the status of an abbey. The final decision on this matter had to be made by the abbots of the Belgian Congregation to which Glenstal was affiliated. The matter had also to be ratified and approved of by the Sacred Congregation for Religious, in Rome. All these preliminaries took place early in 1957. The Apostolic Brief of Pope Pius XII, *Insula Sanctorum*, dated Rome, 10 January

Fig 4: Glenstal Abbey
church

1957, was the official document by which Glenstal was made an Abbey. On 11 April 1957 the monastic chapter of Glenstal met and elected the first abbot, Dom Joseph Dowdall.

Abbot Joseph Dowdall was blessed in the new abbey church on 29 June 1957. The ceremony was performed by Dr Kyne, Bishop of Meath, in whose diocese Abbot Joseph was born. Dr Kinnane, the Archbishop of Cashel, was unable to officiate, owing to illness. Among those who came to Glenstal for the occasion were the President, Mr Seán T Ó Ceallaigh and the Taoiseach, Mr Éamon de Valera.

Glenstal was by now a flourishing and buoyant community, numbering more than forty monks. Some of the monks were already making a name for themselves in different fields of work. Brother Benedict Tutty, a specialist in silver and metal work, had designed and executed much of the copper and other ornaments for the new church. Brother Benedict went on to produce much fine artwork for churches and public buildings throughout the country and beyond.

In September 1966, Abbot Joseph left Glenstal for Rome to attend a congress of Benedictine abbots. While in Rome he became seriously ill and his condition was so weak that he was unable to face surgery. He died in the hospital of San Stefano, in Rome, on 11 October 1966. He was only thirty-nine years of age, and had been abbot of Glenstal for just over nine years.

Father Augustine O'Sullivan, a native of Limerick city, who had served as prior and novice-master in Glenstal under Abbot Joseph, was elected the second abbot of Glenstal on 18 December 1966. His abbatial blessing took place on Sunday 5 March 1967. A very large congregation attended the ceremony, which was performed by Archbishop Thomas Morris. Abbot Augustine continued the work begun by his predecessor. The annual ecumenical conference, begun in 1964, drew greater numbers each year, and fulfilled a useful function in the life of the Irish churches. The twenty-first liturgical congress

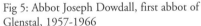

Fig 5: Abbot Joseph Dowdall, first abbot of   Fig 6: Abbot Augustine O'Sullivan, second
Glenstal, 1957-1966   abbot of Glenstal 1966-1980

was held in Glenstal in 1975, and it was felt that, while such meetings were
interesting to some of the Catholic clergy, they could perhaps now be dispensed
with. The monks of Glenstal were able to serve the Irish liturgical movement
in other ways. Two of the monks were involved in bringing out the English
translation of the Divine Office. The work lasted from 1971-74. Fr Placid
Murray was chairman of the working committee, while Fr Gerard MacGinty
acted as one of the team of editors preparing the volumes for publication.

Abbot Augustine resigned in 1980, after holding office for 14 years, and
was succeeded by Fr Celestine Cullen, who received the abbatial blessing on
Sunday 1 February 1981, at the hands of Dr Thomas Morris.

Abbot Celestine soon showed that his main concern was to guarantee a
proper celebration of the monastic liturgy, and especially of the daily community Mass, which he transferred from an early morning hour to a midday
concelebration. Abbot Celestine encouraged and inspired several building
programmes over the next ten years, including a new school sports hall and
a new residential wing in the monastery. One section of the new building was
set aside as a home for the homeless, the 'Men of the Road', who find food
and shelter there.

Fig 7 Icon Chapel

In April 1988, work on the Icon Chapel, situated in the crypt of the Abbey Church, was completed. This beautiful Russo-Byzantine Chapel was designed by Jeremy Williams (architect) and James Scanlon (artist). It contains some noteworthy stained glass, with a concrete fresco floor, but its main attraction is the monastery collection of Russian and Greek Icons, given to Glenstal in the early 1950s, by the Grattan-Esmonde family. The Icon Chapel provides an ecumenical focal point, as well as a quiet place of prayer.

Abbot Celestine Cullen was elected Abbot President of the Congregation of the Annunciation (formerly The Belgian Congregation) in September 1992 and in December 1992, he resigned as abbot of Glenstal. Thus an election was held in mid-December 1992, when Fr Christopher Dillon was chosen as fourth abbot of Glenstal. Abbot Christopher set himself a number of goals, many of which were close to his heart. As Andrew Nugent describes below, Glenstal had made a foundation in Eke, later transferring to Ewu, in Nigeria in the mid-1970s. Abbot Christopher hoped to set the Nigerian monastery on a firm footing, and with this in mind, sent a number of his younger monks to Nigeria. He obtained financial backing for an extensive water scheme in Ewu, to be installed not only in the monastery, but also in the nearby village. The work was master-minded by Fr David Conlon. This proved to be a great boon for the people of the locality.

In recent years, the community has successfully undertaken a large-scale building programme. To date, a new guesthouse and library have been completed. The Guesthouse was opened and blessed on 19 September 1999. It is situated on the north side of the church, on the edge of the woods, and provides accommodation for about twenty people. The library was blessed and opened on 22 June 2001. It is situated near the church, also on the north side. The architects of both the library and guesthouse were Richard Hurley and Associates. At present (2005), work is underway on a major refurbishment of the monastery buildings.

Today, the monks of Glenstal Abbey continue to operate the boarding school, the guest house and a dairy farm. In addition to these works, individual members of the community are involved in many different activities, including academic research and lecturing, writing, recording and other artistic endeavours, together with the many tasks associated with maintaining the house and grounds. All these occupations find their context in and are nourished by the 'Work of God' – the faithful chanting of the hours of the Divine Office and the celebration of the Eucharist.

CHAPTER ELEVEN

Irish Benedictines in Africa

Andrew Nugent OSB

Nigerian Monasticism

If, in the history of the church in Europe, the work of primary evangelisation and the process of monastic implantation often went hand in hand, the story in sub-Saharan Africa has been more one of consecutive than of concurrent developments.

The primary evangelisation of these countries has been the work of the specialised missionary congregations and societies which played such an enormous role in the universal church from the middle of the nineteenth century to the close of the second millennium. The monastic life has arrived into those young churches, more as a sign of their own consolidation and rootedness than as an expression of missionary dynamism. This is not to deny that each of these monasteries has become a major spiritual resource for the missionary personnel still active within its ambit and a focus for the ongoing work of evangelisation both in its own hinterland and further afield in this vast continent.

The scope of this essay will be to give a brief account of the beginnings of Benedictine life in Nigeria, in so far as this has been the work of Irish monks. It is necessary, however, to acknowledge from the outset that this Irish male Benedictine initiative has been only one of several which, together, are writing the first pages in what, by God's grace, will be the golden history of Nigerian monasticism.

The Irish Cistercians have played and are playing an inspired role in this new flowering of monastic life. The Cistercian Nuns of St Mary's Abbey, Glencairn, Co Waterford, founded St Justina's Monastery at Abakaliki, Ebonyi State in 1982. This foundation has gone from strength to strength and is now an independent priory. It has been generously assisted by Cistercian monks from several of the Irish monasteries. The Irish Cistercian monasteries, together with the other houses of the Cistercian Region of The Isles, notably Nunraw in Scotland, have also given wonderful support to the Cistercian monastery of monks at Nsugbe, in Anambra State.

The major role which Nigerians themselves have played in monastic foundations in their own country must also be acknowledged. Several of these monasteries are, in fact, native foundations rather than implantations from Europe or the USA. This is true of St Scholastica's Abbey, Umuoji, and of Queen of Peace Monastery, Ozubulu, both founded by Abbess Patricia Alufuo. It is also true of the Word Incarnate Abbey, which was founded by Abbess Charles Anyanwu, who is currently developing a new foundation at Idah. The same is true of Holy Cross Monastery, Illah, founded by Fr Abraham Ojefua, who also played a major part in the foundation of Mount Calvary Monastery, Awhum.

There are three other names which deserve to be recorded in the list of monastic founders in Nigeria. The first is Sr Justina Anigbo of Glencairn, who had been designated as first superior of the projected foundation at Abakaliki in her native land, when she became ill and died tragically in 1981. Her life and death were strongly inspirational in the foundation of St Justina's Priory. Sister Margaret Mary Hanron, who replaced Sr Justina and remains with the Abakaliki community to this day (2005), must also be acknowledged in a very real sense as co-foundress. The other name is of Fr Vincent Mordi, first novice and first African superior of the Benedictine monastery at Ewu-Ishan. He has been at the heart of that community from the very beginning.

Benedictine Beginnings

One non-monastic figure who deserves equally to be recorded as a monastic founder is Bishop Godfrey Okoye CSSp who, in both dioceses where he served, first at Port Harcourt and subsequently in Enugu, was a staunch sup-porter and indeed, in the literal sense, a founder of monasteries, both Cistercian and Benedictine. His first venture was at Eleme, Port Harcourt, where, with the help of American monks from New Subiaco Abbey, Arkansas, he founded St Mukasa Priory in August 1964. This was the first Benedictine monastery in Nigeria.

Fr Anselm (Abraham) Ojefua, who was to become such an important fig-ure in Nigerian monastic history, was the first novice of this new foundation. A further interesting connection is that Fr Anselm, in his days as a member of the diocesan clergy, had been Parish Priest in the parish of Irrua, where the Ewu-Ishan Benedictine monastery would one day be founded. These inter-connections between the monastic houses of Nigeria are providential and prophetic. It is in continuity with this connectedness, that the Benedictine and Cistercian Association of Nigeria (BECAN) has become one of the clos-est and most vibrant in the monastic world.

Sadly, St Mukasa Priory did not survive the tragic Civil War of 1967-1970. Situated strategically at the very eye of the storm, the monks' position became quite untenable. The remaining two monks finally left in Holy Week, 1968. Their spirit survives in Ascension High School, which the monks had continued to run for as long as they could, until it was taken over by the military and eventually turned into a refugee camp.[1]

A New Beginning: Eke

Bishop Okoye was not one to give up. During 1974, having heard that the Benedictines at Glenstal Abbey were beginning to talk about the possibility of making a foundation in South America or in Africa, he journeyed to Ireland and persuaded the Glenstal community to help him to found a Benedictine monastery in his new diocese of Enugu. On Monday, 28 October 1974, the Glenstal chapter passed the following motion: 'We accede to Bishop Okoye's request to help establish monastic life in his diocese.' It is interesting that what was envisaged at that stage was not so much a found-ation as the cultivation of a truly native growth.

Already, since June 1974, Fr Columba Breen of Glenstal and Fr Columba Cary-Elwes of Ampleforth Abbey, Yorkshire, who had been helping together to set up a diocesan seminary in Bamenda, Cameroon, and Fr Ambrose Tinsley of Glenstal, who had been prospecting for a suitable site for a monastery in East Africa, had assembled at Nsukka, a university city then part of the Enugu diocese. When, after six months, no suitable property had been found, they moved south to Eke, twelve miles from Enugu, where they occupied a large colonial-style mission house belonging to the diocese.

Abbot Augustine O'Sullivan of Glenstal visited Eke in June 1975 and finalised an agreement with the bishop. In line with the Chapter resolution of the previous October, this agreement provided that the Nigerian members of the community would form an association of the faithful or *pia unio* under the jurisdiction of the bishop. The monks of Glenstal would be, in accord-ance with their own constitutions, *monks on loan,* that is to say, a group per-mitted to live outside their home community for an apostolic purpose. Such were the humble canonical beginnings of what was to become in time a fully-fledged foundation of Glenstal Abbey.

By December 1975, Fr David Conlon (a former SMA missionary) and Br Colman Hingerty (an ex-soldier) had joined the three pioneers. During the following year, Fr David was to complete a water scheme for the monastery and to build a simple but attractive guesthouse for the increasing numbers of retreatants and prospective candidates who were arriving.

---

1. For an account of St. Mukasa Priory, see Hugh Assenmacher OSB, *A place called Subiaco: a history of the Benedictine monks in Arkansas* (Little Rock, Arkansas 1977), Chapter 43.

Eke was a friendly place. The local Igbo people were mostly Catholic and very well disposed towards the monastery. But there were difficulties. The land assigned to the monastery was, in African farming terms, extensive, 180 acres, but very sandy and largely infertile. The brethren were also fearful that a proposed major motorway to be built nearby would lead to noise levels incompatible with monastic living.

Bishop Okoye died on St Patrick's Day 1977, seven years to the day since he had become Bishop of Enugu. Within months there was a dispute about the monastery lands. The monks' security of tenure seemed much less assured, especially when important title documents disappeared mysteriously from the relevant archive. This was a further reason to envisage a move to another site. Another argument in favour of such a move was that the other five monasteries in Nigeria, whether of men or of women, were all within the boundaries of Igboland. In a vast country with a population already in excess of 100 million, it did seem desirable to reach out to other areas as well and to enrich the monastic life of the country by attracting vocations from more than one region.

On 16 January 1978 the foundation group decided unanimously that it was desirable to leave Eke and to move elsewhere.

Prospecting
The search for a new site concentrated on three areas, the diocese of Kaduna in the largely Muslim North, the diocese of Issele-Uku, just across the Niger River and still culturally within Igboland, and Benin City diocese, a sort of compromise middle ground between those first two possibilities and a meeting point for many different faiths and cultures. Fr Columba Breen, Fr Columba Cary-Elwes and, especially, Fr David travelled extensively, meeting bishops, kings and chiefs, and the ordinary people of each locality, assessing the advantages and disadvantages of the many proposed sites.

Fr Dick Wall, Regional Superior of the SMA Fathers, and a man with unrivalled knowledge of the area, strongly recommended Ewu-Ishan as the best site within the Benin City diocese for the new monastery. His advice and influence were crucial. Fr Wall has always, and very justly, been regarded as one of the major founders of St Benedict's Priory, Ewu-Ishan. On 20 January 1978, Fr Wall and Fr David were received at the palace of the Onogie (King) of Ewu. There were twelve Muslim and four Christian chiefs forming the council, and these very graciously agreed to grant the community –*gratis* – a site of forty acres in Muslim farmland on the old Agbede farm road, which is, in fact, the historic road from the ancient kingdom of Benin to the North

Fig 1: St Benedict's
Priory, Ewu-Ishan,
construction work on
the new monastery.

and to Mecca. The Onogie sent four Chiefs to show the visitors the approx-
imate site and the stream where the community would source their water.

Two days later, on Sunday 22 January, for the first time, a Benedictine celebrated Mass at Ewu. Fr David heard confessions for two hours and two hundred people received communion. The local Christians were overjoyed to
hear that the monks might well be coming to stay.

Four days later, on 26 January, Fr David met with Bishop Ekpu at Benin
and agreed on the terms of a five year contract to found monastic life at Ewu.
The terms were the same as those previously agreed with Bishop Okoye at
Enugu, with the additional undertaking that the diocese would, during an
initial period, make up any shortfall between current income and expendi-
ture. The bishop also put his own house at Uromi at Fr David's disposal to
use as a temporary residence, from where he could supervise the building of
the monastery.

Abbot Augustine O'Sullivan came to Nigeria in April 1978. He had very
cordial meetings with the new Bishop of Enugu, Dr Eneja, Bishop Ekpu of
Benin City, and the Onogie of Ewu, Igiefo II. On 13 April, he visited the site
of the monastery for the first time, where he was to spend the last two
decades of his own life and where he now lies buried.

On 18 August, the formal signing of the documents handing over the land
for the new monastery took place at the Onogie's palace. The signatories
were, on the one hand, His Highness the Onogie of Ewu and the Odionwele
(Chief) of each of the principal villages making up Ewu, and, on the other
hand, Bishop Ekpu of Benin City. Clearing of the site began on 6 October,
and the contract for building was finalised at Benin on 26 October. This was
to comprise two community blocks with five rooms and a common bath-

room in each, a novitiate block, and a library, which, subdivided, would serve as temporary chapel and refectory. The total cost was to be Naira 72,000, the equivalent in those days of stg £40,000.

The Transition Period

Meanwhile, life went on at Eke. On 7 November 1978, Vincent Mordi arrived to begin his postulancy. There was one other candidate who would survive to come with him to Ewu the following year, though he left shortly afterwards. 14 January 1979 marked the official opening of the novitiate at Eke. As the full monastic habit had never been worn at Eke, the two novices had to wait for the transfer to Ewu before receiving their scapulars.

Building work and preliminary farming were going ahead at Ewu. The first maize was planted on 26 March. Next day, the first yams were planted and the first building was roofed. On 15 May, Mass was celebrated for the first time on the site of the future monastery. A commemorative tree was planted near the new novitiate building. It would be nice to report that it has grown tall and stately over the years: the unromantic truth is that it has long since disappeared.

Back at Eke, the first monastic seminar was held on 17 April. This was the forerunner of BECAN which, as previously mentioned, has played such an important part in the consolidation and development of monastic life in Nigeria.

The Great Move

We had intended to leave Eke for Ewu on Monday 9 July, but the truck sent to transport our goods proved too big to climb the sandy hill to the Eke monastery, so we had to postpone our departure to the following day. The smaller truck, eventually procured and duly loaded, arrived at Ewu at 9.00 pm on Tuesday 10 July. By the time that the landing party had secured water, food, and light, and had unloaded the truck, it was 1.00 am on the morning of 11 July 1979 which, by happy coincidence, was the Feast of St Benedict. So it was that, on our patronal day, we assembled in the oratory for the very first time and sang the *Magnificat*. Monastic life had begun at Ewu-Ishan.

We had not long to wait for acknowledgement from the Benedictine world. Abbot Primate Victor Dammertz arrived on a three day visit on 22 August in the same year. Twenty-five years later, in 2004, the Abbot Primate, this time in the person of Abbot Notker Wolf, again visited the Priory as part of its Silver Jubilee of celebrations (Fig 2).

The First Twenty-five Years

On the day we arrived at Ewu-Ishan, the community numbered five
Irishmen and two Nigerians. On the Feast of St Benedict, 2004, twenty-five
years later, one of those Nigerians, Fr Vincent Mordi, is Prior (since Easter
1996) and there are thirty professed members of the community, all Nigerian
– except for one Togolese. These brothers come from as many as thirteen different tribes, which is a unique situation in the monasteries of Africa.
Twenty-one of the thirty are solemnly professed and eight of these are priests,
and there are nine in simple vows. There are also two postulants.

Canonically, the ties between Glenstal and Ewu-Ishan have been strengthened over the years. Having started as a co-operative venture between a team
of formators and a diocesan *pia unio*, St Benedict's became a 'cell' of Glenstal
in 1981 and a 'simple priory' in 1990. The next canonical stage, which cannot
be long delayed, will be for the monastery to become a fully-fledged, independent 'conventual priory'.

Over the years the residential accommodation of the monastery has more
than doubled. A small guesthouse was built in 1987, which was replaced, just
in time to mark the silver jubilee, by a magnificent new guesthouse. Two
particularly handsome buildings, designed in the African idiom by Demas
Nwoko, a celebrated Nigerian architect, are the community room, which
doubles as a library, and a reception-cum-refectory/kitchen complex, which,
pending the building of a permanent church, serves very decently as a place
of worship.

Fig 3:
Monastic community,
St Benedict's Priory,
Ewu-Ishan

There are also numerous workshops, a poultry unit, fish farm, bakery, and an extensive herbal clinic, pharmacy, and factory for the production of herbal medicines, soaps, and tea. Several of the brethren and very many local people work in the clinic, attending to patients who flock from near and far, as well as compounding the herbal products which are marketed in several major cities throughout Nigeria.

The community provides for its own needs in fruit, vegetables, poultry, eggs, fish, and bread, and also markets these products to outsiders. They also make and sell candles, honey, and art works.

In earlier days, the monks were heavily engaged in parish work and took the lead in the building of four fine churches in the neighbourhood. With the creation of a new parish in Ewu and the arrival of a Parish Priest, they are less needed in this area. The community remains alive to many pastoral needs and is conscious, too, that the spiritual quality of its activities must remain primary.

For several years, the monks have been trying to establish a reliable water scheme to bring water to the people of Ewu from the two relatively inaccessible and distant streams on which they all depend. Just in time for the jubilee, it seems that these persistent and costly efforts have, at last, been crowned with success.

The Glenstal monks who laid the foundations of this noble work are now either gone to their reward or growing old gracefully. They include Abbot Augustine O'Sullivan who, upon his retirement as Abbot of Glenstal, served as superior at Ewu from 1981 to 1996 and remained on in the community as a living sign of God's love and gentleness until his death on 7 December 1999. He is buried at Ewu. So too is Fr Kevin Healy, who had died four months earlier, at the height of his powers. He had served from 1992 until 1999 as bursar, chanter, and prime inspiration of the rich liturgical life of Ewu. Those two graves under the palm trees of Ewu are venerated as holy ground, a sacred guarantee that the monks have come to stay.

The two Fr Columbas and Br Colman Hingerty have also gone to their reward. So has Fr Bernard O'Dea, first monk of Glenstal, who had known the first monk of Maredsous – Ewu's grandmother house. Fr Bernard set out to join the first monks of Ewu in 1972. He stayed for three years and returned twice subsequently. As well as those six who have died, there survive at least a dozen other monks of Glenstal who have spent longer or shorter periods at St Benedict's.

In recognising the contribution that Irish monks have made to the Nigerian monastery, we must also reckon the enrichment they have received for their own spiritual lives and for the life of the Glenstal community through their contact with our African brothers. The traffic has not been all one-way: six of the Nigerian monks have come to stay at Glenstal Abbey at various times.

As we look back on those hard, and yet so wonderful, early days of Eke and Ewu, we thank God with all our hearts for *everything!*

CHAPTER TWELVE

They Make the Valley a Place of Springs (Ps 84:6)
The Story of the Rostrevor Benedictines

Mark-Ephrem M Nolan OSB

Go to the land that I will show you (Genesis 12:1)
The monks of the foundation community of the most recently established
Benedictine monastery in Ireland, at Rostrevor, Co Down, all made their
monastic profession in the famous French abbey of Bec (founded in 1034).

Fig 1: Holy Cross
Monastery,
Rostrevor

Among the most illustrious sons of Bec are to be counted the great
reformer of ecclesiastical life in England, Blessed Lanfranc, and the even better known philosopher-theologian, St Anselm. Both these men were to
become Archbishops of Canterbury in their turn.

Building on the historic links between Bec and the See of Canterbury, as
well as with so many other English bishoprics and abbeys, Dom Paul
Grammont (1911-1989), who led the restoration of monastic life to Bec-
Hellouin in 1948, sought from that time onwards to foster and develop
ecumenical relationships with the Church of England.

In recognition of the contribution the Abbey of Bec had made to the establishment and growth of ecumenical relations with the Anglican Communion, Dom Grammont was invited by Archbishop Robert Runcie to participate in the historic meeting between John Paul II and himself at Canterbury Cathedral on the eve of Pentecost 1982.

A chance encounter at Canterbury between the abbot and the then Archbishop of Armagh, Cardinal Tomás Ó Fiaich, made a profound impact upon the former, awakening within him a spiritual intuition which would eventually lead to the establishment of a 'cell' of Bec in the Diocese of Down and Connor. From August 1983 until May 1987, monks from Le Bec-Hellouin lived a hidden life of prayer in the region of Downpatrick and the Ards. A retreat made with the Protestant monastic community of Grandchamp in Switzerland during the Week of Prayer for Christian Unity in January 1983 was a decisive moment and led to the undertaking of this gesture of communion. In this first outreach to Northern Ireland, the monks were given the encouragement and help of the then Bishop of Down and Connor, Most Reverend Cahal B. Daly.

Expressing the inspiration behind this first initiative of the Olivetan Congregation in Ireland, Dom Grammont said:

> To undertake to pose this gesture of communion is about honouring our ecumenical vocation. This concrete gesture is to be understood as being in profound accord with and in the true spirit of our monastic calling. Our intention is to establish in Northern Ireland a discreet presence of prayer, where the monks will live in profound communion with the local church, creating a place of reconciliation in this martyred land, interceding for the unity of the church and the peace of this people, together with that of the whole world.[1]

Due to a change in circumstances at Bec, one year after the retirement of Dom Grammont, the 'cell' in Northern Ireland was closed. This closure was deeply regretted by the local church and those Christians with whom the small Benedictine community had managed to enter into contact.

Hope does not disappoint (Romans 5:5)

Despite their bitter disappointment at the withdrawal of the monks, many people in Northern Ireland retained and expressed their firm hope that one day, in God's own good time, a monastic presence of Benedictines would be re-established in their midst. Writing in the *Irish News* at the time of Dom Paul Grammont's death, Bishop Cahal B. Daly spoke of the passing of this

---

1. Dom Paul Grammont, Abbey of Bec-Hellouin, 31.03.1983.

great figure of the French church and twentieth century monasticism as the loss of a distinguished abbot and friend to Ireland. Expressing his personal opinion and that of so many friends of the monks of Bec in Ireland, Bishop Daly spoke of their return to France as something deeply unfortunate, while going on to state his fervent hope that one day their presence would be resumed.[2]

Speaking at the Eucharistic celebration to mark the twentieth anniversary of the date Bec monks were first sent to Ireland, on the solemnity of the founder of the Olivetan Congregation, Blessed Bernard Tolomei, 19 August 2003, Dr Daly spoke of the fulfilment of Dom Grammont's dream and the realisation of God's promise, summed up in the deceased abbot's abbatial motto: *Spes autem non confundit* (Hope does not disappoint).

The call of the Irish … Come and walk among us once again
(Confession of St Patrick)
The return of Olivetan Benedictine monks to Ireland came about as a result of a very specific call addressed to monasteries of contemplative life by John-Paul II:

> In a special way, I entrust to monasteries of contemplative life the spiritual ecumenism of prayer, conversion of heart, and charity. To this end I encourage their presence wherever Christian communities of different confessions live side by side, so that their total devotion to the 'one thing needful' (cf Lk10:42) – to the worship of God and to intercession for the salvation of the world, together with their witness of evangelical life according to their special charisms – will inspire everyone to abide, after the image of the Trinity, in that unity which Jesus willed and asked of the Father for all his disciples.[3]

Dom Michelangelo M. Tiribilli, Abbot General of the Benedictine Congregation of St Mary of Monte Oliveto, recognised this call of the church to correspond to the earlier intuition which had led the Abbey of Bec to engage itself in Northern Ireland.

During the course of the canonical visitation of Bec-Hellouin in November 1997, the possibility of taking up the challenge of establishing a monastic presence in Northern Ireland was examined anew. A process of dialogue with those who felt willing to respond to the Pope's call led the Abbot

2. Bishop Cahal B. Daly, 'Dom Paul Grammont, Distinguished Abbot and Friend to Ireland', *The Irish News*, 01.08.1989.
3. John Paul II, Apostolic Exhortation *Vita Consecrata*, n 101.

General to designate the five monks who formed the foundation community of Rostrevor for this specific monastic mission. Their being sent to Ireland was to be the Olivetan Congregation's response to the invitation of *Vita Consecrata.*

Speaking to the Rostrevor foundation community at Monte Oliveto Maggiore, the Mother House and cradle of the Olivetan monastic family, Dom Michelangelo stated:

At the end of your pilgrimage to the source of our congregation, which is the Archicenobium of Monte Oliveto Maggiore, I feel the need to assure you of my paternal proximity as you set out upon your monastic experience in Northern Ireland. (…) To give a testimony of reconciliation in the martyred land of Ulster, as monks, is a mission of great importance in line with the intuition of the renowned Abbot Paul Grammont. Especially at the early stages difficulties will not be lacking. A constantly renewed spirit of sacrifice will be required of each one of you. With the most intense prayer I confide you to the intercession of Our Lady of Holy Hope, our Holy Father, Saint Benedict, and the Founder of our congregation, Blessed Bernard Tolomei … along with those great Irish saints, Patrick and Columbanus. You go forth with my blessing![4]

May all be one (John 1:21)
Ecumenical engagement is very much in accord with the Olivetan charism, which particularly emphasises the promotion of a spirituality of communion. Each Olivetan community seeks to be a foyer of fraternal communion in itself, bound to all the other communities of the congregation in a strong family spirit of solidarity, forming *unum corpus,* one body.

Already over a long period, many of the Olivetan monasteries throughout the world have shown a real commitment to participation in the church's ecumenical endeavour. Some communities have really been pioneers and precursors in this domain of the church's mission, showing commitment to ecumenical outreach long before the Second Vatican Council. Consideration of this important aspect of the Olivetan congregation's monastic ministry led the General Chapter of 1998 to make a resolution whereby it engaged itself to further promote ecumenical endeavour in response to a frequently renewed call of the magisterium to the Benedictine Order.

The Rostrevor foundation, which is the fruit of a long and rich tradition

4. Dom Michelangelo M. Tiribilli, Monte Oliveto Maggiore, 30.12.1997.

of ecumenical engagement, was designated especially for this ecumenical mission. The foundation decree of Holy Cross Monastery states:

> The aim of the community of Holy Cross Monastery is to live the monastic life according to the charism of our Benedictine Congregation of St Mary of Monte Oliveto. Its particular mission is to contribute to reconciliation between Catholics and Protestants in a land marked by reciprocal violence and stained by the blood of Christian brothers and sisters.[5]

Wherever they make you welcome … stay there (Luke 10:9)

Mandated by the Definitory of the Olivetan congregation, Dom Mark-Ephrem M. Nolan OSB (first superior) and Dom Eric M. Loisel OSB, were sent to Ireland to make an exploratory visit and consult with the bishops of the North. They received a particularly warm welcome from the Bishop of Dromore, Most Reverend Francis Gerard Brooks. With the bishop's accord, the five monks designated for the foundation arrived in Northern Ireland in January 1998 and took up residence in the former retreat centre of the Missionary Sisters of Our Lady of Apostles, Rostrevor. In September 1998, Dr Brooks issued, for the attention of the Olivetan General Chapter of 1998, a letter of recognition of the new community, temporarily established at the OLA convent, Rostrevor, and expressed his hope that, as soon as a permanent location be found for the establishment of the community, the canonical erection of the monastery would take place.

The monks had to learn patience, for it was some time before a permanent home could be found to house the community. Indeed, the decision was eventually taken to proceed to the canonical erection of the monastery even before the monks acquired their own property.

The waiting time spent in the former retreat centre of the OLA Sisters proved to be greatly beneficial to the monks – especially the French brethren who were introduced to the Irish way of life by this group of missionary sisters who had retired to Ireland, having spent lifetimes in Africa. These former missionaries were deeply conscious of the importance of helping the French monks adjust to life in what had become their adopted land.

They won the favour of all the people (Acts 2:47)

Within a very short space of time, the monks' presence in Rostrevor came to people's attention. Not only local Catholics, but Christian brothers and sisters from across the denominational divide, soon started frequenting the

---

5. Foundation Decree, 29.09.2000.

daily liturgies celebrated by the community. Contacts were made with the local Protestant clergy and these have led to a remarkable fellowship which has seen former walls of separation fall. Since the beginning of 1999, ministers of all the local churches have been meeting with the Benedictine monks on a fortnightly basis for the shared prayer of the sacred scriptures in the monastic tradition of *lectio divina*. Out of this initiative, at clergy level, relationships have developed among all the People of God. The monastery has become a focal point and place of encounter for all the churches of the area and from far beyond.

The people rejoiced, God having given them good cause for rejoicing (Nehemiah 12:43)

Events in the life of the Benedictine community since the monks' arrival to Rostrevor have been regarded as celebrations for the wider Christian family and welcomed by all as an eloquent testimony to the monks' commitment to live in communion with the local church. The solemn profession of one brother and the ordination of another were particularly striking in this respect. Both these liturgies were celebrated in Kilbroney Parish Church, given the limited space in the OLA convent chapel. A large delegation from the other Christian churches participated in these liturgies. An ancient ninth-century bell from Saint Bronagh's monastery, which is now enshrined in St Mary Star of the Sea Church, was rung at the opening of both these celebrations, recalling the rich monastic heritage of the area in time past, while looking forward to its renewal through the Benedictine community's establishment in the Valley of Kilbroney. On the first occasion, little did the congregation gathered suspect that hope had been given to the monks that they would in fact be staying in the parish of Rostrevor, where they had already experienced such a warmth of welcome. Within a short space of time they were to learn this good news.

I will give you the land on which you lie (Genesis 28:13)

On 23 October 2000, feast of Our Lady of Holy Hope, a patronal feast for the French branch of the Olivetan congregation, a local farmer and his wife made an extremely generous offer of land to the monks for the building of a monastery. In all approximately nine acres (about half of the farmer's small holding) were given to the community. Having discerned this gift to be a sign of the Lord's providential care, and the indication of his will that a new monastery should be built in Kilbroney, the monks accepted this donation and set out in faith on a fund-raising campaign. On 21 March 2001, encouraged by their Abbot General to seek first the kingdom in the assurance that a good providence would supply for their needs, the Rostrevor Benedictines launched their initial appeal for help. At the same time they drew up architectural plans for the new monastery.

'Let us build', and with willing hand they set about the good work
(Nehemiah 1:18)
The first monastic office was sung on the site of the future church on 14 September 2001, for the solemnity of the Exaltation of the Holy Cross, patronal feast of the community. Building work began on 6 November 2002, after the turning of the first sod by the superior, Dom Mark-Ephrem M. Nolan. Rapid progress saw the building soon taking shape. By 29 June 2003, the walls and roofs of the monastery in place, the corner stone of the church could be blessed. The blessing was performed by the local bishop, Most Reverend John McAreavey; many Christian ministers and faithful from the area and beyond also participated in the celebration of this historic event.

The overall building project was completed just on time for the official opening of the monastery and solemn consecration of the church for the first day of the Week of Prayer for Christian Unity, 18 January 2004.

Hear the entreaty of your people as they pray in this place ... hear and forgive
(1 Kings 8:29-30)
The eve of the solemn dedication was marked by an ecumenical prayer vigil. The service opened with the icon of the Holy Cross being carried into the new church building by the Roman Catholic Bishop of Dromore, Most Reverend John McAreavey, and the Church of Ireland Bishop of Down and Dromore, Right Reverend Harold Miller (Fig 2). This symbolic gesture spoke of their commitment to bear witness to Christ together and demonstrated their mutual appreciation of the role the monastery seeks to play as *a house of prayer for all peoples.* Lord Carey of Clifton, former Archbishop of Canterbury, preached the first sermon in the monastery church, in which he concentrated on the vital role this place and the community it houses would have to play in furthering understanding and encouraging encounter between Christians of different traditions. Canon Trevor Williams, former leader of the Corrymeela Community of Reconciliation, spoke movingly of his experience of the community of Holy Cross as:

> a safe space where people from different backgrounds have already been led to come together and in their meeting share their stories with one another in an atmosphere of confidence and trust. This sharing has

helped many not only to grow in mutual understanding and respect but also to experience healing of deep wounds from their troubled past.

Testimonies to the power of forgiveness through the experience of the cross were given by Revd Bert Armstrong, a Methodist, whose brother and sister-in-law were killed by the IRA in the Enniskillen bomb (1987) and Mr Michael McGoldrick, a Roman Catholic, whose only son was killed by the UVF as part of the Drumcree stand-off (1996). Many victims of over three decades of violence in Northern Ireland were present at this prayer vigil and found it to be a profoundly healing experience. An act of repentance and a joint commitment to peace-making was led by the superior of the monastery and the local Church of Ireland and Presbyterian Ministers.

My house shall be a house of prayer for all (Isaiah 56:7)
The solemn dedication, the following day, brought together many distinguished representatives of the church in Ireland and the church universal, of both the Roman Catholic and Protestant traditions. Representatives of the monastic communities of both the Benedictine and Cistercian Orders, together with representatives of other forms of consecrated life, including sisters from the Protestant monastic community of Grandchamp in Switzerland, also came to express their solidarity with the nascent monastery. This Eucharistic celebration opened with the presentation of the original stone water font from Down Cathedral by the Dean of the Chapter, Very Revd John Dinnen, 'as a sign of love and prayerful communion in one Lord, one faith, one baptism'. The Roman Catholic and Church of Ireland bishops united to sprinkle the people, walls and altar of the church with the blessed water. The ambo of the new church was consecrated by Archbishop George Carey, followed by the proclamation of the scripture readings by ministers of

Fig 3: Holy Cross
Monastery Church

the Presbyterian and Methodist traditions. In his homily, Bishop John
McAreavey expressed his hopes and expectations for the community in these
terms:

> The Benedictines value in a special way stability, stability in the long trad-
> ition behind them and stability in the place where their monastery is sit-
> uated. It seems to me that this stability gives them freedom to set out on
> journeys that involve risk and that break new ground. And so the wider
> church looks to this community to become a community of reconcilia-
> tion and, in a way, to blaze a trail that the rest of us might follow. We look
> to you to help us to journey from an attitude of separateness to one of
> partnership; we look to you to help us make the journey from detachment
> from the fate of other Christians to a sense of deep care about what is hap-
> pening to them. There is a journey that we have to make from privacy to
> trust that allows us to share our own personal and church concerns with
> our brothers and sisters in other church communities. Above all, we have
> to journey from a tolerance of division to a deep sense of the scandal of
> Christian divisions. We look to you to make us uncomfortable in many
> of the attitudes we take and to show us the way to a better future.[6]

6. Bishop John McAreavey, Homily, 18.01.2004.

After the anointing of the altar table, the consecration stones of the church were anointed by the local bishop, the Apostolic Nuncio Dr Giuseppe Lazzaroto, the Roman Catholic Primate of All Ireland. Archbishop Seán Brady, Bishop Francis Gerard Brooks, the Olivetan Abbot General, Archabbot Michelangelo M. Tiribilli, and the monastery's founding father, Dom Mark-Ephrem M. Nolan. It was Cardinal Cahal B. Daly who inaugurated the Blessed Sacrament Chapel, placing the reserved sacrament in the tabernacle at the end of this first Eucharist to be celebrated in the church.

They are happy who dwell in your house (Ps 84:4)

The community is now happily settled into its permanent home.

An ever increasing number of visitors to Holy Cross Monastery is delighted to discover this fine complex of buildings nestled in the picturesque foothills of the Mournes. The monastery fits into the landscape as if it has always been there. The exterior and interior design are, at one and the same time, stark in their simplicity and noble in their beauty. The building is filled with light throughout and the strategic placing of the windows has, as it were, established a kind of on-going dialogue with the natural surroundings of the valley. Everything about the design speaks of harmony. This is particularly true of the interior of the church building and is fitting for the place of worship of a community which has for mission 'to live a parable of communion'.

Here God alone will be my intention … His love the subject of my contemplation (St Anselm)

More important than the buildings which house a community is the life it seeks to lead. Having been engendered by the French Benedictine tradition, the monks of Rostrevor lead a monastic life without any outside pastoral ministry. The sung liturgy is central to the monks' daily horarium – Gregorian chant and contemporary music in the vernacular are used. A strong emphasis is placed upon *lectio divina* and personal prayer. Periods of silent prayer after the morning and evening offices are shared in common. Manual work and study are also important features of the monks' daily routine. The community supports itself by the making of handmade decorative candles and the production of greeting cards. All domestic duties are undertaken by the monks themselves. Hospitality is a significant aspect of all Benedictine life and this is also true at Rostrevor. The monastery has a guest house where men and women can make a time of private retreat in silence, sharing in the prayer life of the community and joining the brethren for meals, which are always taken in silence in the refectory. Given the community's particular vocation, the hospitality it offers is availed of by Christians from all traditions.

While the community at Rostrevor is fully engaged in the church's ecumenical endeavour, its approach is less that of *doing* ecumenism than seeking *to be,* by its whole way of life, a living parable of reconciliation and a call to restored unity in Christ.

Dr McAreavey summed up his impressions of the contribution the Benedictines of Rostrevor have to make in the Irish church in these lines, written to endorse the monks' appeal for support:

> At this point in the history of the Irish church, I believe that this monastic presence is a gift of God to us. It enriches us with its tradition of contemplation nourished by the scriptures, prayerful liturgy, a commitment to ecumenism and the task of reconciliation. I am confident that this community, which has put down roots in the Diocese of Dromore, will flourish and bear fruit abundantly.[7]

Remember the rock from which you were hewn (Isaiah 51:1)
The late Dom Paul Grammont always emphasised the importance of remembering the first steps made in any project, so as to remain faithful to its original intuition. The story of the post-Reformation restoration of Benedictine life to the North of Ireland began at Ballykilbeg in the Parish of Downpatrick, 800 years after Benedictine monks came to Down Cathedral from Chester, a Bec foundation. In a letter addressed to Dom Paul Grammont to express his joy that monks from Bec had come to Northern Ireland, the late Cardinal Tomás Ó Fiaich explained:

> Ballykilbeg, where your monks have arrived, is associated with notable figures of Irish history. It was the birthplace of Archbishop William Crolly, the first Archbishop of Armagh after the penal times to reside in the city of Armagh and the prelate who began the building of Armagh Cathedral. It was also the place of residence of a famous Orange leader of the nineteenth century called Johnston and is therefore a name which is rich in memories for the Protestant people of Ulster. Please God it will be possible for your community to link together the two traditions, i.e. that of Crolly and that of Johnston, into one single Irish Christian tradition.[8]

Such is the fervent prayer of the monks of Rostrevor, who gather for worship several times a day below the icon of the Cross which adorns their monastic church and which bears the inscription: *May all be one.*

7. Bishop John McAreavey, 21.03.2001.
8. Cardinal Tomás Ó Fiaich, Letter, 22.11.83.

CHAPTER THIRTEEN

Saint Benedict's Priory, Cobh

M. Angela Stephens OSB

St Benedict's Priory, Cobh, Co Cork belongs to the Congregation of the Adorers of the Sacred Heart of Jesus of Montmartre, a cloistered contemplative Benedictine congregation whose Mother House is Tyburn Convent, London.

The congregation was founded in 1898 at Montmartre in Paris by Marie-Adele Garnier. She was born in 1838 in Burgundy. As a young woman she taught as a governess and was greatly loved and esteemed by both parents and children. From her youth, she felt deeply the love of Christ touching her heart, drawing her to surrender herself totally to him, especially through the Eucharist.

In her own words, the Mass was the 'sun of her life' and devotion to the Eucharist became the centre of her spiritual life. Flowing from this, she felt drawn to establish Perpetual Adoration of the Blessed Sacrament, in order to express fully her desire to offer to the Sacred Heart of Jesus an unceasing homage of love and reparation. Thus it was that the Eucharist – the sacrament and the sacrifice of the love of Christ, and the Sacred Heart – symbol of the love of Christ for his Father and all humanity, could never be separated in her soul.

She sought to live this eucharistic life as a solitary at Montmartre. Her health failed and she was obliged to abandon this way of life. Several years later, she felt called to establish a religious family consecrated to the worship and praise of the Holy Trinity through liturgical prayer and eucharistic adoration in the contemplative life. She established this form of life within the monastic tradition of the church under the Rule of St Benedict.

In 1901, the young community fled to England on account of the laws of France against religious orders. The foundress settled her new community at Tyburn in London, at the site of the martyrdom of more than one hundred Catholic Reformation martyrs. A few years later, Blessed Columba Marmion visited Tyburn and became her spiritual director, giving much help and support. Drawn to the Rule of St Benedict from the outset, Mother Marie-Adele's vision was for a congregation comprising houses in various countries, while remaining one closely-knit family under a Mother General. In 1914, Blessed Columba Marmion presided over the General Chapter which carried this into effect, giving the congregation juridical status as a Benedictine congregation.

St Benedict's Priory was founded in 1916 in England, at Royston, in Hertfordshire to be the novitiate house for the English-speaking sisters. In 1961, the community transferred to Wadhurst in Sussex. Some years later, the novitiate was transferred to the Mother House at Tyburn and a small retreat centre was opened.

In 1992, Bishop John Magee of Cloyne approached the congregation requesting a foundation in his diocese, as there was no con-

templative community there. The community at Wadhurst volunteered to go as their own diocese of Arundel and Brighton already had several contemplative communities.

It took some time to find a suitable property, one that would be accessible to the local people to become a eucharistic centre, while at the same time providing the environment necessary for contemplative life. Eventually, the community was able to purchase a convent from the Sisters of Mercy in Cobh. This property is ideally situated, having sufficient grounds yet being very close to the town centre. The house has a very interesting history dating back to 1886, when it was built for the British Admiralty. It was set on fire in 1922 after the Admiralty had vacated it. In 1930, the derelict building was purchased by the Bishop of Cloyne and it became the novitiate house of the Mercy Order.

The property in Sussex was sold and the community moved to Cobh in May 1993, receiving a very warm welcome as the bells of Cobh cathedral rang out to greet their arrival. The Mass for the official inauguration on 31 July had to be celebrated outside, to accommodate the large number of people. Some twenty priests, including representatives from all the Benedictine and Cistercian monasteries in Ireland and many of the diocesan priests, concelebrated with Bishop John Magee. During his homily, the bishop expressed his happiness at having another centre of eucharistic adoration set up in the diocese:

A new star has come to shine in our midst. The star will shine throughout the night looking down on the cathedral of St Colman and the dear
people of Cobh. May its light ever be a reminder to us all never to forget
the Lord our God and may it join with the many lights that have been
enkindled in the eucharistic chapels of our diocese, and thus help in
establishing an ecclesial constellation which will illumine the pilgrim way
of our people.

A centre for private retreats was opened at the same time and also a small
monastic heritage centre, depicting the history of monasticism in Ireland, the
latter being particularly popular with school groups. A small craft and coffee
shop was also opened. The property at Cobh included two large fields, covering about two acres. One was immediately put into use as a fruit and veg-
etable garden. As the town had no public park, it was decided to make a Bible
garden in the second field, growing trees and shrubs that feature in the Bible.
This was officially opened in 1995 and since then has continued to grow and
develop into a very peaceful garden, much appreciated by the local people
and visitors. It includes a small walled garden, the Resurrection Garden,
which has a tomb, modelled on a first century sepulchre near Jerusalem. Here
there is an outdoor oratory where Mass is sometimes celebrated. The Stations
of the Cross, made locally, were erected along the full length of the garden,

finishing in the Garden of Olives, which leads into the Resurrection Garden, giving the whole area an atmosphere of prayer and peace.

In 1994, on the feast of St Oliver Plunkett, the relic of the saint was brought in solemn procession from the cathedral where it had previously been housed, to a small oratory, specially prepared in the monastic heritage centre. This was particularly appropriate, as St Oliver was the last of the martyrs to be put to death on the Tyburn gallows.

While the sanctuary and choir of the chapel were adequate, it soon became apparent that a larger area was needed for the many people coming to pray before the Blessed Sacrament. Building work began in 1995 to enlarge the public part of the church and also to provide some parlour space and work rooms for the community. A local builder matched every detail of the nineteenth century exterior, so that it is difficult to see which part was built in 1886 and which part in 1996. The renovated church, which holds about eighty people, was consecrated by Bishop John Magee on 31 August 1996. Once again the other Irish Benedictine and Cistercian houses were represented. The next day, the bishop presided at solemn vespers, as it had not been possible to invite all the friends of the community to the consecration.

In 1997, the community was approached by a group from the town who had the idea of making a memorial garden for children who have died and a place for people who have experienced the loss of a child. They saw the priory with its peaceful gardens as an ideal setting. The work, which includes a pool with a limestone carving and inscriptions, was completed and blessed by Bishop John Magee in 1998. The names of the children can be inscribed in a Book of Remembrance, which is kept in the sanctuary. Each year there is a liturgical celebration in June and a Mass in November and large numbers come, obviously finding comfort and support in their loss.

Almost as soon as the community arrived in Cobh, several local people expressed a wish to be more closely associated with their prayer life. Within the first year, oblates were accepted and now there are about twenty. The oblates follow the spirit of the Rule, usually meeting together at the priory several times a year. There is also a small group of lay eucharistic adorers, who come once a week, covering two hours of the adoration. On the First Friday of each month, there is an all night vigil and every Monday evening, after compline, the local Divine Mercy group hold their holy hour.

Thus, within a relatively short space of time, the community has become an integral part of the local parish and diocese. A centre of liturgical prayer and spirituality has developed almost naturally, with little direct initiative from the community, apart from the regular life of prayer, *lectio divina* and work; an important part of the latter being hospitality of various kinds. In his homily on 31 July 2003, when Bishop Magee celebrated a Mass of Thanksgiving for the tenth anniversary of the community's arrival in Cobh, he commented: 'Their vocation is a vocation to love, to recognise and proclaim the presence of Jesus among us – what Mary was about when visiting Elizabeth, loving, caring, nurturing.'

St Benedict places Christ at the centre of his Rule: 'To prefer nothing to the love of Christ.' The greatest expression of this love is found in the Eucharist, where Marie-Adele Garnier discovered her call. In 1897, a year before the actual foundation of the congregation, she wrote that it was 'the desire to respond to the heart of Jesus living in the Eucharist' that inspired the founding of her religious family. And it was the Rule of St Benedict that attracted her, because it would give a 'solid foundation' to her inspiration – a Rule that also puts the liturgy at the centre, 'let nothing be put before the work of God'. Thus, she brings to these twin principles of the Rule the fruit of years of reflection and contemplation on the person of Christ, giving her congregation its particular charism within the Benedictine family. This can be summed up in the introduction to each of the liturgical hours: 'O blessed Trinity, we give you glory, praise and thanks, now and for ever. We give unending blessing to you, O Heart of Jesus!'

Afterword

Celestine Cullen OSB

Facing the future was not, I think either a preoccupation or a problem for St Benedict. The Prologue or Introduction to the Rule is totally timeless and the Latin original is largely in the present tense: 'Let us open our eyes to the divine light, and with startled ears let us listen to what the divine voice is calling out every day, urging us: today, if your should hear his voice, harden not your hearts'[1] – either by obduracy or by a reluctance to read the unfolding scroll of human history, 'to hear what the spirit is saying to the churches'.[2]

Benedict's time frame was the twenty-four hour clock, each day in its symbolic significance of light and darkness, of death and resurrection, of combat and victory: *dies, hodie, cotidie* – day, today, daily and their derivatives are the resonant and oft repeated words of the Rule: 'Seven times a day have I given you praise';[3] 'day by day to fulfil by deeds what God commands';[4] 'to make peace with an opponent before sunset';[5] and this consciousness that life is a daily gift, *dies ad idutias*, a daily reprieve, is particularly evident when the Rule legislates for each day's work, as it is in the realistic view that no day is complete without its call to forgiveness: 'forgive us as we forgive'.[6] The only future Benedict envisages is eternity: 'let them prefer absolutely nothing to Christ who will bring us all alike to everlasting life.'[7] The key principle and the only goal that matter are there. Benedict has no other programme, no policy, no mission statement, no testament other than the Rule, no masterplan; no strategy other than to forge ahead on the path to life *per ducatum Evangelii* – under the guidance of the gospel.[8]

This non specific character of the monastic way was admirably highlighted by Fr Timothy Radcliffe, Master General of the Dominicans as he then was, when he addressed the Congress of Benedictine Abbots in Rome in 2000:

---

1. Rule of St Benedict (henceforth cited as RB) Prologue, 9:10.
2. RB, Prologue, 11.
3. RB, 16:1.
4. RB, 4:63.
5. RB, 4:73.
6. RB, 13:13.
7. RB, 72.
8. RB, Prologue, 21.

The most obvious thing about monks is that you do not do anything in particular. You farm but you are not farmers. You teach but you are not teachers. You may even run hospitals, or mission stations, but you are not primarily doctors or missionaries. You are monks who follow the Rule of Benedict. You do not do anything in particular. Monks are usually very busy people, and are rarely idle, but the business is not the point and purpose of your lives. Cardinal Hume once wrote that 'we do not see ourselves as having any particular mission or function in the church. We do not set out to change the course of history. We are just there almost by accident from a human point of view. And happily we go on just being there.' It is the absence of explicit purpose that discloses God as the secret, hidden purpose of your lives. God is disclosed as the invisible centre of our lives when we do not try to give any other justification for who we are. The point of Christian life is just to be with God. Jesus says to his disciples: 'Abide in my love.'[9] Monks are called to abide in his love.[10]

It is interesting to note that no less a figure than W. B. Yeats sensed this fruitful vacuity of the monks' calling. In the wake of a visit to Mont-Saint-Michel in Normandy in the early twentieth century, he wrote: 'Only that which does not teach, which does not cry out, which does not persuade, which does not condescend, which does not explain, is irresistible.'[11]

All this was confirmed for me in the course of ten years travelling as Abbot President around the monastic world. The kingdom of God is not only beyond our best efforts; it is also beyond our limited vision. We monks accomplish in a lifetime only a fraction of the magnificent enterprise that is God's work:

> I remember the deeds of the Lord,
> I remember your works of old,
> I muse on all your works
> And ponder your mighty deeds.[12]

That is our task: to ponder the past in prayer, to keep alive the memory of that past, whether it be 75 years or 750 years: a past that is the surest augury of more wonders – and indeed more rapids – ahead.

Nothing we do is complete, which is another way of saying that the kingdom always lies beyond us. No ministry of ours is ever wholly successful; no

9. John 15:10
10. Timothy Radcliffe OP, *I call you friends* (London, 2001), pp 101-2.
11. W. B. Yeats, 'Synge and the Ireland of his time' in idem, *Essays and introductions* (London, 1969), p 341.
12. Psalm 76.

programme accomplishes or exhausts the church's mission. We do not deal in solutions, rather in mystery; in deep designs where we are quite literally out of our depth. We speak of the unknown God of the Acropolis, who only reveals himself to be our abiding mystery. Authentic faith, now or in the future, has to be awestruck, filled with wonder, humbling.

The Prologue to the Rule sees us thus humbled, tools in the master crafts-man's hands: 'Such men glorify the Lord, who is at work in them';[13] they do not boast of their faithful service but 'say with the prophet: Not to us Lord, not to us, but to your name give the glory'. We praise the Lord working in and through us; we are surprised that we have been deemed worthy of his trust.

> Lord what is man that you care for him,
> mortal man that you keep him in mind;
> man who is merely a breath
> whose life fades like a shadow?[14]

And from this sense of surprise, which focuses on the past, is born trust or confidence in confronting a future that is hidden from our eyes.

That is what we are about. We lay foundations for others to build on. We cannot do everything and there is a sense of liberation in realising this. It enables us to do something, and to do it well. It may be incomplete but it is a beginning. That has always been the Benedictine way. We shall never see the end result, the final destiny of our monasteries, but that is the difference between the master builder and the workmen. We are his labourers. The Lord seeks his workers in every age, the Rule says,[15] and he has sought us in ours. We are not the architects of the future; we are simply part of the scaffolding. We are called to continue to do the work of God, to live together in unity, to pray in wonder, gratitude and trust for the coming of the kingdom. This is, and always has been, the task of a monastery. And so it will continue to be. As Abbot Augustine O'Sullivan, whose serenity tided Glenstal over the tur-bulent seas of the late sixties and seventies, would have surely added to con-clude: 'all shall be well, and all manner of thing shall be well.'[16]

13. RB Prol 30.
14. Psalm 143.
15. RB Prol 14.
16. Julian of Norwich, *Revelations of Divine Love*, Chap 27.

Index